Donald L. Wells

SHIFTS IN THE SOCIAL CONTRACT

PINE FORGE PRESS TITLES OF RELATED INTEREST

Sociology of Work: Concepts and Cases by Carol Auster

Adventures in Social Research: Data Analysis Using SPSS for WINDOWS by Earl Babbie and Fred Halley

Sociology of Work by Richard H. Hall

Race, Ethnicity, Gender, and Class: The Sociology of Group Conflict and Change by Joseph F. Healey

Diversity in America by Vincent N. Parillo

The McDonaldization of Society, Revised Edition by George Ritzer

Expressing America: A Critique of the Global Credit Card Society by George Ritzer

Sociology: Exploring the Architecture of Everyday Life by David M. Newman

Sociology: Exploring the Architecture of Everyday Life (Readings) by David M. Newman

---

The Pine Forge Press Series in Research Methods and Statistics
Edited by Richard T. Campbell and Kathleen S. Crittenden

Investigating the Social World: The Process and Practice of Research by Russell K. Schutt

A Guide to Field Research by Carol A. Bailey

Designing Surveys: A Guide to Decisions and Procedures by Ronald Czaja and Johnny Blair

How Sampling Works by Richard Maisel and Caroline Hodges Persell

---

Sociology for a New Century
A Pine Forge Press Series edited by Charles Ragin, Wendy Griswold, and Larry Griffin

How Societies Change by Daniel Chirot

Cultures and Societies in a Changing World by Wendy Griswold

Crime and Disrepute by John Hagan

Gods in the Global Village by Lester R. Kurtz

Constructing Social Research by Charles C. Ragin

Women and Men at Work by Barbara Reskin and Irene Padavic

Cities in a World Economy by Saskia Sassen

SHIFTS IN THE SOCIAL CONTRACT:
UNDERSTANDING CHANGE IN AMERICAN SOCIETY

Beth A. Rubin
Tulane University

PINE FORGE PRESS
Thousand Oaks, California •
London • New Delhi

For information, address:

 Pine Forge Press
A Sage Publications Company
2455 Teller Road
Thousand Oaks, California 91320
(805) 499-4224
E-mail: sales@pfp.sagepub.com

SAGE Publications Ltd.
6 Bonhill Street
London EC2A 4PU
United Kingdom

SAGE Publications India Pvt. Ltd.
M-32 Marker
Greater Kailash I
New Delhi 110 048 India

Production: Rogue Valley Publications
Designer: Deborah Davis
Typesetter: Rebecca Evans & Associates
Cover: Paula Shuhert and Graham Metcalfe
Production Manager: Rebecca Holland
Printed in the United States of America

96 97 98 99 10 9 8 7 6 5 4 3 2 1

Library of Congress Cataloging-in-Publication Data

Rubin, Beth A., 1955-
      Shifts in the social contract : Understanding change in American
society / Beth Rubin.
          p.   cm.
      Includes bibliographical references and index.
      ISBN 0-8039-9040-5 (p. : alk. paper)
      1. Social change—United States. 2. United States—Social
conditions—1980- 3. United States—Economic conditions—1981-
I. Title.
HN59.2R83   1995
303.4'0973—dc20   95-13200
                                                                   CIP

*To the best of my students whose questions
generated the answers that became this book*

About the Author

Beth A. Rubin (Ph.D., Indiana University-Bloomington) is Associate Professor of Sociology at Tulane University in New Orleans. She has published in the areas of labor sociology and the sociology of homelessness and housing. Her current research focuses on the interconnections among economic, workplace, familial, cultural, and political transformations and their implications for social organization and stratification as we move into the twenty-first century.

About the Publisher

Pine Forge Press is a new educational publisher, dedicated to publishing innovative books and software throughout the social sciences. On this and any other of our publications, we welcome your comments and suggestions.

Please call or write to:

Pine Forge Press
A Sage Publications Company
2455 Teller Road
Thousand Oaks, California 91320
(805) 499-4224
E-mail: sales@pfp.sagepub.com

CONTENTS

PREFACE

Over the years, I have ended many of my classes with the claim that my students will raise their children in a world that will be profoundly different from the one in which they themselves were raised. I gave this last lecture with the passion of a fire-and-brimstone preacher. But my final message was always, "There is nothing that humans socially construct that they cannot socially change." The message was that yes, things are changing dramatically, but we as social actors must all be authors of that change.

The world today is characterized by a range of changes that are often disturbing and alienating, particularly to college-age people who must face a world so different from the one in which their parents grew up. This book is my effort to explain these changes and to place them into a single coherent framework. In the absence of any guide, changes in the economy, workplace, families, polity, and culture can appear unrelated and overwhelming. A sociological lens, however, provides a way to view not only each institutional change but the interconnections among institutions. These changing institutions are linked together and are part of a great social transformation.

I view the breadth of these changes as comparable to the changes that characterized the transformation from agrarian precapitalist society to industrial capitalist society. That process occurred over hundreds of years and resulted in a society based on markets and contracts instead of superstition, tradition, and agricultural cycles. The transition from industrial capitalism to postindustrial, flexible, global capitalism is happening within a century—in fact, within decades—and it is transforming the basis of social organization away from long-term contracts as the bases of social organization. Instead, transitory relationships and the instantaneous transmission of information, money, and images characterize our daily transactions.

I argue in this book that the movement away from long-term contractual relations, most visible in economic and workplace relationships, causes similar changes throughout society. To understand the often confusing, sometimes threatening, and rapidly shifting forces that affect our daily lives, we need to make connections between those large-scale changes and the more immediate institutions within which we work, play, and live. The focus of this text is on the implications of these changes for the basic institutions of social life.

I have taken an unusual approach to my presentation. Although the contents of the book present a substantial body of sociological theory and research, each chapter begins with a personal story. By the end of the book, some readers may think that they know far more about my life (my father-in-law, my nephew, my grandparents—even my first boyfriend!) than they care to. But I begin each chapter that way because, for most of us, the effort to understand the social world grows out of the effort to understand our own lives. Thus, while each chapter begins with some story about a particular person I know, it goes on to locate that person's own experience in a social-historical context. In doing so, it illuminates the connections between social structural changes and individual experience.

I begin chapter 1 with a series of events drawn from the media. These events dramatize some of the most disturbing and disruptive changes occurring in the economy, the workplace, families, politics, and the culture. Chapters 2–5 discuss the changes in the economy, workplace, family, and polity. Each chapter examines the institution in question in different historical periods—typically, the late nineteenth century, the first half of the post–World War II period (roughly 1947–1972), and the early 1970s through today. My basic claim is that each of these periods is characterized by different social contracts—those implicit, shared understandings that structure social interaction and thus structure each institution.

Thus, chapter 2 examines the changing implicit and explicit contractual relationships between the two main economic actors in society, workers and their employers, in the context of the changing U.S. economy. Chapter 3 examines the ways people actually work and the ways workplaces are organized. This chapter focuses on the factors that have segmented the workplace in different historical periods. It ends with a discussion relating the changing workplace to education.

Chapter 4 examines the transformation of families from colonial times to the present, focusing on the connections between family roles and structures and the economic and workplace changes described in the previous chapters. In this context, I explore how families of different social classes experience and respond to changing social and economic conditions. Chapter 5 explores the changing role of the government during the three periods of interest (pre–World War II, roughly 1947–1972, and post-1972) and focuses on the different ways government intervenes in economic and social life.

Chapter 6 is about culture, and it proceeds differently from the previous chapters. Covering cultural changes in this broad historical context is beyond the scope of this book. Instead, I focus on some of the most visible and frequently controversial cultural characteristics of the current era—the rise of fundamentalism, the role of technology (particularly television and computers), immigration, and multiculturalism. This chapter also explores the creation of meaning in a period of social transformation. The final chapter attempts some crystal-ball gazing and, extrapolating from current trends, suggests worst- and best-case possible futures.

In all instances, I have relied heavily on the extant sociological theory and research found in the references at the end of the book. However, I have sought to keep the text relatively free of excessive citations, jargon, and the typical qualifiers that characterize much scholarly writing. As a result, some of my arguments and conclusions may seem particularly bold or controversial. Nonetheless, I hope that this writing style makes the book interesting and useful to a broad range of readers. Obviously, the references provide the means to pursue topics in greater detail. My greatest hope is that what is between these covers answers some questions, raises others, and stimulates thought.

I will include the usual disclaimer: While the people I thank deserve credit for much that is right with this book, they deserve none of the responsibility for what is wrong with it. I suppose that my greatest debt is to all of the students that I have taught over the years, who really are the inspiration for this book. But also right up there is Steve Rutter, publisher and president of Pine Forge Press. Although I have continued to teach much of what is in this book and have published bits and pieces of it in scholarly journals, I would never have pulled it all together into a book had Steve Rutter not encouraged me to do so. I am indebted to him for doing so, and also for all the gentle pushing, prodding, and demanding that brought this project to fruition. Similarly, I am grateful to Rebecca Smith, whose deft editing helped me say what I wanted to say as clearly as possible.

I owe considerable thanks to the individuals who read various chapters and provided feedback. Thanks to Marlena Studer, Tulane University, for her comments and very valuable suggestions on chapter 4; to Laurie Joyner for her comments on chapter 1; and to various students who read early drafts of chapters 2, 3, and 7. I am also indebted to the reviewers of this manuscript, whose suggestions were indispensable to the revision process.

George Ritzer, *University of Maryland, College Park*
Katharine Donato, *Louisiana State University*
Jonathan Epstein, *Kent State University*
Margaret Brooks, *Terry, Baldwin-Wallace College*
Stephen Zehr, *Illinois Institute of Technology*
Idee Winfield, *Louisiana State University*
Amy Wharton, *Washington State University*
Cynthia Woolever, *Midway College*
John Hartman, *Columbia University*
Barbara Gutek, *University of Arizona*
Steve Legeay, *Shaw University*

I would also like to thank Shira Adams, my most trusted nonsociologist, an informed and intelligent reader who read most of the chapters in their roughest stages and weaned me away from the comfort of sociological jargon. I am also grateful to the students in the honors seminar I taught in the spring of 1994: Emi Bromberg, Matt Giovonizzi, Laura Loventhal, Brian Penzel, Romina Sosa, Angela Vitulli, and Laura Weinstein. Discussions with them gave me the opportunity to work out many of my ideas and concepts even as I was writing, and their patience with my thinking out loud is deeply appreciated. Chapter 6 grew directly out of their words. Various graduate students also have my gratitude, particularly Anna Popova and John Baugher, whose research and secretarial efforts (as well as computer skills) are embedded in this book. Also thanks to Ye Luo for help during the final stages of this project. Donna Listz deserves much thanks for heroic typing assistance.

My greatest, deepest, heartfelt thanks goes to my husband and colleague, Brian T. Smith. His support, intellect, and time—for he has read and given me feedback on every page of this book, usually more than once—have been essential. Moreover, I appreciate and value his willingness to shoulder many of the day-to-day responsibilities of maintaining a home so that I could work on "the book." He has the patience of a saint.

Beth A. Rubin

SOCIAL CHANGE IN THE TWENTIETH CENTURY

In 1992 in Ohio, a disgruntled former cook went into a family restaurant and fired 15 shots from a 9mm semiautomatic handgun, wounding several employees. The first week of 1995, a Michigan automobile factory experienced its third shooting (January 8, 1995, *Times-Picayune*); an employee killed his estranged wife, her boyfriend, and then himself. Such incidents are not as rare as one might suppose. According to the Bureau of Labor Statistics, workplace homicides tripled between 1980 and 1988, making them the third leading cause of death on the job. Moreover, researchers suggest that this trend will worsen. One study found 16 incidents of mass murder in the work-place in the 1980s and 18 in the first two years of the 1990s (*Times-Picayune*, November 8, 1992). Another study indicated that "an American woman is more likely to die on the job at the hands of an attacker than by accident" (*Times-Picayune*, September 5, 1993).

While work may have become increasingly perilous for many, most people still prefer it to the alternative: unemployment. Unfortu-nately, workers who once felt relatively immune from unemployment are discovering that a college degree and a big paycheck are no guarantee against it. Consider the example of IBM, which has long offered many of its workers essentially lifetime employment. In April 1993, in response to declining business conditions, IBM laid off 7,700 workers. Many of these workers were well-paid professionals in their 50s who thought they were at the zenith of their careers. Unlike many blue-collar workers, none of them had ever had to cope with layoffs and employment insecurity. This security was, after all, why they had invested in good educations at colleges and universities. Now, these well-educated, highly skilled, and highly paid workers—who were accustomed to a high standard of living—meet in support/prayer group meetings to discuss their lost careers, provide emotional support for one another, and develop strategies for job hunting and survival. Such support is necessary. In Dutchess County, New York, where three huge IBM plants are located, social service workers report an increase in drinking and family violence (*New York Times,* December 22, 1993). Roughly a year later, a *New York Times* editorial (The Rise of the Losing Class, Louis Uchitelle, November 20, 1994) claimed that the changing economy was linking the white-collar, skilled, college-educated workers with blue-collar, unskilled, high school educated workers through a shared experience of "uncertainty, insecurity, and anxiety about their jobs and incomes."

Surprisingly, unemployment and layoffs were occurring in a period characterized by economic recovery. But this recovery was an unusual one. Despite economic growth in the early 1990s, economic inequality (the gap between the rich and poor) continued to grow. While inequality has been increasing since the late 1970s, for perhaps the first time in America's history economists were faced with the puzzle of falling **median income*** (the income level that half the population is above and half below) at a time of increased economic growth (*New York Times,* October 9, 1994).

The economy and the workplace are not the only institutions that appear to be changing dramatically. The meaning and definition of "family" are also increasingly contested. Working mothers are now the norm, and latchkey kids are old news. Newer, perhaps, are other variants of the family. Increasing numbers of universities are offering health insurance benefits to the gay partners of faculty and staff. In the summer of 1993, a superior court judge in New Jersey found that "a child should have two parents—even if they're both women" and allowed a lesbian couple to legally adopt a child that one of the women had borne (*Times-Picayune,* August 11, 1993).

In contrast, Louisiana courts gave children the legal right to divorce parents who abuse (*Times-Picayune,* April 29, 1993), severing the parents' legal claim. Such a decision probably makes sense given the apparent increase in child abuse cases. In South Carolina, a young mother, apparently unable to cope with the stresses of her life, strapped her two young children into the back seat of her car and released the parking brake, letting the car roll into a lake. The two children drowned.

In Antelope Valley, California, an isolated and economically depressed community, there was an unprecedented number of abuse and neglect cases. Authorities indicated that a number of parents had

* Boldfaced terms are also defined in the Glossary/Index.

been abusing alcohol and taking a cheap form of methamphetamine. This substance abuse was, they speculated, a response to their economic situation and a cause of the child abuse. Authorities argued that while Antelope Valley might be a particularly hellish place for children, rather than being unique it is a microcosm of national conditions (*Times-Picayune*, August 11, 1993).

Of course, parents are not the only ones whose behavior of late seems to depart considerably from social norms. Children, too, increasingly act violently toward themselves and others. In Georgia, for instance, seven sixth graders were sentenced to 48 hours of community service, put on probation, and forbidden to associate with one another. Their crime? They had plotted to kill their teacher by poisoning her and tripping her downstairs. They also had a handgun and a knife. The teacher's "crime"? She was too strict (*Times-Picayune*, July 3, 1993). Or consider the two children in Chicago, aged 10 and 11, who dropped a 5-year-old boy to his death because he would not steal candy for them (*Times-Picayune*, October 20, 1994).

As in the family, great change and seeming contradiction characterize government and politics. The midterm elections of 1994 produced the first Republican Congress since Harry Truman was in the White House—but in an election in which less than half of the electorate voted. Also odd are the political coalitions that are emerging in the current era. GATT (the General Agreement on Tariffs and Trade) evoked a unified protest from the very liberal Reverend Jesse Jackson, consumer activist Ralph Nader, and ultraconservative media commentator Patrick Buchanan (*Times-Picayune*, December 4, 1994).

Turmoil is not, of course, confined to the United States. Economic insecurity is so great internationally that the International Labor Organization calls it a "global crisis." One out of three workers in the world's labor force is either unemployed or earning insufficient wages to allow a decent standard of living (*Times-Picayune*, March 7, 1994). Persistent long-term joblessness affects both industrial countries like the United States and developing countries like Mexico.

Global economic hardship has a number of consequences. It can increase competition for resources, engender political conflicts, and foster immigration. Former Secretary of State Lawrence Eagleburger called the current period one of global revolution (*Los Angeles Times*, February 18, 1993). Unchecked, such instability can lead to massive economic depression and even war. In fact, the 1990s provide evidence of such. As the countries that once constituted the Soviet Union struggle to redefine themselves, hatred, ethnic conflict, and bloodshed have often filled the gap left by a once strong centralized government.

How can we make sense of these images of disorder? For the remainder of this chapter, in an attempt to explain the forces at work, I summarize both the type of society that we were and the changes that have occurred in that society. I'll touch briefly on the institutions covered in the rest of the book, and I end with a brief suggestion of the implications of these changes, a topic to which I return in the final chapter.

SOCIETY IN TRANSITION

Clearly the United States, along with most other countries in the world, is undergoing massive social change. Such change is related to a systematic transformation in the basis of social relations and social institutions (such as the economy, the government, the family). The argument of this book is that *contemporary American society is changing from a social world characterized by long-term, stable relationships to one characterized by short-term, temporary relationships*. This social change alters the **social contract** that underpins society. By *social contract* I mean the underlying shared social understandings that structure cooperation within a world of self-interested people possessing unequal resources. (See Blau, 1993, for a modern analysis of social contracts.)

This shift results from changes in the economy. Specifically, economic relationships are changing to emphasize flexibility rather than stability in the use of resources. In a larger context the relationships among countries are growing increasingly complex. The result is a kaleidoscope of economic and social changes. The images of disorder that I present reflect two very different things. On the one hand, they reflect the disorder that grows out of a society in transition. But, as this book will show, in some other instances they reflect a society that has *institutionalized* continual change. (**Institutionalization** refers to the process of making something permanent, either by law or because people take it for granted.)

Economic Transformations

All societies must ensure that their members produce and distribute enough food, goods, and services to allow the society to survive.

Heilbroner calls this **the economic problem**. Historically, the three major solutions to this problem have been traditional, command, and market economies. In traditional societies, such as feudal Europe, status and tradition determine production and distribution. In command societies, a centralized authority (such as the Communist party of the now defunct Soviet Union) makes decisions about production and distribution. In market societies, such as the United States, production and distribution emerge from unregulated market forces of supply and demand. (See Heilbroner, 1968, for an extensive discussion of the economic problem and these three strategies.) At the end of the twentieth century, many nations discovered that traditional and command economics were inadequate for meeting society's needs. To solve their economic problems, they turned in impressive numbers to the market system. The *Los Angeles Times* (February 18, 1993) reported that more than 65 countries were trying to change from command economies to market economies.

Historically, societies have pursued their solutions to the economic problem in *relative* isolation. For example, The People's Republic of China has experienced profound change in its economy since the communist takeover in 1949. Mao Zedong's Great Leap Forward forced industrialization on an agricultural economy. While these changes were catastrophic for the internal conditions of the Chinese people, they had little consequence for Americans. Now, however, the Chinese are experimenting with markets. Such experimentation makes China a vast new target for *American* business investment. Advanced communication technologies and the **globalization** of economic and political relationships mean that one country's solution to the economic problem has consequences for other countries. *Globalization* refers to the processes that create a global network of interdependent actors and activities that are unconnected to a specific place or national economy. For example, if countries that were once command societies develop market economies, there will be 65 more countries with which we will forge greater economic, political, and cultural ties. There will also be 65 more countries to which American workers may travel and from which foreign immigrants may come.

Countries' attempts to forge new forms of economic and political organization also create major disruptions in individuals' day-to-day lives. Many Russians who were once eager for freedom from centralized economic control now yearn for the days of economic security as prices skyrocket and wages drop. Under such conditions, extremists of various types can emerge (such as Vladimir Zhirinovsky, the ultranationalist Russian politician). Citizens of what was once East Germany are also experiencing deepened economic hardship. In response, many youths have turned to neo-Nazi organizations, whose members have harassed Turkish immigrants and other members of German society. Obviously, any solution to the economic problem has the potential to affect other social institutions.

Shifts in the Social Contract

This book concentrates on the United States, in which competitive, unregulated **markets** (sites of exchange) determine the demand for and supply of goods. In this type of system, people with one type of resource (say, money) want or *demand* another type of resource (say, fresh fruit) from people who can *supply* it. An exchange is made for some mutually acceptable price. This type of system is called *unregulated* because neither tradition nor some centralized authority determines what kind of goods or services will be supplied or demanded. Nor does either tradition or a centralized authority determine the price for the service or good. This system is called *competitive* for the same reasons. In the absence of traditional authority or centralized state command, only lack of resources, opportunity, or will prevents multiple economic actors from participating in the exchange relationship.

What makes those with resources respond to *needs* within a society? What forces create cooperation, given scarce resources and individual self-interest? Market societies, such as the United States, work, in part, because of *explicit and implicit social contracts* underlying exchanges. We sometimes develop explicit, or overt, contracts that create boundaries around the supply and demand of goods and set the price for the exchange. An example of such a contract would be a written document that specifies that over the coming year one person will pay another person x dollars for x bushels of fruit. Such a contract protects both parties and allows long-term planning. The seller knows she will receive a certain amount of money that will allow further development of her orchard. The buyer knows that he will have enough fruit for his pies. The implicit contract (mutually understood but unspecified) could be, for example, that the buyer gets only ripe and undiseased fruit.

In market societies, many types of institutions often use explicit or implicit contracts that mirror those of the market. For instance, in American society, the explicit contract in a marriage is the marriage license and, often, the religious vows. The implicit contract may be something like, "If you are a supportive and sharing spouse, I will give up my career in favor of yours."

Another example of a social contract is the historically implicit contract between children and their parents. In twentieth-century Western society, childhood is often a protracted period in which children are nurtured, socialized, and financially supported by their parents. Implicit in this parental nurturing is conservation of resources so that these resources will be available for the children's future. Obviously, the extent of the support depends on the resources available to parents. Nonetheless, the **norm** (implicit rule of behavior) is that parents will care for their children. In exchange for this extended caretaking and the conservation of social, economic, and environmental resources on the part of parents, children would care for their parents when the parents could no longer care for themselves. Like the fair exchange that occurs in the market, the implicit contract across generations also has assumed a similarly fair exchange (see Bengston and Achenbaum, *The Changing Contract Across Generations,* 1993).

A central claim of this book is that the implicit social contracts underlying much of social life are breaking down as the explicit contracts shift. While these processes are global, this book will focus on the United States' efforts to restructure many components of social life. In the process, this book demonstrates the utility of using a sociological lens through which to view these changes. Since sociology provides a way to link global social change to the changing conditions that affect individuals, it is uniquely equipped to explain these disparate changes. In addition, rather than focusing on only one aspect of society (such as its economics, politics, or culture), this book demonstrates the interconnections between large-scale social change in major institutions (the economy, workplace, family, etc.) and the day-to-day conditions in which individuals must live their lives.

THE AMERICAN DREAM

For over 200 years, a central part of American culture has been the belief in the American Dream. When people talk about the American Dream, they are talking about a belief in a society characterized by political and religious freedom in which anyone, regardless of family background, ethnicity, or race, can "make it." By *making it,* we mean that people can—by virtue of education, hard work, luck, and motivation—have a good job, a home, a happy family, and leisure time. Moreover, they can have these in a social climate free from oppression.

This dream pulled my grandparents from Eastern Europe and my husband's grandparents from Scotland and Italy. It drew others from Ireland, England, China, and elsewhere throughout the world. The children and grandchildren of forced immigrants, such as African-Americans and European indentured servants, whose immigration was neither voluntary nor enriching, came to share this dream as well. Most of these immigrants began in this country with little education, money, or other resources. Yet many in each generation experienced upward mobility. Despite humble beginnings, the children and grandchildren of many immigrant families became successful homeowners. The dream became reality.

This dream continues to motivate people from all over the world. Waves of immigrants continue to come to the United States seeking the same mobility and opportunity that earlier generations sought. Achieving these goals, however, has grown increasingly difficult since the paths to upward mobility have altered.

ACCORD IN THE POST–WORLD WAR II ERA

By the beginning of the twentieth century, America was on its way to becoming one of the richest, most successful countries in the world. During the two and a half decades following World War II, America was, in many ways, at its zenith. No country appeared richer, more powerful, more sure of itself. The American Dream seemed a reality for unprecedented numbers of Americans. For both blue-collar industrial workers (such as assembly line workers in automobile or electronics plants) and white-collar businessmen (such as managers at Dow Chemical or Metropolitan Life), upward mobility, comfort, and security appeared to be the norm. Secure workers married, had children, and bought houses. Those who were excluded from this expanding middle class, particularly African-Americans, placed demands on the government for civil rights and equal opportunities. The government responded with a variety of social programs. American culture also reflected the optimism of this period of expansion and growth.

Economic Growth and Workplace Security

Security and affluence grew out of a period of international economic supremacy. After World War II, Europe and Japan were both economically devastated. The United States, through the Marshall Plan (formally the European Recovery Plan), put millions of dollars into helping rebuild Europe and Japan. We loaned money under conditions that favored United States' economic expansion. There was enormous demand throughout Europe and Japan both for aid in rebuilding their basic infrastructures—roads, building, factories—and for investment in those factories. American government, through loans, business, and direct investment, addressed that demand and made a fortune in so doing. In addition to favorable loan terms, interest rates, and access, the United States ensured long-term military and economic compliance throughout this period. The United States government also supported governments that would be friendly to American political (noncommunist) and economic (free market, cheap labor) concerns.

During this period, manufacturing, construction, and transportation industries in the United States employed an ever-increasing number of Americans. Importantly, these and similar industries required little education of their workers; at most they required a high school diploma. Although these jobs were physically demanding, and actual work conditions were often loud, dirty, and dangerous, they paid well and provided workers with long-term stability. The unions representing most workers in these industries negotiated employment contracts that often protected workers' jobs even during business slowdowns. Unionized jobs also provided workers with seniority systems (which for many workers allowed a certain amount of upward mobility within the job) and expanded job benefits, including health insurance, retirement, and disability. To prevent union growth in their own firms, nonunion employers often offered similar contracts to their own workers.

Economic growth did not just result in the proliferation of well-paying blue-collar jobs; it also expanded the availability of white-collar jobs. As businesses grew, offices grew, and so did the white-collar work force. Large organizations needed more managers to manage the activities in different departments. Those managers needed staffs of co-managers, accountants, clerical workers, and others. Like blue-collar workers, many of these workers also worked in environments that rewarded not only hard work but also stable, long-term employment. Thus, college graduates in the 1950s and 1960s had little trouble stepping into jobs that promised long-term security and the ability to buy a house, a car, and the other amenities coming off American assembly lines. And, as has historically been the case, as people's lives improved, so did their ability to support families.

Of course, it is important to remember that all were not equally privileged in this period of affluence. Deep poverty still existed in rural areas (Appalachia being one of the poorest), and African-Americans were still far less privileged than white Americans. Figure 1.1 shows the distribution of families by income level and race in 1955 and 1967. These data show, for example, that nonwhite families were represented at much higher levels in the lowest income brackets than were white families (e.g., 19% versus 6.6% in 1955 and 4.9% versus 1.8% in 1967).

Still, during the 1960s, civil rights legislation (e.g., the Equal Pay Act of 1963 and Title VII of the Civil Rights Act of 1964, which prevented employment discrimination based on race) provided a very real first step in eliminating structured barriers to opportunity for black Americans. One study of the movement of black women into the professions argued that this period was one in which the combination of economic expansion and civil rights legislation "contributed to the creation of a new black middle class and a new group of black professionals within it" (Sokoloff, 1992, p. 2). So, although black Americans were far behind white Americans in the quest for the American Dream, this was an era in which attaining it, and overcoming the past, seemed possible.

Marriage, Family, and a House in the Suburbs

The expansion of the economy provided a certain lifestyle to thousands of American workers. My father-in-law left the army after World War II with a high school degree and got a job with the telephone company. He moved to Santa Barbara, California, and was able to buy a house for $12,000. That house today would cost at least 10 times as much, something a worker with only a high school education is unlikely to have. However, the postwar economy provided him (as it did so many Americans) with a welter of opportunities, such as to marry and raise a family in economic comfort.

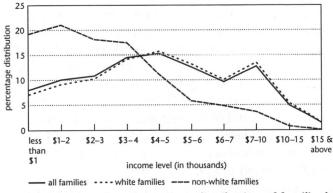

Figure 1.1a. Money income—Percentage distribution of families by income level and race, 1955

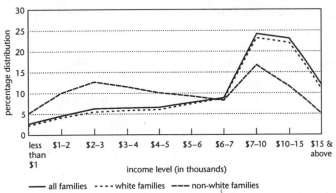

Figure 1.1b. Money income—Percentage distribution of families by income level and race, 1967

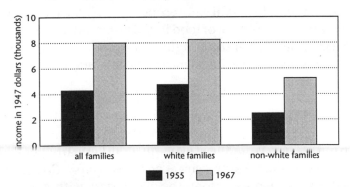

Figure 1.1c. Money income—Median income of families by race, 1955 and 1967

Adapted from *Statistical Abstract of the United States: 1969* (Table 473, p. 322), 1969, Washington, D.C.: U.S. Bureau of the Census.

After World War II, marriage and birth rates soared. The marriage rate reached a peak of 16.4 marriages per thousand Americans; during the 1960s it dropped to around 10–11 per thousand. From 1946–1964 (the baby boom years), women had on average 3.7 children, an extremely high fertility rate; by the mid-1970s the fertility rate fell to below 2.1 children per woman. Moreover, during the 1950s half of all women who married did so in their teens and had children within 15 months of their marriage (Ahlburg and De Vita, 1992).

Many women who had filled in for absent male workers during World War II returned home, and men filled the jobs in their stead. Those jobs, however, paid well enough to allow a single income to provide for a family. Thus, although later generations of white, middle-class women would fight for the right for equal employment, postwar affluence freed many working-class women from participating in the paid labor force. The breadwinner–homemaker model of families that had dominated the middle class was now a possibility for large portions of the working class as well. In 1940, 70% of families were male breadwinner–female homemaker families. For the next 25 years, more than half of all families conformed to this norm.

The dominance of the breadwinner–homemaker model was supported by clearly delineated gender roles. When I graduated from high school in 1973, I was given a copy of *McCall's Cookbook* that had been published in 1963. It began with the following:

> It is true that preparing three meals a day remains the homemaker's biggest chore, and one she strives to accomplish with variety, originality, skill and economy. . . . Social relations radiate from the service of food in the home. So does the most fundamental kind of social status. Thus, the woman who can cook well and serve food graciously is a successful homemaker. (p. 4)

On the next page, the book went on to warn, "You will undoubtedly shed some tears of frustration along the way; but once you achieve your first perfect cake and serve your first dinner party perfectly, you will be a new woman, ready to meet any new recipe" (McCall's, 1963, p. 4). The section on outdoor cooking began with the following words: "We dedicate these recipes to the Great American Mister, who stands, cap on head, fork in hand . . ." (McCall's, 1963, p. 729). Clearly, men should stay out of the kitchen, and real women don't build fires; their greatest challenges are baking a successful cake and throwing a dinner party, and their most difficult chore is preparing *three meals a day*. A quick perusal through some other cookbooks (like the classic *Joy of Cooking*) sends similar messages about gender role expectations. While concern with dinner parties and soufflés was a focus of the middle and upper class, it was one the popular media presented as universal and one to which working-class women could aspire.

Note that throughout this book I often refer to the *working, middle,* and *upper classes*. I use these terms in a fairly loose sense as used by the German sociologist Max Weber. Weber viewed people with similar life chances and economic conditions—such as property ownership, income, education, and skill—as sharing class positions. Thus, here we can loosely think of the upper class as those who inherited their position or who possess great wealth (let's say in the top 5% of the income distribution). The middle class comprises, by and large, college-educated, professional, technical, and managerial workers (Ehrenreich, 1989). The working class is the traditional blue-collar worker. The poor are those who fall below the official poverty line (see chapters 2, 4, 5). This class schema is a heuristic device; there is considerable research that attempts to develop more precise class models (cf. Wright, 1985, 1989). (A *heuristic device* is a teaching strategy that promotes understanding by generating discussion.)

Activist Government

Just as economies and families grew and flourished in a climate of affluence, so too did government. The most notable characteristics of the U.S. government during the two and a half decades following the end of World War II were its increased size and involvement in "solving" economic and social problems. During this period, the government developed a set of policies that were explicitly geared toward improving the economic well-being of the disadvantaged.

Researchers writing about the government during this era describe President Kennedy's "discovery" of the continued existence of the poor when he read Michael Harrington's *The Other America* (1962). The fact is that the country was so affluent and successful during this period that the poor were relatively invisible, and poverty seemed a surprising holdover from an earlier period. It became a problem for government to solve. The idea that the social problem of poverty *could* be solved reflected the optimism that characterized this period. For example, Kennedy's Peace Corps sought to bring modern education, technology, and progress to impoverished third world countries. Similarly, VISTA (Volunteers in Service of America) attempted to bring many of the same things to the newly discovered inner-city poor. The most ambitious and far reaching of these efforts was President Lyndon Johnson's "War on Poverty."

The **ideology**, or belief system, that characterized all these government programs was that America was strong and rich and that there was no problem that we could not solve. While it is certainly true that this period was marked by considerable conflict, including an undeclared war (Vietnam) and an upsurge in social movement, the nature of the conflict reflected this optimism. For example, the various movements for civil rights and equality all appealed to the government for redress of perceived grievances. The implication of such organized social protest was that the government was able and potentially willing to respond to demands. Why launch a March on Washington, as Martin Luther King and civil rights activists did, unless there was a belief that Washington had the will and resources to meet demands? Why mobilize voters unless people believed that voting can bring about social change?

Thus the politics of the era, despite their sometimes conflicted appearance, reflect a public perception that the government was a source of redress. In addition, there was a clear sense that there were resources to redistribute. While there was considerable debate about the best way to reach certain goals or solve certain problems, rarely was there a claim that these goals were unattainable or the problems unsolvable. There was also a strong consensus within the government that an activist agenda could solve problems.

This commitment to government intervention had an international as well as a national component. With Europe and Japan devastated by World War II, America had emerged as the world's economic and political leader. Our international role was to continue to "keep the world safe for democracy" and for American economic activity. Consequently, another prong of government activity was a deepening commitment to halting the spread of communism. We tried to do this through military intervention (in Korea and Vietnam), propaganda (Radio Free Europe), and economic aid (AID, the Agency for International Development). While America may have been interventionist, there was a sense at home and abroad that we had a right to that stance.

Culture and Counterculture

Nostalgia about the 1950s and 1960s focuses on the emergence of beatniks, hippies, and the **counterculture** (a culture with meanings, norms, and practices that run *counter* to the dominant culture). The most visible counterculture of the 1950s was the Beat Generation, and that of the 1960s was the hippies. Both countercultures challenged the legitimacy of the dominant culture from a self-embraced *outsider* **status**, or social position. Ironically, the drama of the 1960s counterculture in particular—and its ability to capture the imagination of so many people—derived from the stability of the dominant culture it challenged.

The dominant culture was still tied to what Alan Wolfe calls a Yankee consciousness inherited from Great Britain (Wolfe, 1991). That Yankee consciousness was embedded in the American Dream. It emphasized hard work, inner-directedness, thrift, honesty, and community. It reflected the dominance of Protestantism in the culture. There was a mainstream, white, Christian culture with a vision of right and wrong, good and evil, American and un-American.

During this era, television emerged as an increasingly important cultural force. Just as it brought entertainment into people's homes, it provided a new medium for the counterculture to exploit. During the beatnik period, television was in its early days, so the Beat Generation never became very visible or influential in the dominant culture. In contrast, in the 1960s, television and other mass media disseminated the images, music, and slogans of the hippie counterculture and in many cases took them over. The popular television show "Laugh-In," for example, appealed to a youthful audience and used the imagery of flower power, marijuana smoking, and other counterculture icons to capture a new audience (not to mention to sell the products of the advertisers during that time slot). Moreover, the 1960s counterculture was far more visible than earlier, similar movements because, as a result of the baby boom, there were so many more individuals involved.

Although the counterculture mocked and challenged the dominant culture, it still reflected the optimism and expansion of the era. The 1960s youth movement in particular was filled with the imagery of joy. To some extent the character of this movement was a response to the earlier anxiety expressed by icons such as the movie actor James Dean and caused by the nuclear threat. Brightly colored, tie-dyed clothing, rock and roll, and flower power became cultural symbols that were indicative of apparently joyous exploration. Free love, sit-ins, communes, and hitchhiking all expressed an openness and optimism about one's fellow (under-30-year-old) beings and possible connections among them.

END OF A CENTURY, END OF AN ERA

While not everyone's experience of life in America during the years 1947–1970 was upbeat, this period was generally one of economic growth, stable work, a liberal and interventionist state, and an increasingly exploratory culture. Once the stability and growth of the economy faltered, however, so too did stability and growth in other institutions. Clearly, the way social life was organized in the period after World War II is extremely different from the way social life is organized at the end of the twentieth century. The next sections provide an overview of how the major social institutions of economy, workplace, family, government, and culture appear to have changed or to be changing.

Insecurity in the Economy and the Workplace

For a variety of reasons that subsequent chapters discuss in detail, the growth of the American economy slowed in the early 1970s. Increased international economic competition and failure to upgrade existing production techniques, among other factors, led to declining business success. As a result, employers experimented with a variety of strategies to maintain their prior economic dominance. All their efforts centered on decreasing the expenses involved in production and finding ways to compete more effectively. The less it costs to produce goods, the more profit businesses can make. Paying workers less, decreasing the number of workers hired, replacing workers with computers, robots, and automated assembly lines, moving to regions of the country and world where production was cheaper—all were ways in which American businesses tried to recoup declining profits.

Moreover, unlike in the decades following World War II, during the 1970s and 1980s other nations were competing successfully with the United States. Whereas American cars, for instance, used to dominate the automobile market, Japanese and German cars now outsold American cars. The increased economic strength of business in other countries also created more economic activity at a *global* level.

The efforts on the part of American business to succeed in the face of newly emerging international economic competitors have changed the national economy and workplace in a number of ways.

- Whereas our economic base previously came from manufacturing (e.g., cars, steel, electronics), it now comes increasingly from services (e.g., education, medical and financial services). This shift in the industrial base of the economy has, like other changes, had enormous consequences for workers and the workplace. Many service-sector jobs (such as restaurant and cleaning services) pay far less than manufacturing jobs. Those that pay well require *at least* a college education. Thus, this change results in fewer opportunities for the non-college-educated.
- Within the workplace, whether goods or service based, production is increasingly based on brainpower and technology rather than muscle power. Computers have been introduced in workplaces as diverse as automobile plants and therapists' offices. Whether on the assembly line or at the desk, more and more workers must have some level of computer literacy. Many workers are simply displaced by robots or automation.
- Fewer and fewer workers are in jobs in which there is the possibility for continuous movement up a career ladder in a single firm. Like the IBM workers mentioned earlier, more and more workers are finding that jobs they thought they would have for a lifetime, or at least decades, are now part-time and temporary. In their efforts to create greater flexibility in the use of workers, technology, and resources, employers are replacing full-time jobs with temporary or part-time jobs, regardless of the skill or education associated with the occupation. Part-time workers are much cheaper since they receive not only lower wages but also few nonwage benefits such as health and disability insurance, paid vacations, and so forth.
- In manufacturing, roughly 75–80% of the workers used to be unionized (other industry groups such as trucking, mining, and construction had almost as many). Unions provide workers with high wages, benefits, and job security, and they provide employers with a well-disciplined work force. However, unions also create limitations for employers; they do not allow employers to fire workers when business conditions decline, for example. Thus, to increase the flexibility of the work force, employers have sought

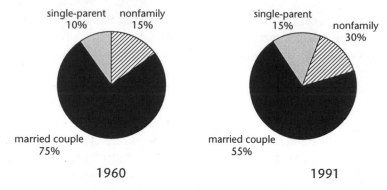

Figure 1.2.   Composition of Households, 1960 and 1991.

From "New Realities of the American Family," by Dennis A. Ahlburg and Carol J. De Vita, 1992, *Population Bulletin, 47*(2), p. 5.

to rid their workplaces of unions, and so fewer and fewer workers have the economic and job stability that unions provide.

In summary, most of the changes in the economy and the workplace have resulted in far more insecurity and instability for workers. In addition, the paths to upward mobility have changed and have become unclear, and so many workers find themselves unsure of their future.

Changing Family Structures and Roles

In addition to economic and political changes, major changes have occurred in another major institution—the family. The nuclear, breadwinner–homemaker family in which husband and wife raise their own biological offspring—once the dominant family form—is now a minority. In 1960, 75% of U.S. households were formed by married couples; 10% were single parents; 15% were nonfamily (singles, roommates, etc.). Based on current trends, the expectations are that by the year 2000, married couples will compose only 55% of U.S. households (see Figure 1.2). More and more of those will be childless. Single-parent households will make up 14% of households, and 31% will be nonfamily. As spectacular in magnitude as these changes are, they only touch on some of the other transitions affecting families. From 1970 to 1990 the marriage rate fell 30%, and the divorce rate increased 40%; and whereas in 1970 only 10% of all births were to unmarried mothers, by 1990 almost a quarter of all births were to single mothers (Ahlburg and De Vita, 1992).

And yet even more changes characterize the family at the close of this century. The increased divorce rate means that many families are now *blended*. That is, families are increasingly composed of biological parents, stepparents, children from multiple marriages, and so on. Similarly, more and more people in their 20s, instead of forming their own marriages and households, are "returning to the nest" (moving home to live with parents).

Accompanying these changes are cultural and political struggles over the meaning, obligations, and limits of families and gender roles. In 1991, only 20% of households were still breadwinner–homemaker households, primarily because more than half of all women are currently in the labor force. In 1960, only 38% were working outside the home. Similarly, almost 60% of mothers with children under six are currently in the labor force. The increased participation of women in the labor force is caused by and causes profound changes in the social constructions of gender—that is, what it *means* to be a man or woman in contemporary society. Struggles over gay rights, abortion, surrogate parenthood, birth control, and family values are all born out of confusion about the family as a social institution.

The changes in family structure and roles often lead to considerable confusion about parenting. Who will raise the children when both parents work? What do children learn about their future roles in life in fatherless families? Can same-sex, homosexual parents effectively raise a heterosexual child? Who has rights over a fetus? The biological mother? The government? The surrogate mother? Who has custody of an adopted child when the biological parents change their minds? Never before have the obligations and rights of parenthood been so confusing.

Distracted Government

As the question of responsibility has become more important in the context of the family, the same thing has happened in the context of government. Whereas in post–World War II years the government was actively involved in solving problems of poverty, inadequate housing, and job and business regulation, in more recent decades it has withdrawn substantially from these commitments. Additionally, with the loss of the Vietnam War and the end of the cold war in the early 1990s, the American government has played an uncertain and vacillating role in international conflicts.

This retrenchment and withdrawal stem from several factors. One is a breakdown of the political coalitions that characterized the earlier period. During that era, the Democratic party *was* the party of the ethnic working class, blacks, and white liberals. The Republican party represented the interests of upper-class white Anglo-Americans. Moreover, the political interests of these two groups tended to coalesce neatly into a "package" of beliefs and preferences. If one knew that a voter was an African-American woman living in New York, one could assume she would vote for a Democrat. If a voter was a wealthy, white, midwestern businessman, one could guess that he would vote Republican.

Now, however, both the Republican and Democratic parties are fragmented by issues of ethnic diversity, gender, sexuality, and religion. Liberal Republicans vote with liberal Democrats; Southern Democrats vote with Republicans. The split is more, however, than a split between liberal and conservative; many argue that the two major parties are so deeply fragmented that they are as divided among themselves as between themselves.

New fragmentations have affected politics as well. Instead of politics being about voting, lobbying, or even organized social protest, it now involves street theater, "zaps," and coalitions based on a variety of identities. One's gender or views about the environment may have become as important in identifying political behavior as one's class used to be.

Additionally, neither party seems to represent the source of solutions to social problems. Whereas once people mobilized to make demands on the government, now there seems to be little activity along these lines. Instead, social protest often seems to take the form of anarchic expressions of violence in an increasingly ugly "war of all against all" (Hobbes, *Leviathan,* 1651/1962) in the streets of the nation's cities.

A second factor contributing to the withdrawal of the government from problem solving at home and intervention abroad is the reduction in resources available to the government to finance solutions. A combination of economic and demographic changes (more elderly and more young people, fewer people at high-paying jobs) has decreased the tax base. Moreover, the increasing national debt absorbs any economic surplus that could be used to finance social programs.

Adding to these is a third factor, the decreased ability of the American government to influence events in other countries. As our global economic competitors grow more successful, they seem less willing to cooperate with and acquiesce in American intervention and political initiatives. Similarly, as American corporations increasingly invest overseas, the American government is less and less able to tax and regulate these corporations. Finally, the lessons of Vietnam make the government reluctant to intervene in situations in which the strategy, commitment, and outcome of intervention are unclear.

The American government is further distracted by tribalistic, ethnic conflicts that have emerged around the world since the end of the cold war. Ironically, the cold war provided considerable stability in international relations. Countries lined up on either side of the line (East Germany on one side, West Germany on the other, for instance), and most international situations were understood in cold war terms. With the end of the cold war, instead of peace throughout Europe and the end to nuclear tension, there seems, in fact, to be greater anxiety, less security, and more fragmentation. In the absence of Soviet protection, for example, countries such as Pakistan and North Korea seek to increase their nuclear weaponry, and in so doing they decrease international stability. The difficulties of negotiating in this fragmented international arena are tremendous. Analysts predict an increasing number of international hotspots, all pulling the United States in multiple directions. Haiti, North Korea, Somalia, Rwanda, Iran, and Bosnia are all countries in which conflicts could potentially entangle United States troops. More than at any other time in history, the American government seems distracted by multiple demands and less sure that it can respond coherently and successfully.

Cultural Confusion

Periods of social change and transformation shake people from their cultural moorings. How we define who we are, what we believe in, what is good and evil, right and wrong—these all become much more complex when everything about our lives is unclear. The late twentieth century is clearly characterized by such confusion.

Contrary to the earlier post–World War II period, the culture of the current era cannot be easily divided into a dominant culture and counterculture. The globalization of the economy—with the mass of images, ideas, beliefs, styles, and cuisines, disseminated throughout the world by the power of television and the swell of immigration—

has created new influences in United States culture. The emergence and proliferation of computers in workplaces has also changed the culture. People are exposed to far more information than they ever have been in the past. This combination of factors has created both new sources of connection and new sources of fragmentation within the culture. Though the dominant culture is contested, it is not contested by a cohesive counterculture. Rather, various groups such as women and minorities are claiming what they see as their rightful place in a culture that has excluded them. There is little sense of a coherent youth culture that was so important to the earlier period. The visible youth counterculture takes a number of desultory forms. On the one hand, there is the inner-city culture of gangster violence and on the other, there are the black-garbed, body-pierced, disaffected youth who embrace images of suicide and despair in their music. Neither group is organized, celebratory, or hopeful.

For some, a return to religion and traditional values that include rigid gender roles, fundamentalist beliefs, and conformity to scripture provides a source of comfort. In the babble of multiple voices, the single voice of an authoritarian church provides clarity. For many others, however, the challenge lies in the weaving together of the multiple voices into a single, richly textured chorus.

The contemporary culture is also characterized by a new mix of real and unreal images, places, and experiences that television and computer technology create. Both technologies allow a greater number of experiences, ideas, and images to reach a greater number of people, yet there is a curious character to these images and experiences. For instance, one of the most popular and pervasive types of television show is the "real-time" police drama. Shows such as "911" and "COPS" offer the viewer the opportunity to witness rescues and drug busts as they are actually "going down." Through video camera footage, dramatizations, and carefully scripted reenactment, viewers can experience "faux" real-time excitement.

The irony of this type of show was highlighted by the weirdly uneventful police chase of O. J. Simpson as he drove down the Los Angeles freeways after being charged with his wife's murder. As a *New York Times* (June 19, 1994) editorial pointed out, Americans found themselves riveted to the television, watching a real, not dramatized event. I was reminded of a line from the futuristic miniseries "Wild Palms." Part of the plot concerned the marketing of a combination of virtual reality television along with a drug that would allow viewers to experience the unreal as immediate or real. "Is it real or is it mimicon?" a character asked, mimicking the old advertisement for Memorex tape (Ella Fitzgerald's singing breaks a crystal glass as the announcer asks, "Is it real or is it Memorex?") As I watched America watch Simpson, I wondered, is it real or is it . . . ?

A similar confusion of reality and image occurred as Virginians protested the Disney corporation's planned "American theme park" five miles from Manassas, a Civil War battlefield. Protesters complained about the degradation of the environment and historical neighborhoods, as well as the artificiality of the theme park itself. The company's plans would allow visitors to witness a Revolutionary War battle, a World War II battlefield, and a slave auction. While the protesters were successful at keeping the Disney corporation from building the theme park in that location, Disney continues to search for an appropriate locale in Virginia. Yet, how real can such representations be? To what extent will students view these images of history as real? To what extent will they visit theme parks instead of visiting the actual sites? How will historical experiences be sanitized for the spending tourist public? The scripted violence and "realities" of television have arguably made imitation of life more palatable than reality to the American public.

IMPLICATIONS

This chapter has provided an overview of the changes that have characterized social institutions in the twentieth century. Chapters 2 through 6 take up each institution in turn. Beginning with the economy, I then turn to the workplace and schools, the family, government, and culture. Throughout the book, I show how the changes in one institution are related to changes in the others. Specifically, I focus on how the changing solution to the economic problem and the changing contractual basis of employment relations (particularly the shift from long-term to short-term) have affected other institutions.

Following a long sociological tradition, this book places the current era of change into a historical context. Each chapter (with the exception of chapter 6) discusses the transition of an institution from the early twentieth century (and sometimes the late nineteenth) to the present. As earlier theorists identified the consequences of social changes that grew out of the shift from a traditional agricultural society to a modern industrial society, this book seeks to accomplish a similar task. The emergence of a flexible global economy, characterized by high levels of service production and technology, represents a new way of solving the economic problem.

I began this chapter writing about the American Dream. The goal has not been to demonstrate the death of that dream but rather to suggest that the path to its realization has changed. C. Wright Mills (1959) tells us that to really understand our own experiences, we must develop a sociological imagination that allows us to see our own experience in a historical and social context. It is easy to see our own day-to-day experiences and to explain them in individual terms; it is much harder to view our lives in terms of the movement of societies and economies. Yet failure to do so means that we are caught in our own limited visions and cannot avail ourselves of the opportunities that social change provides.

FROM INDUSTRIAL ECONOMY
TO FLEXIBLE ECONOMY

When I graduated from high school in the Washington, D.C., area in 1972, I went to college, but my old boyfriend Ricky didn't. He looked for a good, unionized factory job. He knew he could make good money and maybe buy a little house in the same neighborhood his parents and sister Sara lived in. His sister didn't go to college, either. She had a job as a typist in a big office building outside the Beltway, in the Maryland suburbs. At the same time, my best friend's father was some sort of researcher. He worked in a big firm located in nearby Bethesda, Maryland, in which he had started out at the bottom and worked his way into one of the nice offices with huge windows. The occupants of those offices had expense accounts, three-martini lunches, and wives at home raising kids like us in well-heeled suburbs.

Now, the factory is gone, and Ricky is trying to figure out how he can keep paying his mortgage on one third of his old salary. The factory moved to Mexico and now employs young Mexican women. The home office is still in Bethesda, Maryland, but it employs only half the number of men it did 20 years ago. Most of the jobs have been taken over by computers or are done on a consulting basis. The only job Ricky could find was as a security guard for one of the new hotels that have opened up in the Washington, D.C., area.

The typewriter Sara used is also gone. When her office switched to computers, Sara had to learn how to use the new system. She thought that when she did, perhaps she could move into a better paying job, but that didn't happen. She still spends all her time typing, but now, instead of getting together with the other "girls in the pool" between typing letters, she sits alone all day in an office with a computer. During her breaks she sometimes logs onto a computer bulletin board on the Internet. There, she pretends that she is a famous artist with an international reputation. Nobody knows differently; nobody will ever meet the face behind the computer identity.

My best friend's father doesn't work in Bethesda anymore, either. His office moved to Japan, and he travels back and forth now doing consulting work. He has also learned how to speak Japanese, German, and a little bit of Thai. He travels a lot and misses his family.

Neither Ricky nor his sister votes; they don't see what difference it makes. Sara is divorced and raising two children on her own. She isn't sure how to answer any of the questions her children ask; so they've stopped asking the questions. Ricky drinks too much and worries about losing his house; he blames his problems on welfare cheats and homosexuals. Neither brother nor sister really understands why nothing worked out the way they thought it would, the way it did for their parents.

Their difficulty comes in seeing how large-scale social changes are affecting their day-to-day lives; but that's what is happening. From 1972, when they graduated from high school, to 1994 the **economy**—that is, the set of institutions and relationships that produces and distributes goods and services—has changed dramatically.

Whereas work once occurred in farms and factories, it now occurs in offices and cyberspace, that nonexistent place in which computers communicate. The change from one set of places to the other as primary sites of economic activity reflects a major change in the economy. When the economy changes, so too do all other parts of society. Not only does the way we work change, but so too do family structures, politics, popular culture, and belief systems. Thus, to understand the other changes in our day-to-day lives, in this chapter we examine the change from an industrial to a global, flexible economy.

Today's large-scale economic changes are as dramatic in their social importance as those caused by the Industrial Revolution, which sent people from farms to factories. Today, economic activity that was once local is now global. Production that was once largely industrial is now characterized by something quite different that has not yet been completely defined. Increasingly, advanced capitalist economies (like the United States) produce services as much if not more than they produce things—they are **postindustrial**. These processes, and the new structures they are creating, are as likely to change the way people live as did the changes that transformed the United States from a lush country of "amber waves of grain" to a hustling, bustling industrial giant.

This new stage of capitalism might be called **flexible capitalism** (as opposed to industrial capitalism). It is characterized by rapid change rather than long-term stability. This type of change affects what the economy produces, how it produces, where it produces, and who is involved in the production. Not surprisingly, as the economy's products and methods of production change, so too do the relationships among economic actors (workers, employers, business owners, and consumers).

To really understand these changes and how they will affect other arenas of social life, one needs to understand the system we had. The story begins with the change in labor–capital relations that occurred after World War II and the benefits of that change. Then it turns to the decline in the system that produced those benefits. It ends with an introduction to the type of economy that is emerging.

THE LABOR–CAPITAL ACCORD

The United States achieved its superior position in the world economy on the basis of mass production manufacturing (Armstrong, Glyn, and Harrison, 1991; Craypo and Nissen, 1993). By the immediate post–World War II era (World War II lasted from 1939 to 1945), U.S. industry had figured out how to make the most for the least and how to distribute it widely. The efficiency of mass production technology allowed unprecedented production of goods such as cars, washing machines, and television sets at relatively low cost, thereby making them accessible to most people in society. Although we had achieved a certain level of manufacturing greatness before World War II, it was after World War II that our economy really took off.

A key element of our post–World War II success was a new approach to worker–employer relations that lasted from roughly 1945 to 1970. One can call this approach the **labor–capital accord** (Bowles and Gintis, 1982) or, simply, **the Accord**. The Accord stage was characterized by a basic understanding between employers and workers, a **social contract** that provided workers with reasonably secure and well-paid jobs and provided employers with reasonably stable and productive workers.

Unions and Big Business

During the latter part of the nineteenth century and the early part of the twentieth century, workers labored under brutal conditions. They worked 14-hour days but received minuscule pay, no safety provisions, and no protection against illness, injury, unemployment, or other things that today we take for granted. Characteristic industries, such as steel and automobile production, exposed workers to high levels of noise, dirt, and, more important, danger.

Workers had very little recourse in the face of such conditions until unions began to protect the workers' pay and to improve the quality of their working lives. Prior to the 1930s, however, workers who attempted to form unions were subject to brutal oppression, frequently punctuated by violence that took not only their lives but those of their families as well. John Sayles, in the movie *Matewan,* dramatized the various methods, including murder, spying, and instigation of ethnic conflict, that employers used to prevent the organization of mine workers in 1920 in West Virginia. Strikers could be jailed, union organizers deported, and rank-and-file workers fired without any recourse whatsoever. These difficult battles are well documented by labor historians (i.e., Boyer and Morais, 1955).

Historically, strikes have been the single most important means by which workers could flex their collective muscles. The ability to withhold labor power and halt production is one of the only ways workers can make demands on employers. During the pre-Accord period (pre–World War II), strikes were frequently expressions of outrage and protest; they were often long-drawn-out battles that were limited only by the brute strength of employers or the sheer number and solidarity of participating workers (Rubin, Griffin, and Wallace, 1983; Rubin, 1986a).

Large-scale industries and assembly line technology (as in the auto industry) gave workers a less violent way of protesting—the sit-down strike. In response to some grievance (such as the employer deciding to speed up the assembly line, cut wages, lengthen the work day, or refuse to recognize the union), workers simply sat down *in the plant.* Since assembly line technology connects different parts of the production process, if a small group of workers in one part of the plant stopped working, they could stop the process in other parts of the plant. Thus, rather than walking out of a workplace and picketing, workers on assembly lines were able to mobilize strikes rapidly and with very little prior organization. Instead of leaving, and thus leaving their jobs open to replacement workers, workers stayed in the plant. In some cases—particularly the historically important industrial union organizing strike in Flint, Michigan, in 1937—the wives and children of workers surrounded the plant to prevent police or national guardsmen from going in and forcefully removing the striking workers. They were attacked by police during the Flint strike, an incident documented in the movie *With Babies and Banners.*

This sort of strike activity helped workers win the battles of the 1930s. To end the disruptive effect of these successful strikes and to ensure a relatively disciplined labor force, managers and employers agreed to recognize unions as the representatives of workers' interests (Rubin, Griffin, and Wallace, 1983; Rubin, 1986a).

All employers, however, were not eager to empower unions; in fact, employers' resistance to unions in the United States has always been greater than that of employers in other countries such as Sweden and Western European capitalist democracies. As a result, the particular form of the Accord in this country included severe limitations on union power. The laws that were passed and the specific organizations that were formed constitute the formal aspect of the Accord. What is most important for our purposes, however, are the ways in which the Accord rearranged relations between the major actors in the economy, big labor and big capital (Bowles and Gintes, 1982; Wallace, Rubin, and Smith, 1988; McCammon, 1990).

Collective Bargaining In exchange for industrial peace, owners, employers, and managers consented to unions and to negotiations (instead of intimidation), which allowed most workers to obtain stable and relatively high wages in exchange for steady and reliable production. The Accord coordinated the interests of labor and capital by exchanging secure jobs and high wages for a stable, reliable, productive, and peaceful work force that unions would provide.

Collective bargaining was perhaps the most important part of the Accord. Collective bargaining agreements are the **explicit contracts** that define the terms of employment for all workers covered by a given contract. These contracts are usually in place for several years. Their contents emerge out of negotiations between union leadership (elected by the rank and file during periodic elections and governed by constitutions) and managers.

The relative strength of each party influences its ability to forge a contract that meets its demands. Employers almost always have the upper hand in any negotiation because of their ability to fire all workers (and replace them with machines or other workers) or to relocate to other parts of the country or the world. In addition, employers have historically benefitted from the strong relationship between big business and the government.

Even if contracts tend to disproportionately represent the interests of employers, workers are still better off with contracts than without them, overall. Remember, in the absence of contracts, employers

could establish almost *any* kind of working conditions they want;
employers could demand that workers work 24 hours a day in smoke-
and toxin-filled rooms, and the workers' only resort would be to quit.
Quitting, however, is often not an option. The protections that stipu-
late working conditions and regulate the work environment, such as
the regulations from the Occupational Safety and Health Administration, are the result of union demands and struggles.

The terms and conditions of employment contracts typically
establish the length of the working day, the number and length of
breaks, the pay for work, and so on. Additionally, collective bargaining agreements also specify the conditions of hiring and firing. For
instance, in the absence of such agreements, an employer could
relocate an employee to an unfavorable shift or lower her pay if she
refused his sexual advances or challenged any harassment. Workers
covered by a contract are protected from these and other arbitrary
behaviors.

Besides working conditions, the major issue over which American
unions and employers bargain is wages and benefits. This focus is in
marked contrast to unions in Western European capitalist democracies,
where unions bargain over such larger issues as the **labor process**
itself, child care provisions, and other matters that affect *all* workers.
(The labor process refers to the way work tasks are organized.) In the
United States, however, workers were not strong enough to include
these broader issues in collective bargaining negotiations. Instead of
broad-based issues, the strategy on which U.S. employers and large
unions relied for maintaining industrial peace and steady production
was to attempt to reorganize labor–capital relations around cooperative rather than conflictive lines. The coordination of employers' and
employees' interests was the goal of the labor–capital accord. At least
three major aspects of collective bargaining agreements created those
shared interests:

- **Productivity bargaining**: Workers' wage increases were often tied
  to increases in productivity. That is, if production stayed high, the
  wage level for all workers would stay high (note that an alternative
  could have tied wage increases to profit increases). The harder the
  worker worked, therefore, the better off not only the employer but
  also the worker. Thus, productivity bargaining matched the interests of workers to those of their employers.

- **Cost-of-living adjustments (COLAs):** As the rate of inflation (the change of the consumer price index) increases, COLAs automatically increase wages to keep up with it. It is important to remember that employers could afford to adjust wage increases to price increases because right after World War II, when these agreements were first developed, our economy was not yet characterized by the persistent inflation that occurred during and after the Vietnam War. In other words, no one was hurt, and the economy benefitted since these wage adjustments not only kept workers happy but also allowed them sufficient income to purchase the goods they produced—which of course made their employers happy!
- **Seniority rules:** Union seniority rules are best summarized by the cliché, "Last hired, first fired." That is, union seniority rules protected workers from the arbitrary discipline that supervisors had used previously. Now, there were regulations structuring who could be fired and when, and the assumption was that the longer the worker had been on the job, the more secure that job would be. In an economic downturn, for example, new workers—not those who had worked at the plant for 20 years—would lose their jobs. Thus, seniority rewarded workers for being stable, reliable, and cooperative.

Thus, union seniority rules, COLAs, and productivity bargaining—and collective bargaining contracts generally—tied employee interests to those of their employers.

Regulation of Conflict It was not enough to create positive incentives to cooperation; employers also had to make sure that when cooperation broke down, the workplace would not return to the open conflicts that characterized the pre-Accord era. Thus, in addition to the explicit provisions structuring the terms of employment, the labor–capital accord transformed the ways in which disagreements and conflicts were resolved.

Basic to the labor–capital accord was the exchange of union security for industrial peace. By *union security*, I mean employer acceptance, grudging though it was, of independent trade unions as the representatives of workers' interests. In exchange for recognizing unions and bargaining with them, employers demanded assurance that unions would police the rank and file and ensure a relatively quiescent work force. In other words, the task of maintaining a well-behaved and controlled work force fell on the unions instead of employers (Rubin, 1986a).

The threat with which employers and their managers were most concerned was the strike. During this labor–capital accord era, workers continued to strike. But instead of unpredictable, costly battles that erupted out of the harshness of workplace relations, most strikes were relatively routine and predictable. They occurred at the end of collective bargaining contracts, and most of them were geared towards increasing wages.

Though the issues over which workers could strike were substantially limited (to wages, hours, and working conditions), workers were still able to use strikes effectively. Throughout this period, they were so effective in improving their wages and benefits (before unions, for example, there were no such things as paid vacations, overtime pay, etc.) that they increased the total income for *all* workers relative to the income received by employers (Rubin, 1986b).

Moreover, even the wages of *nonunion* labor increased owing to **threat and spillover effects**. Employers of nonunion labor, to avoid union-organizing drives by their workers, raised wages when union wages increased (threat effects). Consequently, though nonunion workers typically received lower pay than union workers, on average they received increases at the same rate as union labor (Freeman and Medoff, 1984; Rubin, 1986a).

Another way the Accord routinized shopfloor conflict was to provide workers with formal mechanisms for handling grievances, to which their employers were supposed to be responsive. Rubin and Smith (1992) found, for example, that within the steel industry (a major locus of the Accord) strikes occurred less frequently and ended more rapidly during the Accord years. Rather than direct confrontation with supervisors (which could easily result in a worker's being fired on the spot), unions established grievance procedures with official channels through which workers with complaints had to go. While increasing the level of bureaucracy in the workplace, such mechanisms served to protect workers.

In addition to formal channels of communication within the workplace, established by collective bargaining, the government created the National Labor Relations Board (NLRB). The NLRB served as a conflict-adjudicating body outside the workplace; it could hear charges of unfair labor practices and enforce existing legislation. Thus, for the first time there was an allegedly neutral outside party whose sole mandate was to resolve difficult industrial disputes. The specific board members of the NLRB (who hear the cases) are appointed by the president.

Shopfloor grievance procedures and the NLRB regulated and channeled shopfloor conflict between workers and their employers. Additionally, they regulated how strikes could occur. That is, laws and NLRB regulations severely limited the strategies available to workers. They were particularly geared toward controlling, if not entirely eliminating, forms of strikes that were most disruptive for business (Wallace, Rubin, and Smith, 1988; McCammon, 1990).

For example, the sit-down strike that was so successful in the organizing disputes of the earlier period was rendered illegal. Similarly, laws regulated specific strike issues as well as which groups could benefit from bargaining or striking. Thus, while industrial conflict still occurred, it did so within a narrow set of rules and procedures. It was predictable but ultimately far less useful to workers than to employers. These were the terms of the social contract, at least for some parts of the economy.

The Accord and the Dual Economy

Remember that the labor–capital accord was a bargain struck between big unions, the government, and big business. Big business had the economic surplus and market power that allowed them to "purchase" good behavior from labor without threatening their own rate of profit growth. Smaller businesses, however, were less profitable and thus less able to rely on these strategies for maintaining industrial peace.

One of the most important things to understand about the structure of the economy throughout most of the twentieth century is that it has been a **dual economy**. That is, not all businesses are the same size or equally important to the economic health of the country.

On the one hand, when you read the *Wall Street Journal* or the economic section of your hometown paper or watch the stock reports on television, you are most likely paying attention to the profitability and health of the largest and most central businesses. On the other hand, in day-to-day experience we all engage in a great deal of local business activity. Buying groceries, going out to dinner, picking up laundry, running down to the corner drugstore to pick up a paper and a pack of gum—all these primarily involve relatively small businesses. These two types of businesses are loosely grouped into what sociologists and economists call the **core** (or **monopoly**) and **periphery** (or **competitive**) sectors of the economy. The businesses in these two sectors differ in size (number of employees, value of assets), profitability, market share, and general importance to the economy. It is important to recognize the distinction between these two sectors of the economy since many of the changes that are occurring are altering the relative size and economic health of these two sectors.

The Social Contract in the Core Those industry groups that operate in national or international markets, employ very large labor forces, are **capital-intensive** (that is, whose production of goods requires expensive technology rather than cheap labor), and contribute significantly to the gross national product (GNP) are core industries. Generally, the workers in these industries are unionized, are well-paid, and have generous benefits. In addition, although these industries are not literally monopolies, they are so large, so powerful, and so few in number that they operate in market environments that are relatively immune to supply and demand conditions. For example, despite declining auto sales, at no time in the past 30 years have the Big Three auto makers (GM, Ford, and Chrysler) *lowered* the prices of luxury automobiles; in fact, they have raised them.

Throughout much of the twentieth century, the core industries included large sectors of manufacturing, mining, construction, and transportation-related industries (such as steel and other metals, automobiles, shipping, airlines, and railroads). These are the industry groups that are directly tied to the economic well-being of the entire country (Hodson, 1978). Thus, the health of these industry groups affects the health of the overall economy. For example, when the steel industry started to decline in the late 1960s and early 1970s, thousands of workers were laid off (see the discussion of structural unemployment displacement in this chapter), and the national unemployment rate (the number of unemployed per thousand nonagricultural workers) increased.

It is in the core that the labor–capital accord between employers and workers was established. It was this labor–capital accord that shaped workplace relationships from World War II until the late 1960s and early 1970s.

The Social Contract in the Periphery   In contrast, the other sector of the economy—the periphery—is made up of industries that operate in local and regional markets, are relatively labor-intensive (production is based on low levels of technology), are small in terms of assets and number of workers, and operate in relatively competitive market contexts.

These industry groups include wholesale and retail trade, services, finance, insurance, and real estate. These industries are characterized by smaller businesses with small profit margins. Workers historically have low wages and few benefits, and are relatively nonunionized. These businesses are relatively responsive to supply and demand conditions, and they appear and disappear with little impact on the larger economy. When, for example, your favorite restaurant goes out of business, it may have an impact on the few employees who worked there and on the few loyal customers who ate there on a regular basis, but its closing has little effect on the national unemployment rate, the GNP, or the general economic well-being of the country.

Businesses in peripheral industries are much smaller than those in core industries. With just a few workers in an office, union organizers have found it much harder to mobilize workers to join unions. Furthermore, many of these employees are white-collar office workers—such as salespeople or workers in financial services—who have identified more with management than with labor. As a result, the appeal of unions has usually been lost on them. The plays *Death of a Salesman* and *Glengarry Glen Ross* show fictionalized examples of how misguided such workers can be. In both plays, older salesmen whose sales have slowed are let go by their companies despite years of loyalty. With no union to protect them, they find themselves alone and treated as expendable.

These characteristics had implications for the social relationships between workers and their employers during the Accord period. Because these businesses were usually relatively small (in fact many were mom-and-pop establishments) the ways disputes occurred and were settled were very different. On the one hand, when conflict did occur in such settings, workers were far less likely to strike and more likely to quit (Cornfield, 1985) or to rely on personal confrontations with management. On the other hand, employers could rely on personal ties of loyalty to control workers or on harsh and arbitrary discipline (Edwards, 1979).

Despite these differences between the core and the periphery, the labor–capital accord *did* affect labor relations in the periphery. In the industrial periphery, the social contract between workers and their employers was *implicit* rather than *explicit*. In other words, while long-term labor contracts were relatively rare, relationships in the periphery often changed in ways that mirrored the changes in the core of the economy. One of the ways in which employers in nonunion, peripheral workplaces emulated relationships in the unionized core was to stabilize employment for their workers. Although nonunion workers continued to experience greater job insecurity, their workplace relations became relatively similar to those in the unionized sector.

For example, more workers worked an 8-hour day than had prior to the labor–capital accord. Similarly, paychecks and pay raises, loose seniority systems, limitations on the oppressiveness of working conditions, and legal structures regulated the general workplace environment. For many workers in the periphery, even nonunion jobs were associated with rising paychecks, benefits, and many of the advantages that characterized union work. In fact, despite lower wages, higher turnover, and more arbitrary discipline, the ability of nonunion employers to "deliver the goods" explains, according to some researchers, the failure of unions to organize even 50% of the nonagricultural work force in the Accord period (Cornfield, 1986).

The Economic Consequences of the Accord

The post–World War II era, then, was characterized by the prevalence of formal contracts (in the unionized sector), as well as the informal contract embodied in the labor–capital accord, that institutionalized on a limited basis the conflicts between workers and their employers.

For at least two decades, the labor–capital accord contributed to the economic growth and affluence of the country. The United States led the world in mass production. Researchers concur that our "mass production system . . . was . . . the basis of the unparalleled success of the United States between 1945 and 1970 as measured both by the competitiveness of U.S. firms in domestic and world markets and by the growth in income and improvements of living standards of workers" (Appelbaum and Batt, 1994, p. 6). The United States produced more for less and thereby became the leader in the world economy. Central to that expansion was the relative material wealth of the American worker. The great majority of workers who had stable jobs were, for the first time in history, well enough off to purchase the very goods they produced. Unionized blue-collar workers, many of whom had only high school degrees, earned enough to buy houses and cars and other consumer durables (washing machines, dryers, television sets, lawnmowers, etc.) for their families.

Moreover, they were often able to afford this standard of living on a single paycheck, thus enabling their wives to fill the role of full-time homemaker, as did their more affluent counterparts in the upper middle class (e.g., educated, white-collar professional and managerial workers). Thus, a perhaps unintended consequence of the labor–capital accord was to facilitate the gender division of labor (see chapter 4) in which men were breadwinners and women homemakers.

The labor–capital accord provided both unionized and nonunionized blue-collar workers (the traditional working class) with sufficient income to create a middle-class lifestyle. This period of affluence bolstered the belief that the United States was a middle-class society in which industrial conflict was a page in history and, perhaps more important, that material well-being and security were available to anyone who worked hard. This period was one of an expanded middle class.

Not all workers, however, were unionized blue-collar workers. Some were white-collar sales, clerical, and supervisory workers. Although their paychecks were often *lower* than those of blue-collar industrial workers, the types of jobs they did (office work) made them appear more middle-class. Nonetheless, the most important component of the Accord—stability—characterized their jobs as well. Under the Accord, the idea of employment stability became one of the most important goals of workplace structures. For clerical workers, low-level managers, supervisors, and sales workers, employers created a variety of incentive systems and career ladders based on long-term stability at the job. This system created incentives for these workers similar to the seniority systems created for blue-collar workers (Edwards, 1979).

The next chapter, on work and education, takes up this issue in greater detail. What is important for our purposes here is that the *hallmark of the labor–capital accord was the creation of labor–capital relations premised on the exchange of job security, monetary gain, and stable employment for industrial peace and ongoing productivity.*

THE BREAKDOWN OF THE ACCORD

The immediate post–World War II era to the late 1960s and early 1970s was a unique period in American history. The Accord produced a period of economic growth and affluence unseen before or since. However, a number of factors made continued expansion impossible and led to the breakdown of the labor–capital accord. All these factors were tied in one way or another to our successes and failures in an increasingly competitive world economy.

Failed Competition and Declining Profitability

One of the most important characteristics of capitalist economies is competition. In a competitive economic environment, unsuccessful competition means slow economic growth. Slow economic growth means loss of sales, loss of market position, and ultimately loss of jobs. Loss of jobs means fewer consumers who are able to purchase goods, which means less profit, which means even less growth. If these conditions continue, a business will falter. This situation creates a crisis in profitability, and the business experiences declining profits to a "life-threatening" extent. This type of failure of competition is what started happening in the early 1970s. Three forces were at work: paper entrepreneurialism, international competition, and rising costs.

Paper Entrepreneurialism Let's say that companies A and B sell automobiles. Company A has successfully sold automobiles for decades; its profits are high, and each year it is able to sell slightly more cars than the year before. Company A sells enough cars each year to have a secure share of the market. As a result, it may not invest its profits in changing the cars it sells or the technology that produces them (why fix it if it ain't broke?).

Company B, on the other hand, is a relatively new producer of cars. Because it is new, it is less secure. Consumers don't really know much about the company, and so far it sells cars only in a very small local market of consumers who are familiar with them. To survive economically and make enough profit to stay in business, Company B must do something to grow; it does this by selling more cars and increasing its share of the market. It develops a new way of producing snazzy cars that are fuel efficient, small, and affordable. This response can be called **productive entrepreneurialism**—that is, entrepreneurialism based on the actual production of goods or services.

Eventually, consumers who have driven the cars from Company A find out and start buying cars from Company B. They discover that "B" cars are cheaper, both to buy and drive. However, Company

A doesn't realize that consumers are switching from their cars to the new cars. Instead, Company A has been busily increasing profits by buying up other, often unrelated companies (jam manufacturers, for example), in a process called *diversification*. Diversification does not expand the number of jobs; it just shuffles the jobs and products into the new parent company. Too late, Company A realizes that while it has borrowed lots of money to purchase other profit-making businesses, its original business (making cars) is no longer making a profit. That is what happened to many American manufacturing firms in the 1970s.

The process of investing in other businesses rather than actually producing goods is called **paper entrepreneurialism**. Paper entrepreneurialism does create short-term profits for companies, but it doesn't help the overall economy. In contrast to productive entrepreneurialism, nothing is actually produced. While the company increases its assets, it does not create new jobs. "U.S. companies spent $22 billion acquiring each other in 1977, but by 1981 that had risen to $82 billion, cresting in 1985 at an extreme $180 billion" (Harvey, 1989, p. 158). In productive entrepreneurialism, things (like automobiles and television sets) are produced by individuals who are put to work. Thus, while both forms of activity increase business profits, only the latter also creates jobs, wages, and therefore consumers (Bluestone and Harrison, 1982; and Harvey, 1989).

International Competition Besides failing to create jobs, paper entrepreneurialism hurt the economy in a second way. This failure to reinvest in original products (such as cars) undermined the United States' competitiveness in the increasingly internationalized market. While American manufacturing businesses were buying up other businesses, businesses in other countries were sinking funds into developing their manufacturing technology. For perhaps the first time in American history, American businesses were competing in increasingly international markets in which they could no longer dominate the competition.

The increasingly competitive international environment is a result, in part, of one of the great ironies of history; some of the greatest threats to our economic reign come from the losers of World War II— Germany and Japan. While the United States sank increasing proportions of research and development funds into military expenditures, Japan and Germany, unable to use their surplus in the same ways (and with the help of the Marshall Plan), put resources into rebuilding their economies. Thus, while U.S. manufacturers rested on their economic laurels (like Company A in the preceding example), Japanese and German manufacturers were learning from the United States' past mistakes and sinking money into capturing consumer markets (as with Company B). Although the United States had commanded the market in products like steel, automobiles, and electronics, it lost considerable economic ground to the Japanese and Germans, who had invested significant profit into upgrading and expanding their manufacturing technologies. From 1960 to 1973, "Japan's annual increase in goods and services produced per person . . . grew four times faster than did that of the United States, and Germany's grew more than twice as fast; during 1973–1988, . . . Japan's grew five times and Germany's four times faster than ours" (Craypo and Nissen, 1993, p. 251, note 2).

Rising Costs   Unions' ability to improve the well-being of their members through collective bargaining grew increasingly problematic to employers as industrial competitiveness declined. For a variety of reasons too complex to discuss here, one result of our involvement in the Vietnam War was to create an inflationary economy—that is, one in which the annual rate of change in the consumer price index grew rapidly (Brittan, 1978).

Inflation results in decreased purchasing power of a dollar. Thus, a dollar indexed to 1982 prices would have purchased three and a half times more in 1955 than it did in 1980, but by 1993 it would not be able to purchase a 1982 one-dollar comic book (see Table 2.1). The decreased purchasing power of the dollar means that a consumer can buy far fewer products with that dollar in 1994 than she could buy in 1974. Inflation increases costs not only for consumers but also for producers since the materials necessary for production are more expensive now than they were when the dollar was worth more. If all the materials necessary for manufacturing an automobile (such as steel, rubber, and plastic) increase, the price of the automobile will have to increase as well. An automobile in 1992 cost one and a half times more than in 1983 (*Statistical Abstract*, 1994, Table 748, p. 490). Inflation made many of employers' economic concessions to workers, which had originally been made when there was little inflation, too expensive. In particular, COLA agreements, those automatic adjust-

Table 2.1   Purchasing Power of the Dollar, 1955–1993

Year	Annual Average Consumer Price
1955	3.73
1965	3.17
1977	1.86
1985	.93
1993	.69

Adapted from *Statistical Abstract of the United States: 1994*, Washington D.C.: U.S. Bureau of the Census. *Note:* (1982 = 100) Annual figure based on average monthly data.

ments in wages that matched wage increases to price increases, simply became too costly; so did certain nonwage benefits (e.g., paid leaves, health care, etc.).

To continue to make a profit and honor labor contracts, employers had to continue to raise prices. To raise them too much, however, would alienate consumers, who were already losing interest in American products. Moreover, markets for consumer durables in the United States had reached their limit (how many cars, dishwashers, and television sets could a family own?).

In an era of declining profits, employers were less willing to provide wage increases to workers; workers were less likely to purchase expensive products; and fewer jobs were available to provide work at all. The labor–capital accord became, for employers, an impediment to responding to their changed economic position. The changed international situation plus rising costs undermined the relationship between employers and workers. Thus, rather than make less profit, employers sought ways to avoid or break their implicit and explicit contracts with organized labor (Bowles, Gordon, and Weisskoph, 1983; Harvey, 1989; Craypo and Nissen, 1993).

Corporate Strategies for Maintaining Profits

In response to unpredictable and decreasing profit growth, business owners explored a range of strategies to maintain profitability. Those strategies included industrial restructuring, union busting, globalization, and technological innovation.

Industrial Restructuring and Deindustrialization Industrial restructuring was one important way employers responded to loss of (or slow growth of) profits. **Industrial restructuring** refers to the shift from manufacturing production and employment to expanding service production and employment. Service industries produce, market, and sell services (such as restaurants, banking, hairstyling) instead of goods (such as cars, radios, televisions) as the source of their profit. Instead of investing in upgrading outdated technology or searching out new markets or cheaper workers, employers in many instances transferred assets to financial and other service-sector interests. Thus, accompanying the shift away from manufacturing has been the expansion of the service sector. Often **deindustrialization** accompanies industrial restructuring. Deindustrialization refers to "widespread disinvestment in the nation's productive capacity" (Bluestone and Harrison, 1982; Wallace and Rothschild, 1988). Disinvestment can take a number of forms, such as investing in mergers instead of production or failing to upgrade technology. The key point is that managers do not continue to invest in basic production. An example of this shift occurred in Flint, Michigan, in the 1970s and 1980s, in which the tourist industry, rather than automobile industry, became a limited source of employment—a process lampooned in the movie *Roger and Me*.

The shift in employment has been so great that many social scientists claim that this factor alone explains the new type of society that is emerging. The term **postindustrial** society (Bell, 1973; Block, 1990) refers to an economy centered on service production and has caught on in the news media. I see this shift as *one* component of the shift to a new type of economy. Although it is only one component, it is an important one. For example, from 1950 to 1990, the percentage of the nonagricultural work force employed in manufacturing industries dropped from almost 34% to around 17%. The percentage of the nonagricultural work force employed in service-sector industries increased during the same period from 12% to 26% (see Figure 2.1).

An important consequence of major industrial shifts (such as the shift from agriculture to industry) is their effect on the relative economic well-being of people who work in the new industrial sectors. The average annual earnings of manufacturing workers in 1990 were $36,503. For service-sector workers the comparable figure was $21,395. So when my old boyfriend Ricky lost his job in the electronics industry and was rehired as a security guard for a fancy Washington

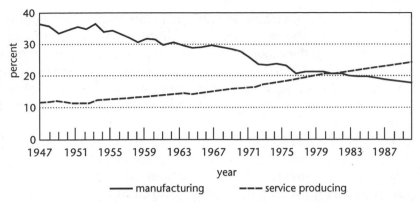

Figure 2.1. Percent of nonagricultural employment in manufacturing and service producing industries, 1947–1990

From CITIBASE, FAME Information Services, Inc. (1946–present), 1978, New York.

hotel, his income dropped to even less than the average of $21,395 a year—hence his difficulty in maintaining mortgage payments.

These averages suggest that the expansion of the service sector is associated with the expansion of low-wage work and that the decline of the manufacturing sector is associated with a diminishing number of higher paying jobs. There is reason to believe, however, that the story is somewhat more complex than these averages suggest. Income averages are useful, but they also can obscure considerable variation; thus it is important to avoid overgeneralizing the consequences of these trends.

Union Busting One of the simplest ways for employers to increase profits is to reduce the cost of labor. In the core economy, that has meant challenging or outmaneuvering the unions. Employers have used a variety of strategies in the past couple of decades, including relocating to the sunbelt, preempting unions, declaring bankruptcy, and enlisting government support.

Many companies have chosen to relocate in areas where unions have traditionally been weak or nonexistent. To that end, plants relocated from the Northeast and Great Lakes areas (the so-called rustbelt) to the South and Southwest (the sunbelt) and overseas.

Southern states were attractive for several reasons. Many are **right-to-work** states. These states have laws that allow workers who are not dues-paying union members to work in plants that are covered by union contracts. These workers thus benefit from union activities, but they neither pay dues nor participate in union activities such as strikes. This kind of situation creates a classic **free-rider problem**, in which nonunion workers have a free ride; they get the gain without the pain. The failure to participate eventually undermines worker and union solidarity.

Another factor making Southern states attractive sites for relocation is, sadly, the often deep traditions of racial oppression. Naturally, workers who are divided along racial lines are much less able to organize successfully. Employers have, historically, pitted black and white workers against one another. One way of doing this, for example, has been to use black workers as replacements against striking white workers. These experiences, plus years of racial antagonism, have made these groups of workers vulnerable to employers' efforts to maintain divisions between these workers. Plants that relocate to the South are often able to take advantage of these conditions and pay much lower wages, offer lower benefits and worse working conditions, and *still* improve the quality of life for black workers, who have historically been excluded from high-paying jobs (Bonacich, 1976).

Employers who did not relocate used a number of strategies to weaken union strength directly. For example, employers hired sophisticated personnel advisors whose purpose was to convince union members that they no longer needed the union or to convince nonunion workers not to unionize. Employers have always used these professionals, but their tactics are far more sophisticated now than they were in earlier periods (Bluestone and Harrison, 1982). Rather than explicitly threaten union organizers with jail or death—or circulate rumors pitting one group of workers against another—professional union busters might encourage employers to run ads in local papers to sway public sentiment against the union. Or they might hold special seminars for workers to allow them to air their grievances, in order to demonstrate the irrelevance of unions as a way to address grievances. Often, once the union is out of the workplace or fails to organize a workplace, these benefits are withdrawn.

Another popular union-avoidance strategy in the 1970s and 1980s was for a business to declare bankruptcy. Companies often initiated bankruptcy proceedings while negotiating new contracts with organized labor. At the end of an existing contract, when unions came to the bargaining table asking for increased benefits or job security guarantees (since wage increases were less frequent demands during this period), employers would claim that such demands would bankrupt them. The benefit of declaring bankruptcy was that the bankrupt business was freed from both debts *and prior contracts*. Thus, bankruptcy reorganization could free a business from union costs entirely (Edwards, Garonna, and Tödling, 1986). When the machinist's union struck Continental Airlines in 1989, owner Frank Lorenzo initiated bankruptcy proceedings, thereby undermining that strike.

Employers had a powerful ally in their union-busting efforts during the 1980s. The Reagan and then Bush administrations were notoriously anti-union. Many argue that when Reagan fired striking air traffic controllers in 1981 and effectively decertified the Professional Air Traffic Controllers' union (PATCO), he declared open season on unions (Edwards, Garonna, and Tödling, 1986; Bowles, Gordon, and Weiskoph, 1993). Employers became much bolder in their efforts to break unions and in their willingness to ignore or sever prior agreements. In the context of expanding unemployment and relocation overseas, unions had little recourse; so these strategies were often successful in weakening them. It is nearly impossible for workers to go on strike when other underemployed or unemployed workers will take their jobs. When employers are able to hire a sufficient number of workers to replace striking workers, they can break the strike.

Not only were the presidencies of Reagan and Bush openly anti-union, but they appointed anti-union individuals to the NLRB. As a result, the number of unfair labor practices suits employers sought against unions (and the number of cases employers won against unions) increased (Goldfield, 1987). For example, the NLRB was more likely during the 1980s to deem a strike illegal, thus rendering strikers ineligible for unemployment benefits. Quite clearly, with the government openly backing management in labor–management disputes, labor is likely to lose.

The antilabor administration, bankruptcy proceedings, and active union busting all weakened unions' ability to engage in successful negotiations. At contract termination, for example, employers increasingly sought to take back previous wage and/or benefit increases. More often than not, strikes in the late 1970s and 1980s were defensive and increasingly antagonistic battles, as labor sought to maintain its past gains (and therefore, its membership). The efficacy of such strikes was considerably weakened, however, when management's response was simply a threat to relocate. In the context of plant closings and increased unemployment, and in the presence of a government that was openly hostile to unions, workers were in an extraordinarily vulnerable condition (Edwards, Garonna, and Tödling, 1986).

For example, in 1994 the United Food and Commercial Workers struck local grocery stores in New Orleans and Baton Rouge, Louisiana, when management sought to eliminate all full-time positions in favor of part-time positions. The owning company was Canadian and had already closed several of its New Orleans stores. After about 8 months it offered the striking workers a contract identical to the one that precipitated the strike and informed them that if they did not end the strike, they would close *all New Orleans stores*. In Baton Rouge they did just that. Not only did they pack up and move out of town, but they made a public display of their move in the local newspapers. Shortly after the strike ended, they moved everything back and re-hired the workers who had not supported the strike. Though President Clinton is not strongly antilabor, Louisiana is a right-to-work state with high unemployment; there is little to suggest that this strike could have succeeded under those conditions.

These conditions put unions in a difficult situation. If, at contract's end, employers seek some sort of wage/benefit concession and union leadership does not call for a strike, members may get disgruntled with leadership and seek to end the union as their representative, for failing to protect them. If they do strike, employers are more able to wait them out. If, in the end, the union basically accepts the original offer, members are often still likely to call for a decertification election. That is, they may elect to decertify the union as their legal representative. One of the major strategies of many employers who want to get rid of unions is to provoke a strike under conditions in which the workers cannot possibly win (for example, when unemployment is high) and then hope to decertify the union after the strike is lost (which means, of course, that striking workers have experienced considerable income loss with little gain).

A major response to the profit crises of the 1970s and 1980s, therefore, was to create a strong anti-union climate, which resulted in union vulnerability and decline. Figure 2.2 shows the percentage of the nonagricultural work force that has been unionized since the late 1940s. At its peak, only about 35% of the work force was unionized; now, however, the percentage is closer to 15%. Thus, one consequence of the declining Accord is the weakening of organized labor and the

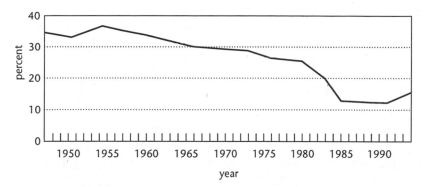

Figure 2.2. Percent of nonagricultural work force that is unionized

Adapted from *Historical Statistics of the United States: Colonial Times to 1970*, 1975, and *Statistical Abstract of the United States*, selected years, Washington D.C.: U.S. Bureau of the Census.

deepening insecurity of all workers as employers relocate or threaten to relocate production overseas (Bowles, Gordon, and Weisskoph, 1983; Edwards, Garonna and Tödling, 1986; Kochan, McKersie, and Cappelli, 1989).

Globalization Employers relocate not only *within* countries as a way to minimize costs and maximize profits; they also relocate overseas. As chapter 1 indicated, **globalization** refers to the resulting alteration of the basic network of economic relations within and among countries. In this altered network, there is no economic center but rather a network of actors, all of whom are competing for dominance on a global level. For example, Liz Claiborne, the highly successful designer of women's clothing, designs clothes in the United States. The garments are actually produced by low-wage workers in third world countries such as Taiwan and Mexico. Similarly, in plants in Marysville, Ohio, Honda produces automobiles that are designed in Japan and re-exported there for sale (Perrucci, 1994). Some of these same companies do many of their financial transactions in Tokyo or Frankfurt, where some of the largest and most powerful banks in the global financial market are located (Storper and Walker, 1989).

Employer efforts to maximize profit have led to an increased reliance on global strategies. Researchers have shown that those companies that experienced the greatest losses in the 1970s were most likely to relocate overseas in the 1990s (Ross and Trachte, 1990).

There, they can pay wages that are a minuscule fraction of U.S. wages, avoid providing benefits, and avoid complex union-determined grievance procedures. Companies can also use the mere *threat* to relocate as a bargaining tool. For example, in 1981 General Motors used the ability to relocate to force concessions from the United Auto Workers that included giving up COLAs for three years and establishing greater flexibility in union work rules (Ross and Trachte, 1990). Additionally, overseas location often releases employers from the costly constraints of environmental controls. (One need only drive along the Texas-Mexico border around El Paso to experience this reality.)

The opportunity for increasing profits has led to unprecedented expansion of production overseas. For example, 71% of all revenue and 51% of all assets that Exxon held in 1987 were held outside the United States. Similarly, 54% of IBM's revenue and 54% of its assets were foreign. These are two of the 40 largest U.S. multinational firms (Braun, 1991, p. 103).

Capitalists in the more advanced nations have always drawn on the cheap labor and raw materials of less developed countries. Now, however, researchers suggest that the extent of internationalization of production (which is a major component of globalization) is *quantitatively* so much more than in the past that it represents a *qualitative* shift in the economic system. Instead of the system that dominated in the previous period (in which core capitalist countries were the center of manufacturing production and peripheral countries provided raw material) under global capitalism, manufacturing is dispersed around the world in a variety of ways (Ross and Trachte, 1990).

One form of dispersion occurs when multinational corporations simply relocate to those countries in which labor is relatively docile, governments are supportive of foreign investors, and regulation of business (e.g., environmental laws) is limited. Another form of dispersion occurs when corporations keep the highly skilled components of production, such as research and development, "at home" but relocate the processing, assembling, and testing of products overseas. Repetitive, unskilled, routinized work (as in the standard assembly line) is exported overseas, particularly to third world countries. There, the workers are paid low wages and work long hours, with minimal to nonexistent benefits. This type of dispersion creates jobs overseas but decreases jobs for unskilled and semiskilled labor in the United States. Researchers such as Frobel, Folker, Heinrichs, and Kreye (1980) refer to this strategy as the "new international division of labor."

Importantly, in either type of dispersion, the docility of workers is often ensured by relying on a largely female work force. For example, the electronics manufacturing work force in Taiwan is composed primarily of women. By and large their jobs are dead-end and pay less than those of their male counterparts. In countries where sons are both highly prized and also the only inheritors of property—and where daughters are considered a liability—women are socialized from birth to view themselves as inferior to men. Similar relationships exist between multinational corporations and female workers in other countries—for example, garment workers in Mexican border sweatshops and female labor in Colombian coffee farms (Ward, 1990).

Women's labor force participation under these conditions is motivated not by a drive toward freedom from this type of patriarchal system but rather by the obligation to *repay* the family for being a burden! Certainly these women will not and do not protest the degraded conditions under which they often work. Thus, globalization not only benefits certain business enterprises, it also often reinforces and benefits from systems of patriarchy that keep third world women working under what United States workers would consider oppressive working circumstances (Ward, 1990).

It is not only production systems and labor forces that are globalized but also markets. That is, manufacturers sell not only to the United States but to markets all over the world, which also intensifies competition. For example, Toyota and Honda, both Japanese companies, make cars in the United States and export them back to Japan! Similarly, U.S. automobile manufacturers must compete not only with one another, but with German and Japanese automakers. Globalization of the economy, then, has created new demands and challenges to existing economic and social relations.

Technological Innovation A number of technological innovations have been implemented in an attempt to maintain corporate profitability. Of course, technology has always played an important role in economic growth. New technologies allow capitalists either to create new products or to produce the products they already make at lower cost and in greater volume. This expanded production gives them an edge in a competitive market. Historically, some technological innovations, such as the three-masted galleon (which allowed transoceanic travel and the expansion of trade) and the printing press (which brought education to the masses), have been so dramatic that they have transformed much of social life.

Arguably, the greatest technological innovation in the past few decades has been the development of information processing technologies—specifically computers. Computers have freed businesses from the limitations of physical place and allow them to operate in **cyberspace**. What that means is that computer technology allows many aspects of a business (i.e., distribution, development, financing) to occur independently of any specific location, since computers allow the almost instantaneous transfer of information from city to city, state to state, nation to nation. For many, it is computerization that has intensified the globalization process discussed previously. Similarly, computers allow the almost instantaneous transfer of money from place to place. (Many blame the stock market crash of October 1987 on these computer-based financial transactions.)

The manufacturing sector has also experienced a number of non-computer-based technological innovations, such as **containerization** and **just-in-time production**. *Containerization* refers to the process of off-loading entire railroad cars full of goods by crane, rather than unloading the contents of those cars by hand. So where 30 men used to unload and load railroad cars, now just 1 man operates the crane to lift containers of goods off the train and onto the boat—and 29 people are out of work.

Just-in-time production is a way of reorganizing production so that suppliers are grouped around the final assembly plant. This reorganization makes all parts necessary for a production process accessible when they are needed. Consequently, manufacturers can avoid the cost of stockpiled inventory (which also makes a strike much less problematic for employers—see Piore and Sable, 1984; Sayer and Walker, 1992). Both these innovations have increased flexibility in production, as the next section discusses.

THE EMERGING ECONOMY

The combination of strategies adopted by corporations to maintain profitability has profoundly altered the divisions of labor, the technology of production, and the fundamental employment relationships that characterize the economy. The picture that is emerging is dominated by flexible production, dualism in the service sector, structural unemployment, and a broken social contract. Although these features have some positive aspects, the disruption they cause in the near future will be painful for many.

Flexible Production and Flexible Accumulation

Historically, manufacturing production relied on either one-of-a kind production (craft, as in custom furniture) or mass production (assembly line, as in automobiles). These technologies were limited to a single product and required direct worker control. New technologies have overcome those technological rigidities and allowed employers to develop methods of flexible mass production (Craypo and Nissen, 1993, p. 21). To do so, they have often relied on computer-controlled machines and robots adapted to specific uses. Besides programmable tools, manufacturers have increasingly relied on computer-based information systems for scheduling and other aspects of business (Craypo and Nissen, 1993, p. 22). Thus, computers provide manufacturers with historically unprecedented flexibility in how they produce what they produce.

Manufacturers are no longer locked into a single product design and can respond rapidly to changing demand and competitive pressures. Whereas previously changes in a product (for example, a car body) would require workers to physically replace machinery, now computer software can adjust the machinery without having to physically rebuild it. This capability means that businesses can respond much more rapidly to changes in consumer demand. Relying on **CAD (computer-aided design)**, for example, means that General Motors can respond to shifting consumer preferences for curvy rather than boxy cars much more rapidly and affordably than in the past. The company can also more easily manipulate consumer demand. By using computer software it can dramatically, but inexpensively, offer apparently new but only superficially different products that appeal to the market but cost little in terms of research and development.

CAD/CAM (**computer-aided manufacturing**) is the use of computers both to design and to produce manufactured items. Shaiken notes that in one automobile assembly line, robots performed about 98% of more than 3,000 welds, and those robots were controlled by computers (Shaiken, 1984; Sayer and Walker, 1992; Craypo and Nissen, 1993; Appelbaum and Batt, 1994).

Computers also allow manufacturers to centralize control of the manufacturing system. This computer-based, centralized control removes limitations of space and time from managers' administration of the corporation. Now, management can maintain centralized control over internationally dispersed subsidiaries with the same knowledge as if they were on the shopfloor (Shaiken, 1984; Harvey, 1989;

Sayer and Walker, 1992). For example, a designer of a machine part in Germany is able to send his design immediately to the computer controlling production in Michigan (or Mexico or Taiwan), thus removing any time or space barrier between conception and execution and completely bypassing any worker intervention.

Thus, computer technology allows business to completely link all aspects of production in a highly integrated system that maximizes productivity and minimizes human intervention (jobs, human error, etc.). Computers are able to control the actual assembly line or robots that make manufactured goods; they allow instantaneous communication between supervisors and workers; and they can monitor and adjust product processing without requiring any human activity. Moreover, they can do this with less error and waste than can any worker.

The changes are so great that together they form a new type of economic production that I call *flexible production*, a major component of flexible capitalism. While flexible forms of machinery are ultimately less important than the flexible uses of labor that chapter 3 discusses, they *do* play an important role in transforming the economy. These trends of industrial restructuring, deindustrialization, and computerization are components of the new stage of capitalism. Many components of economic relations are still inflexible; but the changes employers have made in the 1980s and 1990s, in response to earlier economic stagnation, have been geared toward making production technologies and workplace relations more flexible and adaptable to changes in the increasingly global economy.

In creating that flexibility, manufacturing is no longer the major employing industry. Service production has grown in importance. Regardless of these employment shifts, both manufacturing and service-sector industries are increasingly characterized by flexible production (meaning *the way work is done*), flexible technologies (*the tools to do the work*), flexible labor forces (*the people who do the work*), and flexible distribution practices—all of which together constitute the system of **flexible accumulation** (Harvey, 1989; Perrucci, 1994).

The essence of flexible accumulation is the organization of all aspects of economic activity so that they are relatively unconstrained. It is unlike the earlier period, in which employers attempted to structure their businesses (their production facilities, their labor forces, and their organizations) along stable and therefore *rigid* lines. Under flexible accumulation, employers focus on flexibility in these matters.

Part of what enables businesses to operate under these new terms is the role of banks or **financial capitalists** (capitalists who make their profits from exchanging financial goods such as loans, stocks, bonds, etc.) in controlling the flow of money. Banks control the flow of money to businesses, and computers (as discussed previously) allow that money to move extremely rapidly to a variety of economic actors. Banks now operate globally, without constraints of time, space, or currency. The increased power of banks, resulting from their ability to control and rapidly switch the flow of capital, is further strengthened by the interdependence of national economies and the rapid expansion of world trade and banking. Accordingly, Wall Street checks in with Hong Kong before the stock market opens, because stock trading in Hong Kong affects and is interconnected with that on Wall Street. One major consequence of the position of banks is that they provide businesses with high levels of mobility and decrease the tie of a business to a given place and a given work force. This mobility severs the social contract between businesses and communities.

Thus flexible production and flexible accumulation constitute a new system, in which banks occupy a position of increased importance; business operates both in production and marketing in a global environment; computer technology frees economic actors from space and time limitations; and, as chapter 3 will show, the work force is reorganized to maximize its flexible deployment (Harvey, 1989). In many ways, the economy is becoming boundless.

Dualism in the Service Sector

Many of the strategies on which employers have relied to maintain their competitive position—and that have created flexibility in their production abilities and labor forces—have converged to create new divisions within the service sector. Computers, for example, create not only flexibility but also a labor force distinguished by computer literacy. These divisions often interact with gender. While it is true that, traditionally, low-wage, low-skill, dead-end jobs have characterized the service sector, there is a strong argument that the service sector is not composed solely of these jobs but rather is fairly heterogeneous in its composition (Appelbaum and Albin, 1990; Lorence, 1991).

The service sector includes producer services (finance, insurance, real estate, professional, business), social services (health, education, welfare and public administration), distributive services (transportation, communication, wholesale and retail trade), and personal services (entertainment, domestic, hotel, eating and drinking) (Lorence, 1991, p. 768). The service sector includes not only the kid who works at McDonald's but also his mother who works as a nurse's aide and his father who works for a bank as a financial analyst.

Popular writers such as Alvin Toffler (1991) and some sociologists and economists viewed the emergence of a service-based economy as a positive trend since it placed knowledge in a particularly central position. Thus, these writers argued, inequalities based on, for example, wealth and property would be replaced by inequalities based on knowledge, and knowledge is easier to acquire than wealth and property (Bell, 1976)! Now researchers such as Appelbaum and Albin (1990) suggest that it is not just knowledge per se but a specific form of knowledge, computer literacy, that may distinguish "good" from "bad" jobs in this sector. The kid flipping hamburgers relies on his speed and coordination to accomplish his work. His mother relies on a mixture of people skills and hard physical labor. His father, on the other hand, uses the computer as the mechanism to track and intervene in international stock markets. Thus, computers vary in their centrality to the work process (see chapter 3).

Certain parts of service-sector industries are particularly dependent on information technologies. In industries such as finance, growth is often predicated on the development of the information system. Thus, this industry is one that researchers call *knowledge-intensive* (Appelbaum and Albin, 1990). These knowledge- and information-based jobs require a more educated and skilled work force than old service-sector jobs.

In an article in *Rolling Stone* magazine, Robert Reich wrote that "in the new economy, success will hinge on the ability to quickly identify and solve problems. . . . The new jobs . . . will demand constant creativity," and he counseled readers to "get a good education" (October 20, 1994). Reich went on to point out that most top earners hold college degrees, and those who don't had post–high school education in technical schools. Of those 16 to 24-year-olds without high school degrees, one half are unemployed.

Arguably, then, knowledge and information technologies divide the service sector into a core of better paid, knowledge-intensive "clean" jobs (financial analyst) and a periphery of poorly paid, knowledge-limited "dirty" jobs (nurse's aide). This segmentation results in disputes about the short- and long-term social consequences of service-sector employment growth.

Writers like Toffler, who focus on the increasing economic importance of knowledge- and information-based services, are optimistic about the future of society. For one thing, these jobs require more education, and usually jobs that require high levels of education (like lawyers, doctors, college professors) provide relatively high incomes, prestige, and security. Moreover, these are clean jobs in nice settings (offices rather than factories), in which smashed limbs or respiratory diseases (results from, for example, industrial accidents in manufacturing or "brown lung" in textile work) are highly unlikely. For these writers, the growth of the service sector means more good, high-wage jobs.

Others, however, view the expansion of the service sector as economically detrimental. In addition to the expansion of the "good" jobs are the household, personal services, recreation, restaurant, and sales positions, many of which require little in the way of technical skills and knowledge. They are labor-intensive and easily learned; workers are relatively interchangeable, replaceable, and ununionized. These are the types of jobs that some call secondary labor market or peripheral jobs (e.g., Edwards, 1979).

Health care, for example, is an area of the economy in which the annual number of jobs is increasing rather than decreasing. According to government figures, home health care aides, human services, and personal and home care aides are some of the fastest growing occupations (see Figure 2.3). That job growth is driven to a great extent by the aging of the population and, arguably, is fueled by the need for more gerontological researchers, doctors, and registered nurses, all of which require considerable education and command considerable pay. Most of the jobs, however, are for orderlies, health aides, and home health care workers, all of which are low-wage, low-skill secondary jobs that have low educational requirements.

Many of these secondary labor market, service-sector jobs represent the occupational groups women are most likely to occupy. Of the service-sector occupations, women are more heavily concentrated in service industries that are not knowledge intensive. Somewhat over 70% of personal service workers (e.g., hairdressers, manicurists, etc.), 80% of social service workers, and 78% of nonhospital health care workers are women. On the other hand, while 47% of business services employees are women, only 36% of computer and data

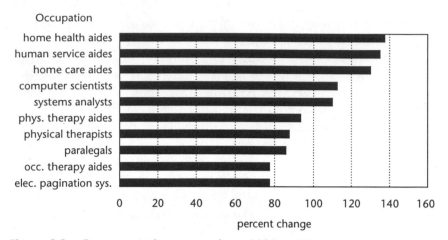

Figure 2.3. Fastest growing occupations, 1992 to 2005.

From *Statistical Abstract of the United States* (p. 394), 1994, Washington, D.C.:
U.S. Bureau of the Census.

processing services employees are women. Computer and data processing service jobs are examples of knowledge-intensive occupations
that demand greater skill and receive greater rewards. Most evidence
suggests that the majority of service-sector employment is lower paid,
is less stable, and has shorter career ladders, weaker unions, and
unfavorable working conditions. Also, it is largely female (Ritzer,
1989; Sullivan, 1989; Lorence, 1991; Smith, 1982, 1984).

Structural Unemployment, Inequality, and the Broken Contract

Industrial restructuring, plant relocation, computerization, and all the
profit-saving strategies on which employers have relied represent efforts
to avoid rigidities or limitations on how, when, where, and by whom
production occurs. These various strategies on which employers have
relied have had the unintended consequence of increasing inequality
and weakening the social contract that employment represents.

In exchange for their relative acquiescence, workers count on
gainful employment that is sufficiently predictable, stable, and routinized so that they can maintain the basic necessities of life (food,
shelter, clothing) for themselves and their families. Flexible accumulation violates this principle. Flexible accumulation strategies have
resulted in relatively high levels of **structural unemployment**

(Harvey, 1989; Mingione, 1991). Structural unemployment refers to unemployment resulting from a change in the base of the economy. In other words, when the structure of the economy changes, certain positions are simply wiped out. For example, the development of automobiles is an example of the **structural displacement** of horse and carriage drivers. If this were the only job people knew how to do, they would be in a very difficult position; they couldn't simply find jobs as chauffeurs.

Similarly, if someone has worked in a manufacturing plant for over 20 years, when that plant relocates overseas or relocates the assembly jobs overseas, that unemployed manufacturing worker is simply out of luck. While it is certainly true that economic reorganization creates new occupations (systems analysis, for example, is a growing occupation), that does an unemployed steel worker, for instance, little good. He (or she, but most likely he) would certainly be unqualified to take one of those new high-tech jobs and would be fairly limited in other jobs that he could take since the skills of a steel worker are of limited utility elsewhere. The jobs that would be most available would be relatively unskilled, low-paying service jobs, many of which are already occupied by women and adolescent workers (who are much cheaper to employ). This worker is, then, structurally displaced.

This type of unemployment is in contrast to **frictional unemployment**, arguably a characteristic of a healthy economy. Frictional unemployment occurs when workers are voluntarily between jobs, presumably in search of higher wages and better working conditions. Globalization, technological change, and industrial restructuring have not, however, resulted in this voluntary unemployment but in the *involuntary unemployment* structural displacement creates. Or, as chapter 3 will show, these newly displaced workers allow employers greater flexibility in hiring and firing.

Recent data in the *Statistical Abstract of the United States* (1994) indicate that of those workers displaced in 1992, 52.1% were displaced because the plant or company closed down or moved, and another 16.3% were displaced because the position or shift had been abolished. These workers, then, lost their jobs not because of their own failures but because of their employers' business decisions. The next chapter discusses displacement further, but here I stress one of its important consequences.

One of the consequences of structural displacement and unemployment is an increase in the number of people living in poverty.

Although a full exploration of the causes of poverty is beyond the scope of this book, the data in Table 2.2 suggest some of the economic consequences of these changes. Table 2.2 depicts the distribution of money income by race and Hispanic origin during the period on which I have focused. "Money income" means money received before payments for personal income taxes and other deductions (*Statistical Abstract,* 1994, p. 443).

Information on the government-determined **poverty threshold** (the income level below which indicates poverty) is useful for interpreting these data (see Devine and Wright, 1993). The *Statistical Abstract* (1994, p. 480, Table 738) shows that in 1980 the poverty threshold for a family of four was $7,732 a year; in 1990 it was $12,292 and in 1992 it was $13,190. (This table does not present data from 1970.)

Given that additional information, what do the data in Table 2.2 reveal? First, income is distributed unequally by race (I am including Hispanic origin here), and the unequal distribution has *worsened in the 22 years for which the data is given.* Compare, for example, the median incomes of white and black families over the period in question. The median income of white families is consistently higher than the median income of black families. (For example, in 1970 the median income for whites was $34,773; for blacks it was $21,330.) Even more striking, however, is that during this period white families experienced some increase in their median income, while black families experienced a *decrease.*

During this post-Accord period, there has been some increase in the percentage of families that are poor (see particularly the "under $10,000" column) and in the percentage of families that are rich (see the "$75,000 and over" column). At first glance, the data for all families suggest that the middle class has become richer. Note, however, that the median income (the midpoint of the income distribution) *declined* from 1990 to 1992. Remember that these data also show more families living in poverty. Additionally, these data reveal that the percentage of black and Hispanic families living in poverty has increased over this period and that the median income of both groups has declined.

Can we link these income shifts directly to displacement? Not easily. However, consistent with studies of displacement (e.g., Perrucci, Perrucci, Targ, and Targ, 1988; Doeringer, 1991), these data suggest that during this period of increasing displacement and structural unemployment, impoverishment has increased and hardship has been distributed unequally by race.

Table 2.2 Money Income of Families—Percent Distribution by Income Level, Race, and Hispanic Origin in Constant (1992) Dollars, 1970–1992

YEAR	PERCENT DISTRIBUTION							Median income (dollars)
	Under $10,000	$10,000–$14,999	$15,000–$24,999	$25,000–$34,999	$35,000–$49,999	$50,000–$74,999	$75,000 and over	
ALL FAMILIES[a]								
1970	8.6	7.5	17.4	20.2	23.1	16.3	6.8	33,519
1980	8.3	7.4	16.5	16.8	21.8	19.2	10.0	35,839
1990[b]	8.6	6.7	15.4	15.2	20.0	19.4	14.8	37,950
1992	9.5	7.3	15.5	15.0	19.2	19.6	13.9	36,812
WHITE								
1970	7.3	6.9	16.7	20.5	24.1	17.2	7.3	34,773
1980	6.7	6.6	16.0	17.1	22.7	20.2	10.7	37,341
1990[b]	6.5	6.2	14.9	15.4	20.7	20.5	15.7	39,626
1992	7.2	6.6	15.2	15.3	20.0	20.8	14.9	38,909
BLACK								
1970	20.8	13.5	24.1	17.4	14.0	8.5	1.7	21,330
1970	21.5	13.7	21.3	14.8	14.8	10.5	3.2	21,606
1990[b]	23.8	11.2	18.9	13.6	15.3	11.2	6.1	22,997
1992	26.3	11.8	18.8	13.0	14.0	10.8	5.2	21,161
HISPANIC[c]								
1980	15.1	12.5	22.7	17.8	16.6	11.6	3.8	25,087
1990[b]	16.8	12.3	20.7	16.2	17.0	10.9	6.1	25,152
1992	17.2	12.6	21.7	16.2	15.1	11.3	5.4	23,901

Adapted from *Statistical Abstract of the United States: 1994* (Table 714, p. 469), Washington D.C.: U.S. Bureau of the Census. [a]Includes other races not shown separately. [b]Beginning 1983, data based on revised Hispanic population controls and not directly comparable with prior years. [c]Persons of Hispanic origin may be of any race.

CONCLUSIONS

Flexible accumulation emerged out of the breakdown of the labor–capital accord, an arrangement that itself had emerged out of the conflicts that accompanied the transition to industrial society. The labor–capital accord—forged in the unionized economic core, dominated by large-scale manufacturing, and mirrored in nonunion sectors of the economy—coordinated the interests of workers and their employers, *in the short run*. Hard work and a stable employment record, in conjunction with a cooperative attitude, translated into long-term, stable employment, as well as growing wages for workers and growing profits for their employers.

Underlying the various strategies on which capital relied during the period of the Accord was the basic mechanism unifying the interests of capital and labor—employment. Simply put, what ultimately coordinated the interests of workers and employers was *the ongoing social contract between workers and their employers that employment represents*. As this chapter has argued, the organization of the employment contract occurred in a context of U.S. international superiority in which U.S. businesses dominated in the world economy, and labor unions contributed to and participated in that economic success.

A number of factors altered the ability of American businesses to maintain their "contractual" position. Expanded competition on a global level made businesses increasingly unwilling to privilege their workers the way they had (with benefits and high wages). Businesses responded to economic adversity with a variety of union-avoidance strategies; they actively sought to bust unions, they relocated to the South and overseas, and they availed themselves of worker-displacing technologies such as automation and robotics (both at home and abroad). Such strategies dramatically weakened unions' ability to protect the wages and benefits, no less the working conditions and jobs, of their members. As a result, unions are at their weakest since the early part of the twentieth century, and workers are once again highly vulnerable to their employers.

Similarly, many companies, rather than attempting to upgrade obsolete manufacturing facilities, shifted their efforts to the production of services. Thus, not only did manufacturing decline both as a source of employment and as a contributor to the gross national product, but service industries increased in importance on both counts.

The growth of the service sector is complex and appears to be creating a new kind of dualism based on the degree to which the service production is associated with knowledge, information, and computer technology. Those services that are more knowledge- and technology-intensive tend to be predominantly male (e.g., engineering, systems analysis) and better paid, while those that are not tend to be disproportionately female and low-paying (e.g., child care, health care, data entry).

These changes have freed employers from the limitations on production, employment, and distribution that the earlier system created. Businesses are able to move around the globe with more rapidity and ease than ever before. Their ability to do so is relatively unconstrained by ties to any place or group of workers. This freedom of movement and flexibility of production, while creating the possibility of new profits and economic growth, breaks the explicit contract embodied in collective bargaining agreements between employers and workers to exchange lucrative and secure jobs for stable and reliable employees. Furthermore, it breaks the fundamental social contract that businesses will grow rich by relying on the labor of workers and that workers will provide that labor power in exchange for the ability to keep themselves and their families at a decent standard of living, so much so that Hal Lancaster, writing in the *Wall Street Journal* (November 29, 1994), claimed that "the social contract between employers and employees, in which companies promise to ensure employment . . . is dead, dead, dead." Most simply, in the absence of employment and stability, the most basic mechanism forging the social contract is sundered.

WORK IN THE FLEXIBLE ECONOMY

When my father-in-law got out of the army after World War II, he moved his wife and baby daughter to southern California. He got a job as a lineman with the telephone company, bought a small house for $12,000, had a son, and knew that in a little over 30 years he would go to his retirement dinner. During his years with the phone company, he moved up the job ladder from lineman to engineer. He did that, moreover, with a only a high school education. He had a unionized job that provided health benefits, sick days, and, most important, security. That security allowed him and his wife to raise their daughter and son, pay off the mortgage, and retire with the health and economic security to enjoy their "golden years."

His grandson (my nephew David) won't have the same opportunities. After graduating from high school David took a variety of jobs, none of which paid much more than the minimum wage. He wants to be a musician and has gone back to school. He knows he should do something practical, but he's not sure what. He can't count on any of the major employers in his area; he can't count on having the type of job security his grandfather had. He doesn't really know what it means when he's told to "get a good job, son." What happened to change his opportunities?

The answer lies in the United States' transition from an industrial economy with a strong labor–capital accord to a postindustrial, flexible economy. That economic shift has altered the definition of good and bad jobs. In the past, a good job was a stable one, one that could be expected to support a worker for a lifetime. Today, a good job is one that requires and rewards high levels of knowledge and promises to keep expanding workers' knowledge so that they remain employable.

As chapter 2 explained, to make the social relations of the workplace more adaptable to the changed international and national market, American employers in the 1970s began reorganizing the workplace around new technologies that would make production more responsive to rapidly changing economic conditions. The outcome of those changes was to create flexibility in the ways contemporary employers use workers and technology. Many telephone operators, for example, were replaced by computers. A major consequence of these changes was to minimize long-term employment contracts. The fundamental security that work provided for people like my father-in-law was lost. Workers getting jobs in corporation X today are highly unlikely to go to a retirement dinner for corporation X in 30 years. In those 30 years they may have long series of jobs, regardless of education or skill level. Their identities won't come from single, long-term employment relationships based on the opportunity to work their way up from an entry-level position.

In an industrial economy, people identify themselves with what they do ("I am a lineman for the county"); work is perhaps the major way people locate themselves in social space. Work during the Accord years provided people with a certain stability. That stability was not just economic but also emotional and familial. The flexible economy, on the other hand, is based on rapid change and adaptability. This chapter will outline the dualism in the structure of jobs, the structure of work in the Accord years, the ways in which that structure has changed, and some implications of those changes.

LABOR MARKET SEGMENTATION

The previous chapter discussed the ways in which the **economy** is segmented into an economic core and an economic periphery. Core industry groups are characterized by operation in national and international markets, concentrated assets, capital intensivity, and centrality to the overall health of the economy. Peripheral industries operate in local markets, have lower assets, are labor-intensive, and contribute minimally to the country's GNP. A similar segmentation refers to the structure of jobs. Sociologists refer to these categories as **labor market segments** (Edwards, 1979; Weakliem, 1990; Bridges and Villemez, 1991).

When people look for jobs, they compete with others in **labor markets** (the arena in which workers are matched to jobs) for the best job they can get, given their qualifications. Employers seeking to fill positions hire the best person they can find for the lowest price—the wage. That is the simplest model of how the matching process occurs. However, labor market segmentation theorists claim that all jobs are not arrayed in a single market. Rather, jobs cluster into distinct market segments, and workers who search for jobs in one market segment are *not* competing with workers in the other market segments. According to these theorists, jobs are grouped into three segments:

- Subordinate primary labor market: unionized, blue-collar, lower-level sales and administrative, and clerical workers. Most workers in this labor market are unionized.
- Independent primary labor market: upper-level managers, professionals (e.g., professors, doctors, and lawyers) and technical experts (e.g., engineers); long-term clerical, sales, and technical staff; and craft labor. Most of these jobs require advanced training or specialized schooling.
- Secondary labor market: low-skill service (e.g., fast food), low-level retail, and low-end clerical jobs—specifically, low-wage "casual" labor (Edwards, 1979).

Although all jobs do not fall neatly into one market or another, labor market segmentation theory is a useful vehicle for examining the changing structure of jobs. Note that the labor markets span both white-collar and blue-collar jobs.

The three labor market segments differ in several ways. One is the way the labor process is structured. For example, white-collar workers tend to have more autonomy, and they work in cleaner, quieter, and less dangerous environments than blue-collar workers, who tend to do repetitive production work. In general, the rewards are greater for the white-collar jobs, which require more education. However, plumbers often do dirty blue-collar work and are paid more than most teachers and secretaries, who are white-collar workers (and not coincidentally, usually female). But the single most important thing differentiating these three labor market segments is the behavioral stability the jobs require, foster, and reward. Behavioral stability refers to reliable and predictable work habits, lack of absenteeism, and a stable employment history (Edwards, 1979).

The concept of labor market segmentation is a useful one. However, as you will see, the definition of the segments is changing along with the economy.

WORK IN THE ACCORD YEARS:
THE STABLE WORKPLACE

The post–World War II labor–capital accord deepened and, in many ways, institutionalized the differences among the segments of the labor market. As employers sought new ways of structuring jobs to accommodate organized labor and increasingly large bureaucratic organizations, they developed good jobs for both blue-collar and white-collar workers in the primary labor market (Gordon, Edwards, and Reich, 1982). What the "good" jobs all shared was their emphasis on stability and security, *for both the employer and the worker*. That stability was what transformed conflict into accord. Employers wanted assurance of stable, uninterrupted production, whether of goods or services; workers wanted assurance of steady, lucrative employment.

Good Jobs: Blue-Collar Jobs in the Primary Labor Market

My father-in-law, remember, was a blue-collar worker, but he was in the subordinate primary labor market. He was a member of the Communications Workers of America. When the CWA called a strike, my father-in-law honored it. When they ratified a new contract, he benefitted from it. When there were layoffs, his seniority protected him. His experience exemplifies the experience of many workers who worked during the labor–capital accord years.

Stabilizing Structures A key component of the labor–capital accord was the institutionalization of unions, productivity-based bargaining, and cost-of-living adjustments. All tied the interests of unionized blue-collar workers to those of their employers. As a result, all union-ized blue-collar workers enjoyed the benefits of being in the primary market. The unions themselves contributed to the stability of the labor–capital accord era. However, unions were not the only struc-tures contributing to the stability of the workplace. The labor process was also a factor.

During this time, corporations designed manufacturing plants so that machinery, rather than the worker, structured the activity of the worker. Assembly line technology, for example, rooted workers to a single spot and made their work process a single repetitive movement all day long. Though the assembly line was not a new technology, during the labor–capital accord era assembly line and related technologies (those in which the production process was linked by machinery throughout large parts of the plant) were used more widely than ever before.

This technique of routinizing and standardizing work originated with the management techniques of Frederick Winslow Taylor in the early part of the twentieth century. Taylor developed a system called *scientific management,* which entailed the systematic study of jobs and the division of jobs into separate tasks. This extended **detailed division of labor** was, for Taylor, the way for managers to exert the greatest control over their employees. He created time-and-motion studies as a way of finding out exactly how much time each part of a job would take—and then tried to minimize any extra movement to make the job more efficient. The key element was to redesign all jobs so that workers had no discretion whatsoever over how they would complete a job. This redesign also allowed the replacement of skilled workers with unskilled workers. Managers have continued to use the logic of Taylorism in organizing the labor process throughout the twentieth century (Braverman, 1974; Harvey, 1989; Sayer and Walker, 1992).

Assembly line and related technologies not only cheapen the cost of production but also create stability in two ways. First, since the workers are by and large limited to a single spot and/or working in a noisy environment, there is little opportunity to talk with one another and possibly create any kind of collective disruption. Second, because the workers often know little about the process as a whole or the final product, they are unlikely to deviate from the specified way of working.

Controlling the pace of work limits worker discretion over what they do and how fast they do it. The classic "I Love Lucy" episode in which Lucy and Ethel are working in a chocolate factory lampoons the assembly line process; no matter how fast Lucy and Ethel might have wanted to work, the speed with which the chocolates flew by determined how fast they had to work. Their employer's reliance on technology was an attempt to ensure steady, uninterrupted production.

The second way to stabilize production, breaking up each task into its most basic components, limits workers' ability to alter the procedures of work. Instead of one worker doing a range of complex tasks, he or she does just one part of the process. Compare, for example, someone who designs a dress, creates the pattern, cuts out the fabric, and then finishes the garment with someone who just sews panel A to panel B on hundreds of dresses all day long. For one worker the process is creative and complex; for the other it is routinized and simple. Although such specialization makes production more stable, it is not always beneficial to workers.

Deskilling and Alienation One result of scientific management, worker specialization, and the use of new production technology is often to **deskill** and cheapen labor. *Deskilling* refers to transforming skilled work into unskilled work. Workers who design and create dresses are drawing on far more of their skills than are the workers who simply stitch seams all day long. The former workers are also more expensive because they know more and are more reliable. Thus, by removing the skill involved in the job, employers have more control over the process, and workers have less.

Any type of job can be deskilled. Think of grocery stores, for instance. When I was a young girl, grocery checkout personnel used more skill in their jobs than they do now. To complete the economic transaction with the buyer, checkout personnel had to have simple mathematical skills; they had to know how to make change. Computerized cash registers have altered that. Now, the checkout person merely runs the item by the electronic scanner. (Watch what happens when the price for a specialty item doesn't make it into the computer.) The computer registers the item and displays its cost. At the end of scanning all the items, the computerized cash register supplies the checker with the amount to request from the shopper. The checkout person enters into the computer the amount that the shopper provides, and the computer indicates the change the shopper is owed. Simple math is now deleted from the skill requirements of being a checkout person.

I once asked a class about their work experiences. Several of my students had worked on an assembly line, and the descriptions converged on something like the following: "I stood in one place all day; this thing went by me and stayed in front of me for a few minutes while I turned some screws, or it stopped at my station and I put it in a box [or something like that]. It was too noisy to talk with anyone else; I had a lunch break and two 5-minute breaks during the day." I asked if it was boring; the answer was always yes. As these students discovered, working under such conditions *alienates* workers. **Alienation** refers to feelings of powerlessness, meaninglessness, isolation, and separation (Blauner, 1964).

Suppose, for instance, that what you love to do is build things; so you start building curio cabinets. You imbue those cabinets with your artistic ability; you sell them. On your own, you do not have enough money to buy the material to continue to build these cabinets and still pay the rent; so you go to work for a custom furniture store. There, you can continue to develop your craft. In time, however, the owner decides that she or he can make more money by mechanizing the process. In no time at all, you are working in a highly mechanized shop producing standardized products. The mechanization of the task has rendered you an extension of the machinery. You are no longer engaged in craft labor but are now engaged in routinized tasks (just like the automobile assembly line worker). The inability to do the work that you love and that expresses your creativity alienates you.

Trade-offs for Blue-Collar Workers While such types of work environments may indeed be alienating in their failure to provide meaningful and interesting work, in many instances there are major trade-offs: job stability, high wages, and generous benefits. Additionally, mechanized work means that plants can produce more in a given period of time, which may free workers for more leisure-time activities. The fact is that for many workers, jobs are means to an end: their paycheck and the leisure time that check will buy. As stultifying as deskilling often was under the labor–capital accord, workers had more leisure time than in earlier periods.

Moreover, it would be a gross generalization to say that all blue-collar jobs are deskilled and alienating. Some of them provide opportunities for workers to learn new skills and enhance the scope of their jobs. My father-in-law began working as a telephone lineman, but over the years he learned about the telephone system and obtained on-the-job training. That training eventually taught him the skills that allowed him to move to an engineering job. By the time he retired, workers hired to do the type of work he was doing were required to have college degrees (which he did not have). By the way, such on-the-job training also creates stability in the workplace. Workers who see a way to progress where they already work are less likely to seek opportunities elsewhere.

Within the blue-collar primary labor market, different jobs have used different strategies toward the same end: to ensure that both production processes and workers operated in stable, predictable ways. The particular mix of strategies depended on the particular job, industry, and so on, but the outcome was more or less the same. For blue-collar workers in the primary labor market, there were ample opportunities to improve their quality of life through job mobility within the company, increased pay, and favorable working conditions. Thus, while work may occasionally have been boring and unrewarding emotionally, it allowed workers to achieve what we think of as a middle-class lifestyle.

Good Jobs: White-Collar Jobs in the Primary Labor Market

Of course, not all workers are blue-collar workers; a great many are white-collar workers. In the era of the labor–capital accord, employers also created job structures to foster stability within the white-collar work force—most notably, career ladders and economic rewards.

Career ladders were one of the most effective mechanisms employers used to ensure stability among white-collar workers. Of particular importance for managerial and, to some extent, clerical workers were **internal labor markets.** Internal labor markets refer to career ladders within firms that fill job openings from within the firm rather than outside the firm. For example, Mr. Black is a manager in the advertising department of a large firm. He has worked there for years and has neither rocked the boat nor presided over declining profits. All in all, he's been a stable, effective manager who plays golf with his boss and goes to church on Sunday. When the head of Mr. Black's department leaves that position to take over another department within the firm, the higher-level position is open. Instead of going outside the firm to look for fresh talent, the firm promotes Mr. Black. They know they can count on him. He is a reliable, normal guy who will represent the firm appropriately. In sum, he's a known quantity, and as such he will be rewarded. That is how an internal labor market works (Edwards, 1979; Kalleberg and Berg, 1987; Jacoby, 1988; Bridges and Villemez, 1991).

Internal labor markets are characterized by finely graded hierarchies that create job ladders with many steps. Each movement up the ladder is associated with some increase in rewards and benefits. There are minute differences between jobs that might be marked by a slightly higher salary, bigger office, and different job title. These job ladders reward workers for their stability and longevity with the firm. For example, an office might have four secretaries, each with a different job title, such as filer, receptionist, administrative assistant, and typist, each with a different salary. A filer might move up the clerical hierarchy into the higher-paid receptionist position as an opening occurs. Reliability and seniority as much as productivity determine advancement. All career ladders are not equally tall. For example, women tend to occupy jobs with shorter career ladders. One study that compared the gender gap in earnings for men and women in the

United States and Sweden (a country with strong egalitarian principles) found that the presence of career ladders had little impact on women's earnings. This finding suggests not only that women's career ladders are often shorter than men's but also that sometimes men's career ladders are completely off limits to women (Rosenberg and Kalleberg, 1990).

Career ladders for professional workers (e.g., college professors, lawyers, doctors) and technical workers (e.g., engineers, high-level computer programmers) tend to cross organizations instead of linking positions in a single organization (Kalleberg and Berg, 1987). For example, I used to teach at a university in the Northeast. I changed jobs several years ago and now work at a university in the South, where rank and pay are higher. Again, reliability and seniority—in the form of a track record in a given field—determine who receives better jobs.

The white-collar primary labor market also rewards workers for their education. For each additional year of school beyond college, a worker can anticipate increased income. Thus, an advertising department may have 10 people working in it, three of whom have some postgraduate training. These workers will undoubtedly receive higher pay.

Bad Jobs: The Secondary Labor Market

The secondary labor market is the antithesis of the primary labor market. Jobs in the secondary market tend to be low-wage and nonunionized. They lack benefits and opportunities for mobility, and they offer little stability. They can be either white- or blue-collar. Secondary labor market jobs also tend to require little skill from workers, thus making workers relatively interchangeable.

The types of jobs students typically have in high school and college are secondary labor market jobs (for example, sales, waitressing, fast-food production). Jobs like these are high-turnover jobs. They do not provide workers with any incentive to stay if the job becomes unpleasant or if a better one comes along. Nor do they penalize workers for leaving. A waitress who gets sick of a leering boss can quit her job and easily find another job waiting tables.

In the absence of career ladders, making more money in the secondary labor market means working longer hours or working a second job. Secondary labor market jobs, unlike the primary labor market, do not reward workers for increased education. A college-educated waitress works for the same pay as the waitress with only a high school diploma.

For college students, secondary labor market jobs are simply a source of additional income. Working in them poses no barrier to future career development. That is not the case, however, for adult workers with job histories in the secondary labor market. These workers may find that their job histories prevent them from moving into a higher paying, stable, primary labor market job. Since secondary labor market jobs do not promote, foster, or reward stability, there is little incentive or opportunity for workers to develop stable work habits. There is nothing to keep them from switching jobs at will. Potential employers often view a multi-job history as evidence that the *worker*, not the job, is unstable. This attribution is particularly likely if the superficial characteristics of the worker (such as race or sex) conform to the employer's preexisting stereotypes (e.g., women are unstable because they will leave as soon as they get married). Indeed, there is evidence that women are disproportionately represented in the secondary labor market jobs (Gordon, Edwards, and Reich, 1982; Blau and Ferber, 1986). Part of what traps workers in the secondary labor market is that they learn few of the work behaviors or skills that will foster future primary labor market employment.

Secondary labor market jobs are unstable in yet another way. They are often part-time or temporary. Part-time work is problematic for many, not only because it provides wages insufficient to stay above the poverty line but also because most part-time workers receive no benefits whatsoever—no health care, no paid vacations, no disability. Thus, secondary labor market jobs may keep workers in an economically precarious position. Not only are their wages minimal, but if a health crisis, car accident, or some unexpected drain on already meager resources occurs, a family on the edge may be plunged into poverty.

WORK IN THE POST-ACCORD YEARS: THE FLEXIBLE WORKPLACE

Today a flexible workplace is developing to complement the flexible economy. Although the nature and status of certain jobs are changing, labor market segmentation remains a feature of the workplace. However, whereas the old forms of segmentation grew out of employers' need for stability, the new forms of segmentation grow out of their need for flexibility.

There are a number of ways in which employers can create flexibility. Some of the ways discussed in the last chapter were the use of technology to create product flexibility (CAD to redesign car bodies with little overall cost and loss of efficiency); the creation of flexible organizations (large firms can outsource labor-intensive jobs overseas—e.g., textiles from Taiwan); and the use of computers to rapidly shift funds. This section examines employers' efforts to create flexible employment and flexible work practices. These new workplace strategies create new segmentations among workers that may overlap or intersect earlier segmentations.

Today's workplace looks very different from its predecessor. The older **organizational structure** (the social relations within the organization) was a large, bureaucratic firm. It had a large, unionized blue-collar work force that remained with the firm through union seniority, and it had a large white-collar work force integrated by internal labor markets. But this type of workplace is disappearing and being replaced with a new workplace that is far more decentralized. One can view the organizational structure of the new workplace as an octopus. It maintains a small core of knowledge-intensive primary workers and *outsources* most of its low-skill jobs. **Outsourcing** refers to subcontracting work that used to be done within a firm to another firm or group of workers (Bluestone and Harrison, 1982). It relies on consultants and temporary workers for accounting, research and development, computer services, and many other functions. Thus many of the workers affiliated with the flexible workplace are affiliated on a temporary basis. As a result employers have more control than ever over some workers, but relatively few workers have good, stable jobs.

Good Jobs: Dynamically Flexible Workers

One of the ways that some employers have attempted to maintain a competitive edge in the flexible economy is to use computer technology to upgrade the skill level of workers. This use of computers is a way of bringing **dynamic flexibility** to a workplace (Colclough and Tolbert, 1992). Dynamic flexibility—or what Piore and Sabel (1984) call *flexible specialization*—is the strategy of constantly changing and innovating production processes and skill levels as new opportunities become apparent. Workplaces that use dynamic flexibility strategies require highly educated and skilled workers who are familiar with computers and other advanced technologies and can respond rapidly to changing markets. Dynamic flexibility relies on employee commitment to the organization and willingness to use their knowledge, skills, and effort to continually improve the product or service.

A dynamically flexible worker is removed from the constraints of routinized mass production techniques and has greater discretion and participation in the production process. For example, a dynamically flexible production worker in the electronics industry might develop new ways to use existing production tools or even design better tools. Instead of penalizing workers for departing from the standard way of accomplishing the work task, management would encourage and reward such innovation. The work day is varied and divided among a variety of tasks. Workers are continually upgrading their skills, gaining new information, and using old information in new ways. This way of organizing work has played an important role in the success of Japanese electronics industries (Colclough and Tolbert, 1992).

Workers in service industries such as education, finance, and business may also be dynamically flexible. In these service industries, "production" often depends on complex computerized processing of information (Appelbaum and Albin, 1990). For instance, a financial advisor might work out of a home office and consult via the Internet with clients all over the world. This type of work setting allows her to spend time with her children, meet with clients, and make transactions—all from her home. Some part of the day might be spent reading, some part advising people, and some part analyzing data. Note that although computers are not a *necessary* condition for this type of flexible worker, they play an increasingly important role. The presence of, absence of, or level of computer skills can thus determine the quality of the job to which a worker has access.

Flexibly specialized or dynamically flexible workers are highly educated and skilled. These are the workers with whom employers maintain the *implicit contract* of long-term, stable employment because their specialized knowledge makes them expensive and difficult to replace. Thus, the new primary sector workers maintain their primary sector status by continually learning and upgrading their own skill levels. While they may have a real measure of stability, they maintain it under constant pressure.

Although the jobs of flexibly specialized workers may be fairly secure, these workers may need to be geographically nimble (Belous,

1989). For example, in the last chapter I mentioned my best friend's father, John. He is a researcher who works for a research and development firm consulted by a variety of companies. John has been with this company for over 20 years. He survived restructuring in the early 1970s because he agreed to spend over 10 months of the year in Asia or on the West Coast; his family lives in Maryland. Thus, while his job is relatively secure, the cost of keeping it has been high.

John is, however, far more fortunate than those workers who lack the skill or opportunity to fit into the new economy. Those workers are more likely to have unstable jobs in the secondary labor market, which unfortunately is expanding.

The new primary labor market comprises a small group of highly educated, skilled workers who are flexibly specialized and highly committed to their employers (Belous, 1989). Most important, only their jobs are as stable as those of the primary labor force under the labor–capital accord.

Bad Jobs: Statically Flexible Workers

Evidence suggests that the majority of workers in the flexible workplace are not in the relatively stable core but are working in an expanded secondary labor market characterized by the *instability* of jobs (Mingione, 1991; Colclough and Tolbert, 1992). This expanded sector is characterized by strategies of static flexibility (or **numerical flexibility**) rather than a dynamically flexible production process. *Static flexibility* refers to the organization of employment around labor demand. Employers attempt to reorganize the labor process so that they have to pay workers only for specific jobs or for short periods of time. Consider the typical secretary, for example. She (about 99% of all clerical workers are female) may be very busy at some times, but under the usual employment contract (8 hours a day, 5 days a week) she may also have long periods when there is very little work to do. Under these conditions, an employer will be paying a worker just to sit around. However, reorganizing the workplace around statically flexible workers might mean that an office does not have a full-time clerical worker but instead uses part-time or temporary clerical workers as needed. This scenario is most feasible where the skills of the statically flexible workers are minimal and interchangeable. In the labor–capital accord era, employers used this strategy only with relatively unskilled workers. In the flexible economy, however, skilled, well-educated workers are used in the same way (Colclough and Tolbert, 1992; Harvey, 1989). In fact, Belous finds that more than half of all temporary workers are employed in technical, sales, and administrative support occupations (1989, p. 28). His research also shows that "at least 17% of the temporary work force is employed in occupations that are managerial, professional, technical or skilled blue collar" (Belous, 1989, p. 29). Those occupations may well include accountants, architects, engineers, financial advisors, lawyers, and doctors, just to name a few.

Technology and Labor Control Computerization is a critical feature of the flexible workplace. Computers facilitate flexible specialization and create dynamic flexibility for the new primary sector workers and numerical flexibility for employers. However, computers are also often used to deskill workers, thereby limiting their discretion and increasing the employer's control. For example, supervisors of clerical workers can keep track (through networked computers) of how many words per minute a worker is producing. If the worker stops typing to fix a shoe or change position, that gap in production is noted. Any time workers are monitored to this extent, their ability to exercise discretion decreases. A secretary who was once able to detect and point out an awkward or incorrectly worded sentence must now just type it regardless of errors. The skills he or she can bring to the task are diminished. Employers use computerization to minimize the discretion of professional workers as well. Garson (1988), in her excellent book *The Electronic Sweatshop*, interviewed social workers who were experiencing computerization of much of their job. One woman claimed that rather than providing the social services her clients needed, she spent her time processing increasing numbers of people through an overly bureaucratic system. Garson also noted that now there are even therapy software packages, in which a computer therapist guides the client through a series of menu-driven questions.

In the flexible workplace, employers also have greater leverage than before in any conflict with workers. While just-in-time practices make strikes in supplying companies more problematic for employers, the computer-connected but geographically dispersed production still gives employers an advantage. If, for example, workers in one plant go on strike, management can easily increase production in a second plant. Additionally, the presence of part-time workers creates a disincentive for permanent workers to engage in collective action. If they strike, they are clearly vulnerable to replacement.

Part-time and subcontracted workers are less likely to be union members. In a workplace with both permanent and subcontracted workers, the workers are usually paid at different rates. In efforts to protect their own well-being, permanent union workers press for legislation limiting the use of temporary or subcontracted workers. In doing so, they are working against the interests of workers who may have access only to part-time or temporary jobs. This conflict is just as great when subcontracted workers *are* unionized since they and full-time workers are usually represented by different unions (Baugher, 1994). The use of numerically flexible workers also undermines worker solidarity, thus further weakening unions. Because most part-time workers are not union members, the move to this type of work makes workers less likely to protest or in any way challenge the prerogatives of management.

Displacement　At the extreme, computerization and automation eliminate jobs. More jobs have been lost to subcontracting than to technology; but technology—in combination with industrial shifts, mergers, and general downsizing—has led to a massive displacement of workers. **Displacement** is the loss of jobs for reasons that are completely independent of how well workers have worked. A worker who is habitually late and is subsequently fired leaves an opening that will probably be filled. But a worker who is out of a job because the factory moves to Mexico has been displaced.

Well-paid blue-collar workers who had benefited from the labor–capital accord constituted the majority of displaced workers in the 1970s. In the 1980s, white-collar financial, professional, and managerial workers were also displaced. Using a broad definition of displacement, evidence suggests that "displacement rates have increased by 20% to 40% since the early 1970s" (Doeringer, 1991, p. 49). Displaced workers suffer far more than the pain and economic costs of immediate job loss. Workers who cannot find equivalent jobs right away often experience permanent wage reductions and repeated job instability. Additional problems may include loss of houses, breakup of families, increased rates of alcoholism, illness, and even homelessness.

In the film *Roger and Me,* Michael Moore interviews a woman who has been displaced from her job in the auto industry. Since there were few alternative sources of employment, she resorted to selling rabbits "for pets or meat" (the title of his next movie). In one particularly chilling sequence, she calmly skins a rabbit while talking about how General Motors hurt her by closing the plant, leaving her with no option but the one so gruesomely depicted in the film. While all workers do not end up selling bunnies as future stew meat, they do end up strapped for work. In their study of displaced electronics workers in Indiana, Perrucci, Perrucci, Targ, and Targ (1988) found that in addition to lost income, a diminished community tax base, and other economic indicators, the displaced workers evinced "high levels of alienation and distrust of the groups and institutions that comprise the social fabric in the community and at the national level" (p. 123).

The displacement process is one factor that has enabled the creation of a numerically flexible labor force. Workers who have been displaced from a job because of industrial restructuring or downsizing are in very vulnerable positions. When an automobile plant closes, what happens to the 50-year-old who worked in the autobody painting department for the last 30 years? There are no other automobile plants in town for him to get a comparable job. And the sector of the economy that is expanding—services—is unlikely to provide him with a job comparable to the one he's been displaced from. He doesn't have the skills or experience to obtain one of the better paid, more secure jobs in the expanding financial and business sector. The types of jobs to which he will have access (security guard, janitor) are likely to be far less lucrative. Displaced workers may be unable to find any job at all and thus join the ranks of the structurally unemployed.

Workers who are displaced have a variety of strategies for coping. Some of the more skilled and privileged displaced workers are able to start their own businesses. The local paper often has stories of people who have turned their labor market adversity into an opportunity. For example, one woman who had been displaced from an administrative position used the skills and contacts she had gained on the job to develop her own temporary employment agency, a business that has relatively low start-up costs. But not all displaced workers have these opportunities. Some fall back on behaviors that are particularly destructive (like alcoholism and substance abuse). Many others end up in the informal economy.

The term **informal economy** can be used in a number of ways. Sometimes it refers to illegal activity such as drug dealing and prostitution; sometimes it refers to income-generating activity that "is unregulated by the institutions of society, in a legal and social environment in which similar activities are regulated" (Portes, Castells, and Benton, 1989, p. 12). For example, domestic and child care workers who receive pay but no social security fall into this category. Garage sales, in which the price does not include sales tax, are also part of the informal economy. The woman selling rabbits for "pets or meat" is in the informal economy. Similarly, computer consultants, tax accountants, fruit vendors, and car washers may also all be part of the informal economy if they neither declare their earnings nor pay taxes. Other options are to become contingent workers or homeworkers.

Contingent Work One member of my family, Peter, worked in the banking industry for years, developing and using new computer software for the bank's information systems. Over the years Pete's job seemed to develop along the lines of flexibly specialized workers. He continually upgraded and used skills to improve the bank's communications network as part of an ongoing process, and he was rewarded handsomely for this work. When the bank merged with another bank, Pete played a central role in restructuring their communication network. Despite massive layoffs, his skills assured him of his position until his boss—and then he—were fired. For 3 years thereafter, despite an impressive array of skills and an equally impressive resume, he was unable to find another full-time job. Instead he has turned to temporary work. Corporations hire him to do a single job; when he completes the job, he has to look for more work.

Pete is not alone in this experience; he represents part of the new and expanding **contingent labor force**. The contingent labor force includes both part-time and temporary workers—some voluntarily contingent and some involuntarily so. Contingent workers receive lower pay, no fringe benefits, and little occupational protection. Their work is contingent on labor demand, and their security is up for grabs. Most would rather work full-time if they could. Research shows that since 1970, involuntary part-time work has grown 121% (Callaghan and Hartman, 1991, p. 4). It is no wonder that it is involuntary, given these conditions. Part-time workers are six times more likely to work for minimum wage than full-time workers. Additionally, the Internal Revenue Service has estimated that up to 30% of employers deliberately misclassify their workers as independent contractors rather than full-time workers to avoid paying unemployment compensation and social security tax (duRivage, 1992, p. 87). duRivage also finds that only one in six contingent workers is covered by a pension plan.

The involuntary, part-time work force is growing more rapidly than the full-time work force and is becoming a permanent part of the

·modern workplace (Callaghan and Hartman, 1991). Recent estimates suggest that contingent workers represent 25–30% of the work force and appear most often in the retail trades and in services, which are low-productivity, low-wage jobs (Callaghan and Hartman, 1991). Women make up roughly two thirds of the contingent work force. Black men in temporary, blue-collar manual work constitute the second largest category of contingent workers (duRivage, 1992). One report indicated that "displaced white-collar workers are told up front that any job they get in any company should not be expected to last longer than three to five years—if they are lucky and stay on their toes" (*Times-Picayune*, October 9, 1994).

In contrast to earlier periods, high levels of what economists call **human capital** (e.g., education, training, and skills) no longer ensure status as a primary worker as firms increasingly hire consultants, accountants, marketing researchers, lawyers, and technical help on a temporary, as-needed basis. The firm of the future is likely to include very few permanent workers and to subcontract out for the rest of its workers, from the low-skill janitorial and cafeteria staff to the highly skilled workers.

Reliance on a contingent labor force has two major advantages for employers. First, it dramatically decreases labor costs. On average, part-time workers earn 60% of the hourly wages of full-time workers (Belous, 1989; duRivage, 1992, p. 87). Most receive neither pensions, health benefits, fringe benefits, nor unemployment insurance. When banks hire Peter on a contingent basis to do work similar to what he had been doing, they get the same work from him as they used to. Now, however, they do not have to pay for the generous benefits workers at his level usually receive.

Second, reliance on contingent workers also allows employers to use workers only as they need them, rather than maintain a stable work force during, for example, periods of slack demand. Ironically, though, there is evidence that employers are not using contingent workers solely in response to shifting demand conditions (i.e., hiring extra sales workers during the holiday season). Rather, they are using contingent workers on a permanent basis (Belous, 1989; Callaghan and Hartman, 1991; duRivage, 1992).

Homework Another part of the labor force that is expanding is the **homeworker** group. These are not workers who bring work home from their regular place of employment but workers whose home *is* their regular place of employment. Some of these workers are part of the informal economy, and some are part of the formal (regulated) economy. My tax accountant, for instance, has a full-time job but also works out of her home doing tax returns for university faculty. She relies on a sophisticated computer service she accesses from her home computer. Similarly, when I pick up the phone and order clothes from certain catalogues, I may be talking to a home-based worker. One company, Deva Cottonwear, includes in their catalogue little biographical sketches of the homeworkers who hand-stitch their garments. These homeworkers are part of the formal economy.

This form of work has emerged in part as a result of computer technology. When personal computers first hit the market, journalists and other commentators predicted that people would no longer have to drive to an office because computers and telephone lines would allow them to work at home. This prediction was particularly compelling in the context of the expanding service economy because so many services do not require an office. Indeed, the number of homeworkers is expanding. According to the Bureau of Labor Statistics, about 1.9 million Americans work exclusively at home (as opposed to those who bring work home from the office) (Christensen, 1988).

What is most germane for the current discussion is the vulnerability and neediness of many of these workers. The lack of benefits associated with their work makes them vulnerable to any misfortune (an accident, sudden illness), as does the instability of their workloads. About two thirds of homeworkers are women who average a 27-hour work week (Christensen, 1988). Since most women who work do so for economic reasons, the limited and uncertain number of hours of work makes them economically vulnerable. The often precarious market position of many of these workers makes them an ideal labor force within flexible capitalism. For example, as demand expands, employers can bring increasing numbers of workers into the production and distribution process without incurring many of the associated overhead costs of a larger work force. As need arises, they can, for instance, hire consultants, accountants, clerical workers, and phone-sales workers on a short-term basis without acquiring the additional costs of office space, cafeterias, phones, and so on.

Flexible work arrangements may, on the one hand, seem particularly appealing to women workers who wish to combine paid work with housework, child rearing, and emotion work in families. Work arrangements that depart from a traditional 40-hour week benefit workers who must negotiate the dual demands of work and family. On the other hand, researchers such as Christensen (1988) find that even most homeworkers end up relying on paid or unpaid child care so that they can get their work done. For other workers, however, flexible hours and the departure from routinized tasks have the potential to increase productivity, decrease stress, and generally improve their job satisfaction (Piore and Sable, 1984; Zuboff, 1984). In any case, evidence suggests that many homeworkers are in that position by default. Women with children, in particular, would often choose to work as full-time, permanent employees if good child care options were available—and if the jobs were available (Christensen, 1988; duRivage, 1992). In the flexible workplace, however, "good" jobs are harder to find than ever. The lack of good jobs goes a long way toward explaining the increased inequality and poverty that the data in chapters 2 and 4 depict.

THE CHALLENGE TO EDUCATION

What prepares workers for the demands of the workplace? Historically, schools have been one of the major sources of that preparation. For the remainder of this chapter, I discuss some of the implications for schooling of these workplace changes.

Education in the Accord Era

During the labor–capital accord era, in addition to teaching basic cognitive skills, schools played an important role in screening potential job applicants and socializing them to their future work roles. This socialization process included teaching the work habits geared toward different levels of jobs. Thus, high schools emphasized the work habits needed for jobs requiring only a high school diploma (i.e., the ability to follow rules, respect for authority). Similarly, colleges emphasized work habits needed for jobs requiring a college degree (i.e., the ability to work independently on a task someone else designs). Finally, postgraduate education emphasized the internalization of the norms and goals of the particular profession (Bowles and Gintis, 1976; Edwards, 1979).

Since stability was such an important component of the labor–capital accord era, it stands to reason that schools would stress stability as a teaching goal. We can see this emphasis in a variety of ways. In kindergarten through high school, for example, an important emphasis in conventional education is on following rules and respecting authority. Although many of the classroom techniques teachers use are aimed at controlling a large group of young children, they also teach these necessary work behaviors. I remember as a child, for example, having trouble in class because I would neither color within the lines, nor use "appropriate" colors. This inordinate emphasis on enforcing arbitrary "rules of art" reveals a focus on rules rather than creativity. Similarly, arranging children's seats into rows also reinforces the hierarchical relations within the classroom. The teacher is in the front, and all eyes must be on him or her. Students sit with their backs to one another, thus (supposedly) minimizing communication. And, of course, many students are told, when they ask a teacher why a certain assigned task is important, "BECAUSE I SAID SO!" Schools like Montessori use very different structures (self-directed work groups, for example) because they seek to stress independent and creative work.

By the time a student is in college, the expectations for work habits change. There, students are expected to work without direct supervision and a welter of specific rules. College teaches students to work hard, on their own, on a task that someone else has assigned— what Edwards (1979) calls "habits of predictability and dependability." A typical college instructor might assign a term paper and provide the student with the topic. Assignments along these lines teach students to work independently on a task not of their own choosing and to do it relatively free from supervision. This type of work process mirrors the work process in which many office workers are involved. Additionally, the motivation for work in school is often the grade rather than the interest. This process also mirrors the typical work situation, in which workers work for a paycheck rather than for the value or necessity of the work. Thus, while college may not teach job-specific skills, it teaches more generalized skills that are applicable in a variety of work settings (Bowles and Gintis, 1976).

Many independent primary labor market jobs require postgraduate education. One of the characteristics of postgraduate education is an inordinate amount of work to do and insufficient time to do it. Learning how to perform complex tasks well, under pressure, prepares workers for the type of work that professions like medicine, law, and scholarship require. The intensity of work demands in graduate school also facilitates the process by which students internalize norms and goals of the profession. One of the reasons rigorous graduate and professional schools place such high work loads on students is, in part, to wear them down. To keep up with the work, they have to simply, and more or less unquestioningly, work. This process hastens students' internalizing of the norms of the profession (Bowles and Gintis, 1976). This internalization process is extremely important. When I go to a doctor, for example, I want her to act as a competent medical professional, not a journalist, business woman, or anything else.

While these traits may have been the ticket to a good job in the Accord era, it is likely that such approaches do not prepare students for the best jobs in the flexible economy. Schools have emphasized order and stability in the structure of classrooms and the organization of knowledge. Progress through the educational system entails the linear acquisition of skills that build on earlier knowledge. The new workplace requires, however, that, to advance, workers learn things that may not be related to prior knowledge. It requires, too, that they learn and apply knowledge in new ways.

Education and the Emerging Economy

The changes in the economy and workplace require changes in both the quantitative and qualitative aspects of education. Analysts have projected that those occupations that require at least one or more years of college are the ones that will grow the most by the year 2000 and beyond. As the data in Figure 2.3 (chapter 2) showed, after home health and human service work, computer engineers, scientists, and systems analysts are the next fastest growing occupations. These are managerial, technical, and professional occupations. The occupations that require a high school diploma or less will decrease in number over the same period. Included here are low-skill blue-collar occupations such as machine setters and operators, agricultural and fishery workers, transportation and material movers, and laborers (Kutscher, 1990). Two things are clear about the workplace of the future. First, the best jobs require at least some college. Second, job opportunities for those without an education are limited.

The *kinds* of education required of workers may change as well. Whereas the labor–capital accord workplace incorporated a range of rigid structures to ensure stability (and so encouraged such reliability and stability among workers), the flexible workplace, at least in the skilled positions, will require the flexible use of knowledge. If flexible specialization requires ongoing learning, one of the things schools will have to do to further prepare future workers is to emphasize *learning to learn* rather than fact-based learning.

The rapidity of technological change decreases the longevity of skills and thus makes frequent worker *re*skilling necessary. These changes suggest the need for an increasingly tight coupling of schooling and work. One consequence may be a challenge to traditional liberal arts curricula and a deemphasis on teaching humanities and social sciences. Another possible consequence is the greater involvement of private business with education. Under these conditions, adult education and reeducation are quite likely to be vocationalized (specific skills rather than liberal arts), traditional entrance requirements will change (experience rather than a certain GPA), and the timing of schooling will become more flexible (periodic returns to school throughout adulthood).

An additional pressure on education results from the globalization of the economy. The global education movement calls for reorganized knowledge that stresses the interconnections of political, economic, cultural, and ecological systems rather than viewing them as separate and distinct (Tye and Tye, 1992).

Information technologies are also changing education. Computerization is changing what, where, how, when, and from whom students learn. At the most basic level, the workplace of the future requires students to use computers as tools. However, technical jobs will require more than just the ability to use word processors and spreadsheets. Computer-aided design and other such innovations will require that more and more workers use computerization with the same facility that they now use calculators. Computers are also changing the structure of educational institutions. On the one hand, computers have the potential to provide students with the information that lectures used to provide, thus freeing teachers to engage students in more seminarlike contact. On the other hand, they might free universities from much of the cost of maintaining a teaching staff— not a prospect I relish!

Additionally, computer technology can create a truly global university. As the knowledge required to function in a global economy becomes increasingly complex, scholars from any single nation are unlikely to possess all relevant information. Computerization allows collaboration among scholars and teaching at the global level. Students and teachers would be freed from the constraints of any particular place. Instead of costly international travel they would commute electronically through computer networks, electronic classes, and computer-based courses, libraries, and bulletin boards. Universities will continue to have branch campuses in other countries, and students will continue to be able to take their junior year abroad. But it is the intellectual exchange that occurs in **cyberspace** that will typify the emerging global university system.

The educational system's future shape, beneficiaries, and participants will ultimately rest on questions of power. While technology makes possible the education of the globe's population in heretofore unimagined ways, the likelihood of this occurring has much to do with the relative power of different groups. If parents on the South Side of Chicago or rural Mississippi or downtown Detroit, for example, have neither the resources nor the power to develop such technologies, then their children will be excluded from the benefits of twenty-first century education. The costs of that exclusion may be reflected in deepening structural unemployment and an expanded and entrenched underclass (Kozol, 1991).

CONCLUSIONS

Industrial transformation has eliminated many of the good—that is, stable and well-paid—jobs held by workers with only a high school diploma. Now, increasing numbers of jobs require a college education. Moreover, they require complex interpersonal skills and computer literacy, something that schools often fail to provide to all students. These differences pose dilemmas for young entrants into the labor market. Students in wealthy school districts have access to a quality of education, both in content and in resources, that can provide them with the human capital necessary to compete in the future workplace. For many more students, however, particularly those in inner cities or economically depressed rural areas—in fact, all communities that lack sufficient tax monies to maintain and upgrade existing schools—the education is of a quality that leaves them increasingly unprepared for the twenty-first century. Those students who are unable to acquire the necessary skills are likely to fall into the secondary labor market. Unfortunately, given the increasingly rapid pace of knowledge growth, initial deficiencies will be even harder for those students to overcome than they were in earlier periods.

The nature of the flexible economy is such that many workers can no longer anticipate long-term employment relationships with a single employer or a small number of firms over the course of their working lives. Instead of anticipating a relatively predictable career path, more and more workers are becoming contingent workers or homeworkers. The shift to flexible employment threatens the well-being of workers in a number of ways. Workers lose access to stable health care, for instance. Correspondingly, low pay associated with the secondary labor market makes health benefits purchased from private providers harder to afford.

Flexible work arrangements also result in loss of access to retirement and other benefits. This problem is exacerbated by the anticipated increased burden on the social security system as the population ages and fewer labor-market entrants support it. Moreover, lower paid workers contribute less in taxes, reducing government's resources for providing health and retirement benefits.

The flexible workplace is less an actual place than ever before. Workers go to a job, but they are less and less likely to have a "place of work." Likewise, the job ladders they used to climb are broken. Now, they may be confronted with an endless effort to upgrade skills and hustle up jobs, just to pay the rent. Finally, work in modern society has been a major source of identity. Without a stable work-place, what will provide the bond that links people to society? What will replace the social contract that used to be formed within the workplace? These are questions to which I return in the final chapter.

FLEXIBLE FAMILIES

When I was growing up there was a television show called "Leave It to Beaver." Beaver was a boy of grade-school age with an older brother named Wally. Beaver's parents were named Ward and June Cleaver. June wore dresses, nylons, and pumps all the time. Her hair was sort of short and styled (it was set and sprayed into immovable place). She smiled and baked cookies a lot. She made dinner for her family every night. She was there during the day to help Beaver get out of his "scrapes." Ward wore a suit and tie to work, but I have no idea what that work was. He went to work and came home at the end of the day, and *he* was the final judge in any disputes between Beaver, Wally, and June. Ward and June kissed each other on the cheeks; they hugged their children; they played bridge with their friends. What the Cleavers didn't do was bear any resemblance whatsoever to my family in any of its permutations.

For much of my life, my family consisted of my mother, my father, his male lover, my mother's second ex-husband (my second father: I had two daddies before the television show was even a gleam in the creator's eye), my second father's wife, and my sister. When my mother and my second father divorced, I was 16 and my sister was 8. My mother had custody of my sister and me, and we grew up in a female-headed household. Parenting was nevertheless shared among my mother, my fathers, and their spouses. When I got married several years ago, all these parents and significant others shared that occasion with me. My own experience with family has included, then, single motherhood, divorce, extended families based not on blood but on multiple marriage (blended families), a gay couple, and my own childlessness in the context of a dual-career marriage. But this family and its myriad family structures is not unique. Increasing numbers— some suggest over one third—of all American households include similar structural complexities. What is a family then? Is it the Cleaver family or the family I grew up in? Actually, it is both—and more. I define a *family* as a set of kinship and gender relationships considered typical in a given society. **Kinship** tends to refer to the ways in which society organizes sexual and property relationships. For example, some kinship structures allow men to have multiple wives; in some kinship structures, property might be inherited only by the eldest son (Collins and Coltrane, 1991). **Gender relationships** are the ways in which societies define and organize women's and men's roles. For example, women may be responsible for all the work inside the home, and men might be responsible for all work outside the home.

What a family is and what it does must be understood in a broader social context in which economic, political, and social forces intersect. Thus a multitude of factors impinge on kinship and gender relationships; it is my argument that economic and workplace changes are some of the most important. Moreover, in each historical period, gender and kinship relationships constitute the implicit contract on which the family centered. For example, the labor–capital accord era (roughly 1947–1972) was associated with a certain ideal of the typical family that was reflected back to us all on television. While never a reality for all families, its image was a powerful one. When people talk today about the death of the family or changes in the family (e.g., Popenoe, 1993), they are talking about changes in that Accord-era family so blandly represented by Ward, June, Wally, and Beaver. However, the relationships that constituted it are often merely nostalgic memories. That family structure is gone for most, if it even existed for more than a few.

The families that are appearing in the Accord family's place may be called **flexible families**. In flexible families, kinship structures, parenting practices, gender roles, and the relationship of the family to the workplace vary with class, occupation, and social possibilities. A range of relationship patterns characterized the family at the end of the twentieth century.

In this chapter I discuss the decline of the Accord family and the emergence of the new family forms that are becoming the social norm. In so doing, I link changing family structures to changing economic and workplace structures because it is the basic argument of this book that, to understand the world we experience, we need to focus on the linkages among major institutions.

FROM PREINDUSTRIAL FAMILIES TO MODERN FAMILIES

To appreciate the myriad of relationships that constitute the family today and to understand how familial relationships are connected to economic relationships, it is useful to look at the dynamism of families as a social institution. Historians of the family have documented many transformations in family relationships over the centuries. In some eras in Western society, elders have held an honored place in families, making the major decisions about the dispersion of property, the marriage of children, and the activities of all family members. In our time, the elderly are often treated as superfluous or as burdens draining families of income and leisure time.

The extent to which families are associated with creating and rearing children also varies across periods. In the current era, children are perhaps of less importance to the formation of families than at any other period of Western history. (For example, think of the time when children used to be central to the success of family farms.) Parenting has also taken on different roles in various historical periods. For example, the notion that parents love and bond with their children and are intensely motivated by and involved in their emotional lives and well-being is a relatively modern view. Contrast this view with that of elite English parents in the 1500s, who upon birth of a child would send it away until it was at least 18 months old (Dizard and Gadlin, 1990)! Obviously, we cannot assume that any one family structure is the human norm. As economic systems have changed, so too have families.

The Agrarian Family as Production Unit

At the end of the nineteenth and beginning of the twentieth centuries in the United States, a majority of families lived in rural farming communities. These families were production units. That is, much of what the family needed (i.e., food, clothing, etc.) it produced. All family members participated in farming. Even in families that participated in manufacturing production (after all, even agricultural societies require some manufactured goods), the entire family was involved. This involvement of all family members in the material well-being of the family is what sociologists mean by family economy. In their study of schooling and child labor in the early twentieth century, Walters and James (1992) found that white children's participation in early textile industries decreased their school enrollment. This research suggests that children's contribution to the family economy was often more important than schooling.

In this era, the exchange of goods occurred not only in markets but along kinship lines (Dizard and Gadlin, 1990). If Mother Jones was a quick and able seamstress, she would be more likely to exchange the garments she sewed for the bread that her cousin baked than to exchange them in a market for money. Care and responsibility also traveled along those broad-based kinship lines.

Perhaps the most important characteristic of the preindustrial family was its rural community context. In preindustrial rural America, large families existed in communities characterized by many kinship ties. Although the notion of the extended family of grandparents, aunts, uncles, mother, father, brothers, sisters, and cousins is increasingly considered a romanticized myth, family boundaries were truly more permeable than they are today. Families expanded and contracted as kin returned and left, and there were strong norms of responsibility and accommodation to the needs of all kin. During hard times, for example, a daughter, her husband, and their children might return home to her mother, with the expectation that the household would simply expand to include them. This pattern was common among working people, who often had little in the way of surplus but who distributed what they had in terms of space, food, and work to include these "new" family members.

During the preindustrial era, elderly and ailing parents and other family members often lived with their children (or with nieces or nephews). Most households did not, however, include elderly parents. While the *ideal* was to aid elderly kin, the *fact* was that in preindustrial society, the average life expectancy was around 45 years! People just didn't live long enough to move in with their adult children.

In the United States additional factors mitigated against the formation of large extended families. Westward expansion lured enterprising sons and daughters to strike out on their own as soon as they were old enough, thus decreasing actual household size. In addition, immigrants from eastern and southern Europe who arrived in the late 1800s and early 1900s often came *without their families*. The intent was to make money that they could then return home with, and many settled in urban communities. Thus, though the norm of responsibility to an extended kinship network was present, in many instances the kinship network itself was not present. In other words, while extended families never dominated rural agrarian American or early American cities, the social context of kin and community ties did (Laslett, 1977; Dizard and Gadlin, 1990).

The Rise of Companionate Marriage   Part of that social context meant that families began differently than they do today. Mate selection in colonial times was based on the fit between the prospective mates' families; marriages were arranged. Given the intermingling of home and work, family formation was primarily an economic partnership. Spouses expected little from marriage by way of emotional support, companionship, and affection. In fact, a marriage could not occur in the absence of a viable business, farm, or some sort of economic enterprise. When young couples did marry, they were beholden to the kinship network. Given the hardship associated with mere survival, love, affection, and romance were frivolous distractions from the rough business of life.

In fact, historians link the emergence of romantic love as a basis for marriage with the modern industrial family. The reasons for the emergence of the **companionate marriage**—that is, one based on love and companionship rather than economic expediency—are unclear. It occurred first in England and the American colonies. As with any social transformation, it took some time for this change to become the norm. The companionate marriage is one of the factors that distinguishes the premodern family from the modern one.

The Role of "Little People" As the basis of marriage changed, so too did parenting and the understanding of children. Children in premodern society occupied a very different social position than they do today. In many ways, children were viewed as little working adults. Children participated in the household economy as early as age three. Prior to that they were simply strapped onto their mother's back or left swaddled in a corner and more or less ignored while the mother went about her work. Given the economic importance of children to rural households, families were much larger than they are today. In 1790, for example, almost 36% of households included seven or more people. Even if one or two of those people might have been boarders, still, the majority were children.

Parenting did not involve the protracted nurturing and sacrifice that it did in later eras. Children were little adults with sinful wills, and the role of a parent was to break the sinful will of the child. In so doing, parents created a moral and disciplined being (Dizard and Gadlin, 1990). This approach clearly differs from one that views parenting in terms of the close, affectionate, and loving relationship that we now (we hope) see between parent and child. Authority and discipline, rather than love and socialization, were the basis of parenting.

The Modern Family as Consumer Unit

While the early settlers and later immigrants to the United States brought many of the premodern family forms with them, from the beginning families in the United States had most of the characteristics of modern families. They were not as extended as many families in the Old Country, and marriage was increasingly based on love, affection, and companionship. It was not until industrialization, however, that the other characteristics of the modern family became more normative. Those changes were associated with the separation of the household from the workplace.

Instead of baking bread, one bought it; instead of making clothes, one bought them; instead of chopping firewood, one purchased energy. As with the other changes associated with the modern family, this transformation resulted from the movement of men into an industrial (rather than agricultural) work force and the movement of families from rural to urban environments.

When families moved from rural to urban areas and men moved into the emerging industrial economy, they demanded a rate of pay that was sufficient to support not only themselves but also the unpaid activities of their wives. This shift gave rise to the notion of the male breadwinner whose labor would provide sufficient income to support his new family unit. In fact, as many have pointed out (e.g., Pahl, 1988), union struggles were often geared to the concept of a **living wage**. That is, unions agitated for wages sufficiently high to allow male union workers to support the rest of the family.

This change did not mean that there was no work done in the home; rather, it meant that paid labor played a much more important role in the survival of the household because much of what had been produced for use in the house was now purchased. This separation, among other things, made the unpaid labor of women invisible (Stacey, 1990). That is, when both husband and wife (and children) participated in the labor necessary for the survival of the household, the efforts of both appeared far more equal. When men went into the waged labor force and women stayed home, their nonleisure activities (e.g., cooking, cleaning, shopping, child rearing, etc.) lost the social status of "work."

Urbanization and the separation of work and family required an economy that was strong enough to allow families to exist independently of their kinship networks. During the early part of the twentieth century, this affluence was exceedingly difficult since employers still sought to govern the workplace with oppressive strategies that relied, in part, on paying workers as little as possible. However, businesses began to recognize that in order to grow they had to sell their products. Although they were not necessarily willing to pay their workers high wages, they were willing to allow these new families to buy against future income. In developing the concept of consumer credit, businesses put considerable energy into creating new desires (and therefore new markets) among the growing urban work force. Now, the Jones family no longer had to wait until they had saved enough money to buy the new washing machine that was available; their local Sears provided them with the opportunity to buy that washing machine on credit. Thus the family came to be seen as a unit of consumption instead of production (Dizard and Gadlin, 1990).

Privatization Changes in the economic base of society created new pressures, new demands, and new opportunities for families. The extended Jones family became Mr. and Mrs. Jones, living in an apartment in the city with their dependent children. They became a **nuclear family**, an independent unit of husband, wife, and children, separated emotionally and financially from an extended family of parents, aunts, uncles, brothers, and sisters. The nuclear family, unlike earlier families, is basically an isolated, privatized kinship unit.

That privatization was not sudden. As the companionate marriage became more normative, couples sought to live in their own home, alone with their children. Remember that these changes occurred in the context of industrialization. In an agrarian economy, a family farm can support only so many members, and this limitation restricted sons' abilities to begin new households. That is, if the family did not own enough land to give part of it to a son to begin his own farm, the son couldn't start another household. Industrialization created, however, economic possibilities that allowed, encouraged, and facilitated new households to form. In other words, industrialization played an important role in privatizing households (Coontz, 1988).

Privatization meant that husbands and wives increasingly looked to each other for emotional and financial sustenance instead of to the larger kinship network in which they had been situated. They no longer followed tradition in deciding how to raise their children, run the household, or work. The historically tight linkage between fathers, sons, and inheritance (even of barren farms from which one could scarcely eke out a living) was sundered in the early to mid-1900s (Coontz, 1988). Of course, as Kain (1990) points out, this isolation of families, while allowing companionate marriage to flourish, also allowed all sorts of pathologies (like abuse and alcoholism) to flourish in the absence of familial social control.

Gender, Domesticity, and Class With the separation of work and family and the privatization of family life, women (at least those whose families could afford it) were confined to the home as they had never been before. Care and nurturance of fewer and fewer children were elevated to the most important activities on which women should concentrate their efforts. Thus, though this period is associated with declining family size, parenting (by the mother) took on an importance that it had not had in earlier years. The success of the child increasingly became a measure of the success of the mother. Rather than rely on discipline and authority to force compliance from children, affection and socialization and the threat of lost love became tools of child rearing (Dizard and Gadlin, 1990). The sphere of women's lives shrunk to home and children and was reinforced by the ideological weight of the cult of domesticity.

The ideological glorification of homemaking and child rearing circumscribed primarily the lives of white, middle- and upper-class married women. In contrast, working-class women (many of whom were African-American and eastern European), single, young middle-class women, widows, and unmarried women found employment in the industrializing economy. The classic example of one of the first manufacturing industries, the mills in Lowell, Massachusetts, was "manned" exclusively by women. Similarly, women increasingly moved into occupations such as teaching and domestic work. They did so, however, in the face of strong normative pressures against such labor force participation. In 1900, for example, only about 18% of the labor force was female, and recent Irish and Italian immigrants (the poor and the working class) were most strongly represented. White, native-born middle- and upper-class women were highly unlikely to work. It was not until the post–World War II era—when the labor–capital accord changed economic, political, and workplace relations—that women started to reach their current proportion of close to half of the labor force.

ACCORD-ERA FAMILIES

The nuclear, privatized, consumer family reached its zenith in the two and a half decades following World War II. These years were characterized by unprecedented economic growth. The stability of the labor–capital accord accelerated the trend toward nuclear families. First, it gave husbands and fathers more time to spend with their wives and children. Second, through the creation of a variety of social programs such as social security and unemployment insurance, families were released from the burden of caring for their own parents and elderly relatives. The state took over that role. Other features of the modern family intensified as well.

The Implicit Contract: Homemakers and Breadwinners

For much of the Accord era, the ideal-typical family was centered on a gendered division of labor. The ideal family was composed of a "stay-at-home mom," a working father, and dependent children. He earned wages; she cooked, cleaned, cared for the home, managed the family's social life, and nurtured the family members. The breadwinning father and homemaking dependent mother dominated the culture, at least normatively. In fact, a man whose wife didn't *have* to work was considered successful.

During the 1950s and first part of the 1960s this extreme gender specialization in roles was at its highest point. During this era unions were at their strongest, and therefore even working-class men received sufficient wages to buy houses, take vacations, and keep their wives at home—cooking, cleaning, and otherwise approximating the alleged leisure of more affluent women.

Small Families and Endless Childhood With that affluence and the gendered division of labor came interesting contradictions surrounding parenting. In the decades following World War II, families had fewer children than they had had in the early part of the twentieth century. For example, in 1900 over 18% of households had six or more members. The average woman had seven children (though there was a much greater probability that some of those children would not live through childhood). During the 1930s and the Great Depression, the average number of children dropped to about 2.1 per woman. But by 1960, about 11% of households had six or more members, and the average number of children was 3.6. While higher than the depression years, these figures were much lower than the early 1900s (Ahlburg and De Vita, 1992).

Despite these smaller families, child rearing was a far more important component of women's roles than it had been in earlier decades. Women spent far more of their time, energy, and family surplus on their children and demanded far less participation in household labor from their children. Yet despite the elevated importance of child rearing, schools took over an increasing amount of childhood socialization as compulsory education was instituted. In fact, by 1940 secondary schools took in children from all social classes; so schooling became the norm for all children, even though working-class children were still more likely to enter the labor market if their family required their wages (Walters and O'Connell, 1988).

One factor in women's roles that increased attention to parenting was the extension of childhood. Teenagers in the early part of the century often had the obligations of laboring and childbearing, but in the Accord-era family wages were high enough to allow children to participate in school full time for a longer period. Extended schooling also extended economic dependence. Adolescence became a separate stage of development and a new category of "child." The Accord family, then, placed the sole burden of maintaining the household financially on the father and made both mother and children economically dependent (Coontz, 1992).

Television, Credit, and Mass Consumption The image of the family whose apparent demise haunts many of us is an image that was presented on television, which itself emerged during a period that may have been unique. Television gave us images of happy nuclear families in which a well-coifed wife reared happy and spunky boys and pretty girls, in a clean suburban house outfitted with a car, a backyard, and a hard-working (usually white-collar) father who appeared in the evenings and on the weekends. Television provided the expanding middle class and increasingly affluent working class with a model of familial and economic success that became a standard against which people could measure their own (often inadequate) family lives.

Key to this life was the expansion of consumption. That is, to live this life, one needed not only a house in the suburbs but a car to get from those suburbs to the workplace (as well as roads on which to drive the car), the furniture to live up to middle-class standards, and washers and dryers and other allegedly labor-saving devices (although research shows that such devices did not actually decrease the amount of time spent at housework—see Berk, 1988).

That kind of consumption was predicated on easily available consumer credit and an economy busy enough to provide the goods and the jobs to allow families to avail themselves of the credit. Thus, family development and economic development were heavily intertwined. While credit expansion began in the early 1900s, it wasn't until the Accord era, in which labor and management accommodated the economic well-being of each other, that even the working class could enjoy an expanded role as major consumers—and that working-class women could emulate the role of homemaker heretofore occupied primarily by middle- and upper-class women.

The sum total of these changes was to reinforce the autonomy, independence, privatization, and perhaps social isolation of parents as they relinquished some control over their children and ceased being responsible to their own elders. Married couples now had the emotional and financial independence to make decisions independent of their kin, and this independence was nurtured by an ever-expanding economy that saw their family type as an ever-expanding market with endless needs (Coontz, 1988, 1992; Dizard and Gadlin, 1990).

Breakdown of the Accord Family

There were a number of factors that challenged the television image of the happy suburban family and families' efforts to live up to those images. Those factors grew out of the intersection of the family, gender, and economic forces. Post–World War II inflation, particularly in the 1960s, created economic pressures, and suburban middle-class life created emotional ones. Women who were isolated at home in the suburbs, but who were increasingly college educated, began to question the assumptions underlying their lifestyle. These conflicts were portrayed in such movies as *Diary of a Mad Housewife,* in which a bored and neglected woman takes on a lover, drinks, and rebels against the stultifying conditions of her life. Similarly, as the economy began changing in response to global competition, economic pressures on the family also started to change. Over time, this isolation and these economic pressures, in the context of other social changes, ultimately challenged the breadwinner–homemaker contract on which the Accord family was based.

Women, Work, and Feminism Women's labor force participation has been one of the most important factors affecting the family. World War II brought us Rosie the Riveter, that cheerful, patriotic woman who filled factory jobs when men went to war. When the war ended, Rosie was sent home. The cult of domesticity and the postwar emphasis on the homemaker role were part of the ideological effort to get women to leave better paying jobs so that returning soldiers would find employment. While women were forced out of those jobs, many of them did not return to the home; instead, they found other, usually inferior, jobs. In 1945, women made up somewhat more than 37% of

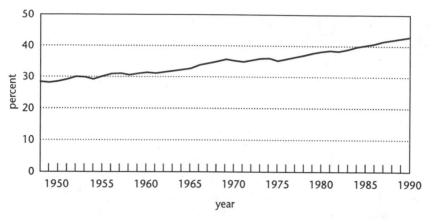

Figure 4.1. Women workers as percentage of total civilian labor force, 1948 to 1990

From CITIBASE, FAME Information Services, Inc. (1946–present), 1978, New York.

the employed civilian labor force. By 1965 they constituted about 33% and by 1990 roughly 43% of the employed labor force (see Figure 4.1).

It wasn't until the 1960s and the rise of the women's movement that women throughout the class structure (though not the most affluent) moved into the labor force in large numbers. The feminist movement challenged the implicit contract between men and women by presenting a broader set of roles and opportunities to women and challenging the legitimacy of the housewife role. Books such as *The Feminine Mystique* by Betty Friedan questioned the level of fulfillment that the homemaker role provided women. For many women, these questions resonated with their own dissatisfaction—and gave it a name. In increasing numbers, highly educated women isolated in the suburbs, frustrated with the limitations of the homemaker role, sought access not only to traditional women's jobs (teachers, secretaries, nurses) but also to the professions (medicine, law, management). The experience of work empowered women both in and outside marriages. Now, rather than stigmatizing such labor force participation, television offered up spunky role models like Mary Richards in the "Mary Tyler Moore Show."

While women, particularly unmarried women and working-class women, had always participated in the paid labor force, now married women and women with young children were doing so in ever greater numbers. Moreover, they were competing with men for positions to which they had little prior access (Kessler-Harris, 1982).

At the same time, the combined income of working couples allowed greater consumption. The two-breadwinner model also increased the need for services that housewives had once provided, such as housecleaning and child care. When the 1960s ushered in an era of fairly rapid price increases, the combined income of both husband and wife became even more necessary to maintain the standard of living to which they had become accustomed.

As women increasingly entered the labor force and sought entry into a wider variety of occupations, they were less willing and able to play the full-time homemaker role that was the norm. While they continued to do most of the housework, they increasingly challenged the legitimacy of this double burden. Generally, though, women have had little success in getting their partners to share the housework (Coverman and Sheley, 1986). Despite their inability to achieve equitable redistribution of household labor, the combined influence of increased labor force participation and changing ideologies about gender challenged the traditional gender roles that were at the center of the Accord family (Coverman, 1985).

These changing ideologies were occurring in an era characterized by a more general challenge to dominant ideologies [as in the antiwar, civil rights, and counterculture movements; see, for example, *Liberation Now!* (Babcox and Belkin, 1971; Matthaei, 1983)]. Those challenges championed equality and freedom for all citizens and in all sorts of ways. Of particular concern was the open discussion of sexuality and pleasure that emerged during this period. A major consequence of that challenge was to separate sexuality from procreation and marriage.

Sex Versus Procreation The first way in which the separation of sexuality from procreation occurred was in the availability of birth control. While women historically have sought to terminate unwanted pregnancies or divest themselves of unwanted children in a variety of ways, it was not until the 1960s that cultural changes and new reproductive technologies gave women unprecedented freedom over their reproductive ability. The advances in birth control also gave women far more control over their sexuality. Freed from the inevitability of an unwanted pregnancy (and in the context of the feminist and counterculture movements), women were able to explore their sexuality with a new and (for many) shocking openness. Books like Erica Jong's *Fear of Flying* (1973), which celebrated a woman's sexual explorations, were read by respectable middle-class women and sold in mall bookstores.

Just as sexual pleasure was separated from procreation, so child-bearing was also separated from marriage. This period also witnessed an increase of births out of wedlock. Although out-of-wedlock births clearly were not completely acceptable, the stigma attached to them declined. In 1960, 5.3% of all births were to unmarried women; by 1970 that figure had more than doubled (10.7%). In 1989, 27.1% of all births were to unmarried women; importantly, most of those were to women 20 years or older, not to teenagers (Ahlburg and De Vita, 1992). Incidentally, although many of the children born out of wed-lock were the result of unplanned pregnancies, they are not necessarily unwanted. This phenomenon speaks to the increased acceptability of nonmarital sex.

The gay rights movement was another major challenge to dominant views of sexuality and the family. In 1969, in a bar called the Stonewall Inn in Greenwich Village, a group of men protesting a police bust of drag queens and homosexuals made history. The incident inaugurated the gay liberation movement. Instead of continuing to remain "closeted"—that is, to keep their sexuality secret—homosexuals and lesbians sought the same kind of civil rights that other groups were seeking. In the process of challenging existing rules of behavior and insisting on their civil rights, they contributed to the sundering of sex and procreation.

The freedom to explore sexuality in a number of ways and with a variety of partners—freed to a great extent from the tyranny of unwanted children—allowed men and women to try new forms of pairing. It also normalized, to a greater extent than had existed, premarital sex and cohabitation. While this process was not universal, it was to have profound consequences for family life. By the time the labor–capital accord unraveled and the economy began its great shift, the landscape of family, parenting, and partnering had changed irrevocably. For example, only about one quarter of people surveyed in 1988 believed that premarital sex between adults is wrong (it was about a third in 1972) (Kain, 1990, p. 130). Homosexuality and abortion remain highly contested issues, but unlike the early 1960s they are now part of public political discourse. By the early 1990s, for the first time in American history, 17 members of the President's staff were openly gay. In addition, Congress was debating the issue of allowing self-defined gays into the military. Clearly, the family ideal that dominated the culture in the early part of the Accord period needs revision.

FORMING FLEXIBLE FAMILIES

Greater sexual permissiveness, reproductive technologies, female labor force participation, changing gender roles, and out-of-wedlock births have all created the impression that families are fundamentally threatened (Popenoe, 1993). By and large, however, family sociologists argue that such is not the case. Rather, the family in the 1990s is a vital institution but is experiencing profound changes and challenges. Unmarried people continue to seek marriage and families and, though in decreasing numbers, continue to have children (Kain, 1990; Stacey, 1990; Ahlburg and De Vita, 1992).

Let's take a look at some of the specifics about families in the 1990s. In 1991, 42% of all families were married couples with no children. Of married couples with children, 19% were in blended, or "step," families. One in eight families was a single-parent family. While only about 20% of families were dual earners in 1940, about 40% were in 1990. Though the United States has one of the highest marriage rates in the Western world, the divorce rate has doubled from the 1960s; it is now about 4.7 per thousand population. To indicate the changing incidence of divorce, Ahlburg and De Vita (1992) report that "14% of white women who married in the early 1940s eventually divorced, almost half of white women who married in the late 1960s and early 1970s have already been divorced. For African-American women, the percentages rose from 18 to almost 60" (p. 15). The age of marriage has risen from 20.3 years old for women and 22.8 for men in 1960 to 24.1 and 26.3 respectively in 1991 (Ahlburg and De Vita, 1992).

Like the economy and workplace, today's family is characterized by a new flexibility that has both positive and negative aspects. Because almost all families are connected to the economy and workplace in one way or another, it is inevitable that those larger changes would also affect family life. Just as the labor–capital accord generated affluence that allowed a certain type of family structure to flourish, so too flexible economic relations facilitate certain types of family forms and challenge others (Stacey, 1990; Gerson, 1991).

Remember (from chapter 3) that flexibility in location, skills, or hours worked will be a component of work in the flexible economy and that a long-term, stable employment relationship will characterize the occupations of fewer and fewer people. Furthermore, flexible capitalism is likely to create a very small core of highly educated, skilled managers, experts, technicians, and workers, and a very large periphery made up of numerically (or statistically) flexible workers throughout the occupational hierarchy. These differences suggest that families will respond differently to social changes. Families supported by workers in the primary labor market will have a somewhat different structure from families supported by workers in the secondary labor market.

Flexible Specialization and the Middle Class

Let us begin with the most highly educated and well-off families— those in which one or both parents are technical experts, professionals, or managers in the core labor market. These families occupy upper-middle-class positions. Under post-Accord economic conditions only the very upper middle class and upper class (those with independent or inherited wealth) can afford to maintain the traditional gendered nuclear family. For example, Mr. Jones works as a surgeon, while Mrs. Jones goes to school and does volunteer work after the kids are in school and day care. For other upper-middle-class families, continued economic well-being requires two incomes. These middle-class families diverge, then, from breadwinner–homemaker families.

The flexible economy intensifies the pressure on these families by requiring even more geographic mobility, which makes sustaining the dual-income marriage more complex. Relocating for a job is always stressful, but what happens when both husband and wife are in professions? It is with these families that we see long-distance marriages. For instance, one professor I know received a good job in a small town. His wife is an attorney in a lucrative position at a large firm in a major city. The problem is that the two jobs are several hundred miles apart. They can afford, however, to maintain a large apartment in the city and day care for the children. The father, who is the academic, rents a small apartment in his small town. He drives into the city on weekends to be with his family. This situation is not all that extraordinary, but notice the level of income it requires; in addition to all of the usual household expenses, it requires sufficient surplus to maintain a second home as well as the transportation costs.

With these working arrangements, many of the homemaking tasks are either neglected or hired out. For those families in the upper income levels, housekeeping, child care, gardening, and even dog-walking become services for which one pays. Similarly, there has been an increase in families paying for the husband's traditional family tasks (e.g., lawn mowing and automobile maintenance).

Additionally, women who pursue careers are likely to forego or postpone childbearing to avoid jeopardizing careers in a business world that is increasingly competitive and unforgiving of non-work-related pressures. In fact, childless families are more normative now than at any period in American history. For upper-middle-class families, then, maintaining occupational position—or the flexibility to respond to changes in their occupational position—often means foregoing or delaying parenting (fewer children, born later, with whom less time is spent) (Bouvier and De Vita, 1991).

On the other hand, there are some possible benefits to the transformation to more flexible work. We know from past research that the structure of relations in the workplace affects the structure of relations outside of the workplace, through the effect of workplace relations on individuals' senses of who and what they are (see Kohn, 1977; Kohn and Schooler, 1982). Thus, families whose jobs are characterized by flexible specialization are more likely to have flexibility in their nonwork roles. For example, more fathers in this group are becoming actively involved with child care. For perhaps the first time in American history, nurturing men are admired (e.g., Alan Alda) rather than vilified as "sissies" (Hunter and Davis, 1992).

Hage and Powers (1992) suggest that one consequence of flexible work is the emergence of flexible selves. When people's lives are very clearly defined by particular roles—for example, breadwinner or homemaker—those roles become fixed and central to one's identity. However, flexible capitalism implies a much more multifaceted set of roles. Even advantaged, highly skilled workers are working for a variety of workplaces. Thus, they are unlikely to develop the kind of single role of the "corporate man" (or woman) with an identity shaped by working for a single employer. Workers will be able to wear more "identity hats"—and change more frequently.

We can perhaps see the influence of flexible identities most clearly in the context of gender roles. The Accord-era family was characterized by, or at least aspired to, highly specialized and separate gender roles that depended on women's absence from the paid labor force. But when women constitute more than half the labor force, earning more of the family income—and increasingly in nontraditional jobs— maintaining the highly circumscribed gender roles of the earlier period becomes untenable. Families in which the adults work in flexibly specialized workplaces are likely to bring that same flexibility into the home. For example, my husband does all of the menu planning and cooking. While women still do most of the housework and parenting, there are certainly strong cultural pressures for men to share in those tasks. As they do so, the mix of roles played by men and women changes (Presser, 1994). In this way, economic transformations challenge traditional family roles (Stacey, 1990; Gerson, 1991; Hunter and Davis, 1992).

Numerical Flexibility and the Working Class

Of course, relatively few families are likely to occupy core positions as dynamically flexible workers. Far more workers experience the insecurity of working as statically (or numerically) flexible workers. That is, they are more likely to obtain part-time, temporary, or otherwise contingent work. Additionally, that work may require few skills and provide little in terms of wages and benefits. The great majority of workers in this increasingly two-tiered work force are in precarious economic positions and thus have difficulty meeting the challenges to the family that the flexible economy creates. For example, those families cannot pay for services that were part of the homemaker wife's role (e.g., child care), and so husband and wife scramble to accomplish tasks both in and outside of the home.

In the post-Accord economy, well-paid male manufacturing workers who have lost their jobs often have been unable to find new jobs that paid as well, if they can find jobs at all (Bluestone and Harrison, 1982; Perrucci et al., 1988). Increasingly, families rely on the labor of wives who are better able to obtain jobs in the expanding service sector. In fact, in many cases, those wives' incomes have been the only income sustaining the household. This shift in income-generating power has undermined traditional gender roles based on male authority and dominance and female dependence and deference. While some families have been able to adjust, some respond less well.

For some families, the pressures caused by deindustrialization, employment uncertainty, and increasing reliance on female employment have resulted in family breakup, alcohol abuse, and violence (see, for example, the study by Perrucci et al., 1988, on the consequences of plant closings). For these families, economic stress severs the bonds of intimacy and support that families provide. The intensity of reactions may well reflect the deeply threatening experience of job loss. If a man's identity and sense of self-worth are bound up in his role of breadwinner (e.g., I *am* a machinist, salesman, pharmacist, etc.) and he can no longer play that role, depression and anger are common responses. Because the objects of that anger are intangible (the corporation? globalization?), the anger and frustration are turned inward. That can lead to depression and substance abuse. When the anger is turned outward, it can lead to spouse and child abuse. Certainly not all men in this situation become alcoholic monsters; rather, they are in situations that can facilitate such behavior.

Another way people translate these feelings into behavior is through efforts to resist change and to hold on to earlier ways of life. The effort to promote "family values" and to control the images and lyrics of popular culture can be viewed in these terms, as can the contentious battle over the issue of abortion. Luker (1984), in her study of the political struggle over abortion, concluded that it was as much about the place of women in society as anything else. Those who were most opposed to abortion rights tended to occupy more working-class positions and tended to have lower levels of education. Those who were most economically threatened also felt most socially threatened by challenges to their beliefs about gender roles. Similarly, I also view the increase in conservative "profamily" politics as a response to the challenge to traditional gender roles (among other things—see chapter 6).

All the responses to the changed economy are not so grim, however. In her analysis of "postmodern" (or in my terms, flexible) working-class families in Silicon Valley, Stacey (1990) argues that these families have created new family strategies. Given the relatively low wages in many service-sector jobs, working-class families have turned to support systems similar to those of the agricultural family— that is, they *un*privatize the family by creating a variety of kin support networks. Children in their 20s are staying at home because they can no longer afford to launch independent households; women with children but without husbands are doubling up in order to share and coordinate the double burden of paid labor, parenting, and unpaid work in the house. Women who remain in seemingly traditional family forms (e.g., nuclear—note the redefinition of *traditional!*) are demanding greater participation from their husbands (Stacey, 1990; Gerson, 1991). Extended families based not on blood kinship but on prior marriages, non-kin families, single-parent families, and friendship are all responses to working in conditions of numerical flexibility. Part of what facilitates these creative responses to economic pressures is the freeing of women from the constraints of traditional gender roles and, by extension, the freeing of men from traditional gender roles. While many may be pushed unwillingly from positions and roles in which they were comfortable, for some the new opportunities and freedoms are ultimately quite liberating.

The New Economy and the Underclass

Economic changes have, however, been unambiguously devastating for the most economically marginal of families, those whose jobs keep them in or near poverty. Particularly problematic has been the industrial shift from manufacturing to service-sector growth. Industrial restructuring has wiped out the well-paid occupational positions in manufacturing that required only a high school diploma—such as an assembler in an automobile plant—in which many urban workers (particularly African-American males) had gained a strong and profitable foothold.

In a major study of the urban underclass, Wilson (1987) has pointed to economic factors to understand the causes of entrenched urban poverty. He links these factors to the family structures of many of the urban underclass. The "tangle of pathology" that includes unwed teenage mothers and unstable family structures results, according to Wilson, from the inability of young African-American men who are from economically marginal families to find jobs that allow them to support a family. Wilson argues that those difficulties are deepened by isolation when those workers live in high-poverty areas in which there are few opportunities for decent employment. In fact, this isolation in impoverished areas is one of the factors that differentiates the urban underclass from the poor who do not live in poverty areas (see also Devine and Wright, 1993).

Part of what has made the situation so problematic is the economic displacement of so many of these men. When General Motors experienced profit losses in the early 1980s, employment in Detroit declined by 69%. The black population in Detroit experienced a 27% unemployment rate (Ross and Trachte, 1990). Since few jobs replaced those that were lost, many of those automobile workers were displaced from the economy. Given Wilson's analysis, the transformation to flexible capitalism within a globalized economy can only worsen the condition of the urban underclass and make the creation and health of those families exceedingly difficult. The increase in poverty and the unequal distribution of that increase by race (blacks and Hispanics are disproportionately represented among the lower income groups) are even more alarming when we examine the increase in poverty and the increase in the percentage of children living below the poverty level. Again, just as income is distributed unequally by race, so too is poverty. And, as before, blacks and Hispanics, particularly children, are most heavily represented among the poor

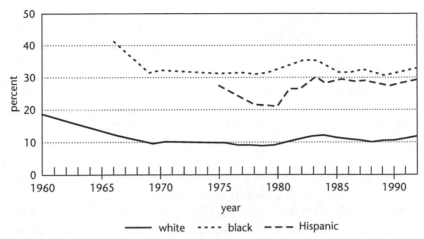

Figure 4.2. **Percentage of people below poverty level by race, 1960 to 1992**

Adapted from *Statistical Abstract of the United States: 1994* (p. 475), Washington, D.C.: U.S. Bureau of the Census.

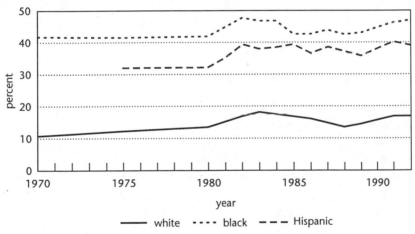

Figure 4.3. **Percentage of children below poverty level by race, 1970 to 1992**

Adapted from *Statistical Abstract of the United States: 1994* (p. 475), Washington, D.C.: U.S. Bureau of the Census.

(see Figures 4.2 and 4.3). Specifically, in 1966, 14.7% of all persons were living below the poverty level. However, examining that figure by race reveals that 11.3% of whites and 41.8% of blacks were living below poverty level. (The government did not collect data on Hispanics at this point.) By 1975 poverty had decreased—most likely a consequence of the anti-poverty programs discussed in chapter 5. By 1975, 12.3% of all races, 9.7% of whites, 31.3% of blacks, and 26.9% of Hispanics lived in poverty. Yet, by 1992, those members were increasing again. Now, poverty was 14.5% for all races, 33.3% for blacks, and 29.3% for Hispanics.

During the years from 1975 to 1992, the percentage of children living in poverty increased somewhat more dramatically. In 1975, 16.8% of children of all races lived below the poverty level. Minority children were much more likely to be among the poor. Living below poverty level were 12.5% of white children, 41.4% of black children, and 33% of Hispanic children. By 1992, however, children living below poverty level included 21.1% of all children, 16% of white children, 38.8% of Hispanic children, and almost half (46.3%) of black children (*Statistical Abstract*, 1994, p. 475).

The presence of unwed teenage mothers, the absence of occupational opportunities, and the antifamily nature of welfare state provisions (highest benefits go to those with no breadwinner, thus discouraging husbands and boyfriends from staying in the house) all worsen conditions for this group. They also lead to what researchers call the feminization of poverty.

The Feminization of Poverty

The feminization of poverty refers to the relatively recent increase in the number of impoverished female-headed households. Between 1969 and 1990 they more than doubled, from 1.83 million to 3.77 million (Devine and Wright, 1993, p. 51). Researchers point to a number of factors, such as teenage pregnancy, low wages in female occupations, occupational segregation, dead-end jobs, the divorce rate, and welfare policies, as causes for this feminization of poverty. Common to most explanations are the economic factors (Scott, 1984; Joekes, 1987; Goldburg and Kremen, 1990). As with the underclass, the current economic changes will only deepen those problems.

Industrial restructuring and globalization have affected women in three ways:

- The decline of labor-intensive manufacturing (such as textiles, clothing, toys, leather goods, and microelectric assembly) and the export of production to cheap-labor areas mean the loss of jobs that women were most likely to occupy (Scott, 1984, p. 34). Many of these jobs are now filled by third world workers, particularly women workers.

- While women have benefited from the expansion of service-sector occupations, as the previous chapter has shown, that gain is limited. Since women are concentrated in the lower wage occupations within the service sector, the expansion of this sector does not necessarily lift these women out of poverty (Reskin and Padavic, 1994).

- The technological innovations that are part of this transformation also directly affect the well-being of women through the deskilling of clerical jobs. Since the 1800s, these have been female-dominated jobs. Similarly, computerization results in fewer entry-level and clerical positions, many of which gave women access to white-collar occupations with possibilities for career advancement to positions that would keep them above poverty levels.

Although a complete explanation of the feminization of poverty is beyond this chapter, it is clear that current economic conditions have worsened the situation for female-headed households and the children born therein.

CONCLUSIONS

Like all social institutions, families are adaptable and fluid, and they are capable of change. Four changes in the essential relationships that define families—the emergence of the companionate marriage, privatization of the household, separation of family from workplace, and the transformation of gender roles—ushered in the modern family. As family structures developed in the labor–capital accord era, relationships became organized around homemaker–breadwinner gender roles, extended childhood, and heterosexual relationships. Flexible capitalism undermined that family.

For many, the decline of the gender contract structuring most marriages is a powerful and positive force for social change. In the absence of traditional gender scripts, greater possibility exists for both men and women to organize their roles around equality and mutual support, each providing what he or she can to the union. At the same time, changing gender roles make sustaining long-term relationships more difficult. In the absence of rigid scripts of behavior, men and women have to continually negotiate their relationships. Inability or unwillingness to do so can create deepened isolation for increasing numbers of people.

Similarly, the decline of the long-term marriage contract has both beneficial and negative aspects. The flexible economy does not "value" children in the way earlier economies have (particularly agricultural economies), and in fact they are more of a liability than in the industrial, Accord economy. Their relatively low societal importance is reinforced by the lack of programs and policies that protect and nurture them. Thus, the flexible economy has not created a child-friendly environment. This combination of economic liability and lack of social support for parenting undermines parenting behaviors within families—yet people, particularly young people, continue to have children (often as a result of inadequate education or limited access to birth control).

On the one hand, the ability of spouses to leave a destructive relationship is positive. Staying together for the sake of the child helps few children. On the other hand, as long as divorce plunges many women into poverty, divorce will add to the deepening feminization of poverty. The solution to that problem lies more in changes in the labor market than in urging women to remain in failed marriages. That is, when women are no longer disproportionately represented in the most secondary of jobs, they will be less dependent on a man's income to keep them out of poverty (Sidell, 1986).

While the severance of some of these implicit and explicit contractual relations has liberating potential, the decline of the parenting contract is more problematic. On the positive side, the diminished sanction against childless couples frees men and, particularly, women from having children out of a sense of tradition or compulsion. It frees them from unwanted parenting. Disturbing, however, are those families that have children but do not parent them. The failure of both mothers and fathers to care for children damages society. Fathers who leave the mothers of their children (whether married to them or not), mothers who leave their children uncared for, parents who do not commit the time to socialize their children—all these undermine the contractual basis of society. Unloved, unsocialized, abused children often grow up to be damaged adults. In the absence of decent child care facilities, however, more and more children will grow up unparented. In the absence of loving and involved caretakers or parents, television and peer groups will fill the gap. In the absence of a connection to a broader social contract, these children will not feel commitment to live by its terms.

Nevertheless, it is possible to imagine a world in which children flourish. Workplace flexibility that allows the integration of family and work life, gender roles that allow full parenting by both parents, and political relations that foster choice in family creation and facilitate high-quality, regulated child care facilities can go a long way toward strengthening the social contract within families and between families and society.

THE CHANGING ROLE OF GOVERNMENT

When my grandfather came to this country from Russia, there was no such thing as social security, unemployment compensation, a minimum wage, or retirement benefits. When his son, my father, retired in the mid-1980s from his teaching job at age 55, his retirement benefits, supplemented by occasional periods of substitute teaching, allowed him to take frequent trips to the Far East. My tax attorney tells me, however, that if I don't want to spend my old age in poverty, my husband and I will need to supplement the shrinking retirement benefits that our jobs and social security will provide. Even worse off is my sister. To date, none of her jobs in the restaurant business has provided her with health, unemployment, or retirement benefits. Her part-time and often seasonal schedule will limit benefits the government will provide (if there is anything left in the social security coffers by the time she retires).

Similarly, one of my teachers told me about the industrial accident in the early 1930s that blinded and crippled his father. The only things standing between this disabled worker and destitution were the labor of his wife and the charity of his community. A few decades later (say, the 1950s or 1960s), a worker in similar circumstances would have received disability payments and other sources of non-employment-based income that would have saved him or her from total impoverishment. These differences in experiences reflect historic changes in the extent and form of government involvement in people's lives.

Contemporary debates about reforming health care (should the government provide it or should private business?), about reforming the welfare state (how should the government—or even, *should* the government—help people who are unable to make enough money to stay out of poverty?), about involvement in the Bosnian-Serbian conflict (should the United States coordinate air strikes and send troops?), and other such political debates center on this very question:

How much should government become involved in social life, and what form should involvement take?

LEVELS OF GOVERNMENT INVOLVEMENT

This chapter examines the way in which government's role has changed in the historical periods I have been examining throughout this book. Specifically, this chapter examines what I call the pre–World War II *uninvolved state,* the post–World War II *involved state,* and the emerging *distracted state.*

Prior to the depression in the 1930s and World War II in the 1940s, the government was relatively uninvolved in the lives of all but the business classes. By the end of World War II, however, the role of government had changed dramatically. The restructured role entailed a set of policies, institutions, and budgets targeting a wide range of the citizenry, previously relatively ignored. What emerged were systematic government attempts to secure the well-being of even the most disadvantaged citizens of society.

The size of government (that is, the sheer number of employees and dollars spent) grew dramatically as government became more involved in citizens' lives. For example, in the years 1906–1910, government expenditures totaled about $720 million a year. By 1951–1955, that number had increased to about $3.2 billion a year. By 1992 it had increased yet again—to about $1.4 trillion! These changes coincided with and were part of the changes in the economy and workplace during those years.

The declining corporate profitability that began in the 1970s (discussed in chapter 2) was associated with a shift in political ideologies from involvement to noninvolvement. The most notable shift was in the government's commitment to aid the needy. The election of Ronald Reagan in 1980 was a culmination of anti-big government sentiment in the business community and among part of the population. Though the size of the government (measured in budget and employment) did not decline, the focus of government activity did. The policy thrust of the Reagan and Bush administrations (1980–1992) was to expand the rights and freedoms of business and property and to shrink government support of individuals, particularly disadvantaged individuals. Their efforts to free business from any potential threats to profitability took the form of decreasing environmental regulation, work and safety protections, and spending associated with welfare—for example, Aid to Families with Dependent Children (AFDC), school lunches, and so on (Piven and Cloward, 1993).

The Reagan/Bush administrations' antispending policies failed to improve the economy because they misdiagnosed the source of the threats to profitability. Unions, government regulation of business, and welfare spending were not to blame; rather, the changing global economy was forcing the big U.S. corporations to compete as they never had before. This failure perhaps accounts for the election in 1992 of President Clinton.

The changed terrain facing the Clinton government included a global economy; an altered geopolitical balance of power because of the end of the cold war; new social movements centered on gender, race, sexuality, and definitions of citizenship rather than class (e.g., big business versus big labor); and technology that reaches beyond political control. These factors created pressures on the government (such as inadequate taxes, conflicts over values, changed demands on government budgets) that led to what I have labeled the distracted state. Thus the current era is one in which the level and form of state involvement are once again the focus of debate. The remainder of the chapter discusses the changes in the role of government that have led to this point.

THE UNINVOLVED STATE

Prior to World War II, the U.S. government was relatively uninvolved in the lives of most citizens. Thus I characterize it as the *uninvolved state*, even though at the same time the government was highly involved in the affairs of business. The basic purpose of government activity in our capitalist, market society, according to those in power, was to support the economy. It is true that when the economy is sluggish or unstable, people can't count on steady work, stable prices, or sufficient consumer goods. In this earlier period, then, the government's activities centered on fostering the well-being of the emergent business class.

That well-being relied on three things. First, businesses had to be able to engage in economic activity wherever they wanted. Creating that freedom required eliminating any restraints on trade (such as tariffs, limited access to raw material, and lack of access to potential markets). Second, the government had to preserve social order by preventing political disruption, riots, and radical social movements.

Finally, government had to protect national boundaries from geopolitical threats; providing this protection was under the purview of the military. Our government's early efforts to protect property and regulate labor played a major role in creating the United States as a world economic leader.

The Protection of Property

Among the Western capitalist democracies, the United States has always been unique for a variety of reasons. For one thing, the United States is much younger than Western European capitalist democracies. In addition, from the earliest days of U.S. politics, "the people" (at first only white men and, in some states, only white male property holders) elected our national leaders. Similarly, our **nation-state** (the state, for short)—the set of institutions comprising the implements of force (the army, police, etc.), the judiciary (courts), the legislature, and the executive and administrative branches—emerged concurrently with our market economy.

From our nation's inception, one of the primary purposes of government action was to protect and conserve the rights of private property, which were embedded in the Constitution. The Constitution originated in a period in which newly developing business classes (Southern planters and Northern manufacturers, merchants, and landowners) were struggling against the constraints the British royalty had imposed.

Our nation-state developed into a modern state during the period from the Civil War to the turn of the century. Prior to the Civil War an alliance between Northern business classes and Southern planters dominated (Lee and Passell, 1979). The Civil War brought an end to that alliance, and Northern business classes remained dominant. The emergence of Northern industrialists removed the last restraint to explosive economic growth of Northern industrial manufacturing interests, such as the steel industry. The activities of government supported that growth.

Military Intervention Although a preoccupation with westward expansion delayed United States entry into international trade, by the early 1900s American businesses were looking overseas for resources and markets. During this period, the government supported American property interests overseas through military involvement. China, for example, was of considerable interest to the American business class.

Access to China required some intermediary points of entry that the Philippines provided. To maintain an "open door policy" that allowed free trade with China, the United States, during the Spanish-American War, established colonies in the Philippines in 1899. By 1899, American businessmen obtained the trade contracts they sought (Williams, 1970). The army flexed its muscles in China in 1911, 1912, 1924, and 1926, when unrest threatened the security of American business concerns. In 1912, the American military interceded in Nicaragua to prevent interference in the financing of a railway. In 1915, United States troops occupied Haiti on behalf of United States bankers; in 1916, troops seized control of the treasury in Santo Domingo to force compliance with earlier economic obligations. Similarly, when oil interests were threatened in Mexico in 1916 the marines secured our interests through a show of force (Edwards, Reich, and Weisskoph, 1986, p. 112).

After the Russian Revolution of 1917, the anxieties of American business interests coalesced around the Soviet threat. As early as 1901, the Socialist party had garnered considerable support among working people in the United States. Although communism reached its ideological zenith after World War II, it motivated considerable state activity in this earlier period. Much of our military involvement throughout the world was to stop the spread of communism, which threatened not only, ostensibly, democratic rights but also capitalist markets (Weinstein, 1968; Edwards, Reich, and Weisskoph, 1986; Armstrong, Glyn, and Harrison, 1991).

Infrastructure In the era of the uninvolved state the government also played a major role in building the infrastructure of the country. Government land grants, financing, and police protection aided the building of railroads, highways, and waterways, all of which were necessary to interstate trade. Thus the "uninvolved" government was actively involved in providing the transportation necessary for economic expansion and growth.

By the mid-1800s, the government had provided financing for road and canal systems that connected the East and the West. Prior to the Civil War, of the $190 million invested in canal construction, the government provided roughly $143 million. To support railroad construction from 1850–1871, the government granted about 131 million acres to developers; the estimated value was roughly $400 million (Lee and Passell, 1979, p. 310). Research suggests, however, that the grants were provided after the railways were built and that the grants were economically unnecessary subsidies for already wealthy industrialists (see Lee and Passell, 1979).

Business Regulation   Perhaps the most dramatic and oft-discussed role of the government before World War II was its role as regulator of business. This role emerged with the set of policies that defined the Progressive era of the early twentieth century. These policies were aimed at controlling big business; in reality, they aided the consolidation and stability of those very businesses they regulated (Kolko, 1963, 1967).

A period of dramatic economic expansion characterized by high levels of business competition had begun in the late 1800s. That competition, in the absence of any controls, led to dramatic fluctuations in prices, massive unemployment, recurring recessions, and the first Great Depression in 1873. Such disruptions took a heavy toll on businesses. For example, during the years 1890–1928 almost 600,000 businesses failed. Many businesses that did not fail *per se* were absorbed by more powerful companies. There were 1,208 mergers in 1899 and 1,245 in 1929, levels unmatched until 1967.

An economy in transition created profound social disruption as well, such as massive immigration from the even more devastated economies of Europe, relocation of black Southern workers displaced by agricultural mechanization, the spread of factory labor, and the proliferation of banking and financial institutions. Out of this cauldron of social changes came a series of movements characterized by efforts to maintain some control.

The Progressive movement demanded that government control the unrestricted growth and competition of large corporations. It was driven by small businesses that were being gobbled up by larger ones, some large industrialists who recognized the failure of voluntary efforts to control competition, and conservative labor unions. Their concerns motivated passage of the Federal Reserve Act, the Federal Trade Commission Act, and the Sherman Anti-Trust Act, which were among the first major examples of government action to stabilize and regulate the economy. The Sherman Anti-Trust Act (1890) attempted to prevent contracts and conspiracies that would interfere with free trade. While early interpretations of the act threatened the growth of big business, later interpretations allowed monopolies to develop as long as they did not create "unreasonable" restraints to trade. In some instances, the Sherman Anti-Trust Act was used against unions, claiming that union organization created restraints on trade. The Federal

Reserve Act (1914) standardized and regulated the banking and financial system, regulated the flow of money and credit, and controlled interest rates (to some extent). The Federal Trade Commission Act (1914) formed a government agency to investigate possible restraints of trade in industries such as tobacco, oil, beef, cotton, and others.

Regulation of Employment Relations

In addition to regulating business, the government also sought to regulate the growth of radical working-class movements and politics. Political reforms and outright repression were used to keep industrial workers, immigrants, and other members of the "dangerous classes" from challenging the growing power of corporations.

Repression of Workers During the late nineteenth and early twentieth centuries, when the government intervened in conflicts between workers and employers, that intervention was consistently on the side of employers. Prior to the establishment of the Wagner Act in 1935, later solidified by Taft-Hartley in 1947, unions had no legal standing, and strikes could often result in jailing. Labor history during this period includes numerous incidents, many bloody, in which government troops were used to repress union organizing and strike activity (Boyer and Morais, 1955; Rubin, Griffin, and Wallace, 1983).

Of particular concern during the early twentieth century were the Industrial Workers of the World, or the "Wobblies." The IWW was an early industrial movement with an unabashedly radical platform. They sought to organize all workers, regardless of skill, ethnicity, or race. They not only demanded decent wages but claimed that "those who did the nation's work should own the nation's industries" (Boyer and Morais, 1955, p. 172). They challenged the strategies of more conservative unions like the American Federation of Labor (AFL) and called for a solidaristic working-class movement empowered by mass strikes.

The Wobblies were beaten, jailed, and executed. Their strikes were stopped with National Guard bullets. Their headquarters were dynamited and members were deported. Still, they had some influence at the local level. By 1915, 25 states had passed laws limiting the working day (there had previously been no legal limit), and states had begun to legislate child labor laws (Boyer and Morais, 1955).

Despite occasional victories, unions faced an uphill battle. Courts during this period were openly and consistently antilabor. They outlawed revolutionary unions, sympathy strikes, closed shops, and boy-cotts. Sympathy strikes refer to strikes by a group of workers to show support for other striking workers. For instance, if production workers in a factory strike for safer working conditions and the sales and clerical workers then strike in support of those production workers (all of which together would bring business to a halt), the second strike would be a sympathy strike. Closed shops are workplaces where employers can hire only unionized labor (where a union is already represented). Outlawing these strategies, all of which were very effec-tive in union organizing struggles, was part of the routinization process discussed in chapter 2. Employers frequently obtained court-issued injunctions against strikes, ending the strike by decree and criminalizing its continuance. Injunctions against strikes over the right to organize were effective means of limiting union membership (Griffin, Wallace, and Rubin, 1986). In the 1920s, injunctions were used 921 times against unions. Also effective were yellow-dog con-tracts, which made the promise never to join a union a condition of employment. The courts upheld the legality of these contracts as late as 1917.

Repression of organized labor was not the only way in which the "uninvolved" government intervened in the affairs of the working class. One target was corrupt urban "machine" politics (Chicago's being perhaps the best known and longest lasting). Think, for exam-ple, of the movie *The Godfather*, in which the fictitious Corleone family, through a combination of violence and beneficence, protected the members of the Italian community. The Corleones took care of their own, punished their enemies, and rewarded their friends.

Machine politicians, like the Corleone family, protected their ethnic constituencies and provided benefits, jobs, and redress of grievances. They maintained their power to provide these services by falsely registering voters within their wards and intimidating critics. Voter registration legislation and other reforms were designed to curb such corruption. Some have argued, however, that these reforms actually limited ethnic and working-class participation in govern-ment (Piven and Cloward, 1993).

By cleaning up urban machine politics, reformers replaced ethnic workers' political power with the more nationally organized and elite-dominated party politics. Similarly, voter registration, while seem-ingly a positive reform, meant that potential voters had to register periodically and meet a variety of criteria in order to vote. Electoral participation decreased dramatically (Greenberg, 1985; Piven and

Cloward, 1993). A combination of force, legal action, and political reform served to diminish the influence of ordinary people on the government.

Relief to the Poor Sometimes the state used a velvet glove rather than an iron fist to quell workers' potential for self-organization and the militancy of ordinary people. **Poor relief** was an example of such a strategy. Though we now associate big government with welfare, social security, food stamps, and other federal programs like these, before the depression there were no comparable policies. By and large, the government in the pre-depression era was *uninvolved* in providing for the poor. The absence of any effort on the part of the federal government to collect data on the extent and composition of the poor reflects the government's indifference to their plight.

In part, this laissez-faire approach was the result of powerful ideologies depicting the poor as victims of their own godlessness or slothfulness. Still, many recognized that the poor among them often were poor because of some happenstance outside their control. Certainly, widows and disabled soldiers could not be faulted for their position. Similarly, some recognized that rapid industrialization had played a role in creating hardship and poverty.

Prior to the 1930s, churches, charities, benevolent societies, communities, families, and the occasional mutual aid society kept the poor from total, unmitigated destitution. **Poor relief**, or the dole, was administered to the "deserving poor"—that is, to widows, the disabled, the sick, and the aged. By and large, any able-bodied poor (including children) were often institutionalized in workhouses (the type of place in which Oliver, the title character in the Charles Dickens–based musical about the poor of England, sings the praises of "Food, Glorious Food"). They were put to work, often under completely odious conditions. Being "on the dole" was highly stigmatized and a source of deep humiliation for people.

There was, however, consistent support for some sort of old age pension, especially for widows and veterans of the Civil War (see Quadagno, 1988, for an excellent study of the origins of old age security). For the most part, aid to the poor was spotty and administered on a state or community rather than federal level. Economic downturns often resulted in complete cessation of any sort of relief.

The other source of old age pension during the pre-labor–capital accord era was union pension funds. World War I had increased the strength and size of unions and allowed them to initiate pension plans for their members. But unions had little legal stability and protection during these years; so after the war, unions lost much of their membership and, therefore, their ability to maintain these pension plans.

Depression, War, and the End of an Era

The stock market crash of 1929 ended the period of the uninvolved government. When the depression and World War II were over, the federal government was committed to making sure that society never again experienced such massive economic and political disruption.

Try to imagine the situation the government faced during the 1930s. One third of the work force was unemployed, banks and major businesses had failed, and the country was in danger from a major war in Europe. Ordinary men and women who had done everything they thought they were supposed to do had lost everything. Many had come to this country, often with nothing but the clothes on their backs. They had worked hard, saving a little bit here, a little bit there, putting those savings into banks, trying to live the American Dream. Suddenly, through no fault of their own, they were out of jobs; their homes were repossessed; the banks wouldn't give them their money; and they could put little food on their soon-to-be repossessed tables. Traditional nineteenth-century solutions of charity and local responsibility were completely inadequate to meet the needs of the millions of people suddenly thrust into poverty, unemployment, and homelessness by the depression. At the same time, the Socialists and the Communist party provided an answer that made sense to many people. They blamed society's distress on exploitation and greed on the part of big business and told working people that they were the source of the nation's wealth but were not rewarded for it (Lynd, 1973; Weinstein, 1973; Stepan-Norris and Zeitlan, 1989).

Besides the threat from the organized left, there were threats from populist and right-wing movements. Father Coughlin was a radio priest who had enormous support for his demands for guaranteed wages and nationalization of industry. The Townsendites of California called for old age pensions of $200 a month for anyone over 60 years old that each pensioner had to spend within a month.

Then there was Huey Long, an enormously popular senator from the state of Louisiana who was elected in 1932. Long was flamboyant, charismatic, irreverent, and outrageous. He built bridges, roads, and schools and bought the loyalty of thousands. His support was tremendously important for mobilizing the votes that brought Franklin D. Roosevelt to power. However, Long's populism increasingly distanced him from national elites. Particularly threatening was his Share the Wealth movement, which demanded a federally guaranteed family income of $5,000 a year. Long had support not only from his own Louisiana constituency but more broadly throughout the impoverished rural South. Many believe that had he not been assassinated in 1935, he might well have made a successful run for the presidency (Amenta and Zylan, 1991; Piven and Cloward, 1993).

During the depression, many responded to economic hardship by leaving their homes and seeking work elsewhere. John Steinbeck's great novel *The Grapes of Wrath* recounts the story of the Joads, who left Oklahoma for California looking for work. The rootless despair of the Joads was one type of response to the depression, but others were less quiescent. In major cities like Chicago and New York, there was a rise in mass lootings of department and other stores. Similarly, often under the radical banners of the Socialist and Communist parties, unemployed workers staged mass protests that ended in violent clashes with the police. People evicted from their homes often staged rent strikes in which they refused to leave and protested for relief. Many of these strikes ended in violence.

Some of the strikes were so dramatic, however, that local officials did indeed respond with funds. Unfortunately, even if these local officials wanted to come to the aid of unemployed citizens, they often lacked the fiscal ability to do so. Eventually, the federal government was forced to confront the faltering economy, the widespread social disruption, and the incessant demands for relief.

The social and economic disruption of the 1930s played an important role in the emergence of the Democratic party. The Republican party had dominated the government since the end of World War I, but as the depression deepened more and more urban voters turned to the Democratic party. In 1932, Democrat Franklin Delano Roosevelt became president, and was reelected three times. Although a product of an elite family, he immediately responded to the demands of the electorate with a program of legislation, now called the New Deal, that attempted to diffuse radical claims by partially responding to their demands (Piven and Cloward, 1977, 1993). These programs included social security, work relief, and unemployment insurance.

The result of protest and economic and political instability was a redefinition of how Americans and their government conceived the government's role. For the first time in history, some part of the responsibility for individuals' well-being shifted to the government. This view was radically different from the one that blamed the poor for their poverty and misfortune.

THE INVOLVED STATE

Clearly the state had been involved in the economy prior to the New Deal, but it had been *uninvolved on a systematic basis with the well-being of ordinary citizens*. However, the political coalition that emerged after World War II devised policies that made the government a factor in people's lives. The involved state combined the social institutions of the New Deal with the military institutions of World War II (including the industries that made military hardware) as a way to protect the economy from future disasters. The range of issues with which government became systematically involved included policies regulating banking; protecting working people from the most odious conditions of employment; providing a certain amount of economic security for the aged, unemployed, and widowed; regulating industrial conflict; and using the government budget to stimulate the economy when its activity slowed. This set of policies structured government activity for the next two and a half decades. The United States thus became a **welfare–warfare state** (O'Connor, 1973).

The Welfare State

Perhaps the most important change in the government's role was its adoption of the set of protections grouped under the label *welfare*. Central to creating this new set of protections was a shift in the political and social understanding of the rights associated with U.S. citizenship in the labor–capital accord described in chapter 2. One significant component of the Accord was the relationship between workers, particularly unionized workers, and their employers. Another major component was what Bowles and Gintis (1982) and others have called the **citizen wage**, payments one receives by virtue of citizenship rather than by employment.

Prior to this era, the rights of citizenship had not included guarantees of minimum levels of employment, health, and employment safety. Rather, the government primarily protected the rights of property. However, as a result of the political and economic conflict that characterized the 1930s and 1940s, the government expanded its protections. The Wagner Act (1935) gave workers the right to bargain collectively through a representative of their own choosing. The Social Security Act (1935) provided, for the first time, a certain level of financial security to entire segments of the population. The Employment Act (1946) indicated commitment to maintaining a certain level of employment. Later, again as a response to social protest, riots, and disruption, the government extended the logic of responsibility with the extension of the Social Security Act known as Aid to Families with Dependent Children (1968), formally, Public Law 90-248. Similarly, the Occupational Health and Safety Act (1970) and the Clean Water Act (1971) also reflected the increased involvement and responsibility of the government in protecting the rights of citizens.

These legislative initiatives represent a very different relationship between the government and the citizenry. But all have come under attack or are threatened by current economic and political conditions. Perhaps the two that are most politically contentious are social security, which is a form of social insurance, and Aid to Families with Dependent Children, which is a form of public assistance.

Social Insurance **Social insurance programs** are linked to participation in the labor market. They distribute income to the aged, disabled, and unemployed, assuming they have worked in certain kinds of jobs for the minimum duration. They thus provide a citizen wage to those who have participated in the labor market. They provide income to poor and nonpoor alike. However, because they are tied to prior earnings and payroll contributions, they provide more income to those with lifetime, relatively high-level employment than to those with a spotty employment history.

Social security, which provides monthly payments to retired workers and their dependent families, is the most successful social insurance program and a prime example of the capabilities of the welfare state. It has been instrumental in saving many elderly persons from dire poverty. The percentage of the poor who are 65 years old or over decreased from 35.9% in 1959 (when data were first collected) to 10% in 1990 (Devine and Wright, 1993). (The government defines *poverty* as an annual income that does not support a minimum standard of living for a family of three or more.)

Social security has been enormously successful in protecting the well-being of Accord families, those consisting of a married breadwinner and homemaker. It has been less successful in helping people who, like my mother, do not fit the mold. Like many women of her age (born in 1932), my mother married in her early 20s and was a full-time homemaker. However, after her second divorce in the early 1970s she entered the labor market as a clerical worker. When she lost her first job she was able to replace it only with a part-time job. In the 1980s she was diagnosed with multiple sclerosis. She worked as long as she could until the debilitating effects of her disease forced retirement, at which point she applied for disability payments. Since she was not yet 65, she was unable to get social security. She did receive supplemental security income (SSI), which provides assistance to the blind, disabled, and aged. But given her late entry into the labor force and the limited years of her payment into the system, she was provided only a few hundred dollars a month on which to live. Moreover, she was informed that once she reached 65 her SSI payments would decrease. When my mother died well before her 65th birthday she was living below the poverty line and dependent for necessities on her friends and few living relatives. My grandparents, on the other hand, had stayed married over 60 years and had a successful business. The combination of social security payments and investments allowed them to retire to a comfortable and pleasant life. Even after my grandfather died, my grandmother has had enough income to enjoy life.

Another important form of social insurance provides benefits to military veterans. Over the years, these benefits have expanded to include medical care, college tuition, and housing loans. Of course, as recent protests by homeless Vietnam veterans make clear, these programs, for a variety of reasons, fall far short of need.

Unemployment insurance and workers' compensation are two other major forms of social insurance. Unemployment insurance provides temporary payments to workers to tide them over during periods of forced unemployment. The size and eligibility of payment are, of course, tied to past employment history. To obtain benefits, workers must meet state requirements and report weekly to employment offices. Workers displaced by industrial restructuring often use up these benefits before they find a new job, and they then fall into the uncounted and unpaid ranks of unemployed workers. Workers' compensation, in contrast, is for those whose work is interrupted by illness, disease, or work-related injury. It is similar to unemployment insurance in its administration (Levitan, 1985).

Public Assistance The other major type of welfare program is **public assistance programs**, which provide support on the basis of need rather than on the basis of prior contributions. There are programs for the elderly, blind, and disabled, as well as for poor families with dependent children. (See Sar Levitan, 1985, for an extensive, detailed, and accessible book on the variety of governmental programs geared toward the poor.)

The most well known and politically contentious of the public assistance programs is Aid to Families with Dependent Children (AFDC). AFDC provides income to single-parent families with young children, presumably to keep those families out of poverty. The AFDC program supported the overall image of the Accord family. It was geared toward supplementing the incomes of women who did not have a male breadwinner and was originally conceived as support for widows with children. In other words, AFDC was not established as a program that somehow would allow women to become economically independent. Such a program would include job training, child care, and other benefits that would allow poor women to obtain incomes sufficiently high to support their families. Because the state played the role of the missing husband, it reinforced women's economic dependency, an aspect of the program that is now deemed one of its greatest weaknesses.

AFDC constitutes a relatively small part of total welfare expenditures. In 1960, for example, AFDC accounted for 4.2% of total federal social welfare expenditures; at its peak in the 1970s, it was only 6.3%, and by 1988 it was reduced to 3.2%. However, AFDC has been the fastest growing of the *means-tested* income programs in the post–World War II era. **Means-tested programs** are those for which recipients must demonstrate need. Such programs are in contrast to entitlement programs like social security. The percentage of all families that received AFDC in 1960 was 1.8%, but by the 1970s it was 5.0% and by 1988 5.8% (Devine and Wright, 1993, Table 6.2, p. 144). Among the reasons for the rapid expansion of AFDC expenditures were the ideological changes that swept the nation in the 1960s, which seemed to relax some of the stigma of accepting help from the government.

Table 5.1 presents the increase in current dollars allocated to AFDC and AFDC expenditures as a percentage of total government expenditures. These data show that during this period, the amount of money allocated to AFDC did grow dramatically. The data also show, however, that as a percentage of total government expenditures, AFDC payments were relatively minuscule.

Table 5.1 AFDC Expenditures in Current Dollars as a Percentage of Total Government Expenditures

Year	AFDC (millions)	AFDC as Percentage of Total Government Expenditures
1950	551	.89
1955	613	.56
1960	991	.65
1965	1,650	.80
1970	4,823	1.40
1975	9,186	1.55
1980	12,409	1.23
1992	24,923	1.00

Adapted from *National Income and Product Accounts of the United States 1929–1974*, 1977, Washington, D.C.: Bureau of Economic Analysis; *Survey of Current Business* (monthly publication), July 1976, July 1978, and July 1983, Washington, D.C.: U.S. Department of Commerce (Bureau of Economic Analysis); *Economic Report of the President*, 1978 and 1983, Washington, D.C.: Government Printing Office; *Statistical Abstract of the United States*, 1994.

AFDC is state administered; so the levels of benefits are highly uneven. In New York in 1991, for example, the average monthly payment for AFDC recipients was $550, while in my home state of Louisiana the payment was $167 a month. While there is little doubt that the cost of living in Louisiana is far less than that in New York, there is also little doubt that even in Louisiana, a family, no matter how small, cannot live on $167 a month! In no state are AFDC payments alone enough to keep families out of poverty.

Some have argued that AFDC payments must be kept unattractively low so that they will not induce young women to have more children out of wedlock in order to get on the AFDC rolls or increase their benefits once on them. There is, however, little evidence to support either of these concerns. Devine and Wright's summary of the data on poverty, welfare, and illegitimacy indicates that women receiving AFDC are no more likely than poor women not receiving AFDC to have more children. They go on to argue that reducing AFDC payments would not decrease the number of children born out of wedlock; rather it would increase the poverty of children who are dependent on AFDC payments. Moreover, the minuscule dollar increase associated with each additional child is scarcely enough to impel women to have additional children (Devine and Wright, 1993, p.141). It is true that there are increasing numbers of out-of-wedlock births; it is not true that the increase is related to the provision of welfare (Levitan, 1985; Wilson, 1987; Devine and Wright, 1993).

All public assistance programs have been successful in reducing poverty, even though they do not eradicate it. There is little doubt that without them the extent of misery throughout society would be much greater. The problem is that the political alliance that led to the expansion of the welfare state and the resources that have funded it may well be absent in the current era. I will return to this issue; however, before I do, I need to discuss the other arm of the involved state—the warfare state.

The Warfare State

The policies of the New Deal alone did not end the depression. World War II also played a role. Wars stimulate economic activity (someone must build the tanks and guns). Business profits and workers' wages increase, and unemployment decreases. When employment and wages increase, so do consumer buying and corporate profits. The problem, of course, is that no one wants a war to go on forever. Though it might be good for the economy (at least if it is a war fought in someone else's country), it is certainly not good for the thousands of men and women who are killed and maimed, nor for their survivors. The coalition of leaders who emerged at the end of World War II recognized the economic role that war had played and sought to continue the benefits of wartime production without the costs. They sought to use the military budget, regardless of geopolitical threats, as a mechanism to stimulate economic activity (Griffin, Devine, and Wallace, 1982).

The continued expansion of the military budget after World War II was fueled in part by the cold war (see Figure 5.1, which shows military expenditures as a percentage of the total budget). Though Stalin had joined the Allied forces during the war, after the war was over military leaders focused their concerns on the possible spread of communism. The role of the Communist party and of Socialists in fomenting social protest, empowering industrial workers' movements, and organizing rent strikes and other forms of civil disobedience had not gone unnoticed by military and political leaders. Thus, after the

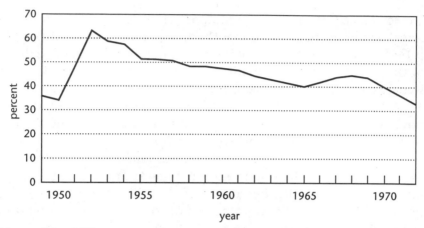

Figure 5.1. **Military expenditures as percentage of the federal budget, 1949 to 1972.**

From *Historical Statistics of the United States: Colonial Times to 1970*, 1975, Washington, D.C.: U.S. Bureau of the Census; *Economic Report of the President*, 1978, Washington, D.C.: Government Printing Office.

war, they also sought to purge all leftist influences from domestic institutions.

The most celebrated examples of this purge were exemplified by the witch-hunts presided over by Senator Joseph McCarthy. Senator McCarthy brought dozens of writers, producers, actors, and others up on charges of engaging in "un-American" activities—that is, being communists. In a country that celebrates freedom of speech, this period of history is deeply shameful. *It Did Happen Here* (Schultz and Schultz, 1989), for instance, includes testimony of a number of victims of the HUAC (House Unamerican Acitivities Committee): Hollywood screenwriters like Ring Lardner, Jr., the singer Pete Seeger, and others, many of whom were unable to work under their own names for years. Actors such as Gary Cooper, Ronald Reagan, and the writer Ayn Rand testified about the "red menace" that was sweeping Hollywood. The screenwriter Dalton Trumbo was vilified, for instance, for writing the line "share and share alike, that's democracy," among other things. Other careers were destroyed, and some, under the scrutiny of the committee and condemned by false accusations, had heart attacks or took their own lives (Schultz and Schultz, 1989; see also, Barnow, 1970). Woody Allen's movie *The Front* dramatized these conflicts.

The McCarthy hysteria was behind passage of the McCarran Act (1950), which forced unions to expunge many of those who had been instrumental in union organizing efforts. This legislation was a component of the labor–capital accord. However, the anticommunist hysteria supported the cold war and provided a powerful ideological tool for justifying continued expenditures on the military budget, even in peacetime.

All the military activity from World War II to 1990, such as in Korea and Vietnam, was motivated by the United States' efforts to stop the perceived threat of communism. While there is no doubt that communism posed a real threat to the expansion of capitalist markets, it is less clear that communists threatened the United States directly. Some have claimed that military spending became a tool to prevent the stagnation of the economy (O'Connor, 1973; Griffin, Devine, and Wallace, 1983).

There is some evidence to back this claim. During the years 1944–1977, for example, when the rate of unemployment increased in the core of the economy, regardless of what the geopolitical situation was, military spending increased. Remember, it is in core industries (e.g., manufacturing, mining, transportation, communication) that unionized labor is most likely to work. And these are the workers with whom business had established the labor–capital accord. To maintain industrial peace and high wages and, therefore, consumption, the government increased spending for armaments and military products whenever unemployment in the core increased. These increases kept business production high, unemployment of the most powerful sectors of the work force low, and wages high.

Using military spending to stimulate the economy is attractive to both business and government for several reasons. First, the government can manipulate it easily—it need only write another armaments contract. Second, armaments become obsolete quickly. The supply never reaches the demand. Third, this kind of spending does not compete with private enterprise. If, for example, government poured money into building schools or hospitals in areas that needed them, such spending would compete with private economic actors such as construction contractors. Such competition is extremely unpopular among big business.

While it is true that President Roosevelt was able to initiate public works projects (for example, the dams of the Tennessee Valley Authority) during the depression and war years, such projects are only politically feasible during rather extraordinary times. In ordinary times, military spending became an acceptable way of stimulating economic activity. It provided employment to the most powerful sectors of the economy (the unionized workers in the economic core) and kept core manufacturers busy producing goods that would not saturate the market.

Tensions in the Involved State

The postwar accord thus included not only the changed relationships with labor that chapter 2 discussed but also a changed relationship between the government and the citizenry. Between 1947 and the early 1970s, the government increased its involvement not only in the affairs of business but in the lives of working people. For the first time in United States history, there was a set of programs geared toward protecting the aged, the young, the disabled, and the impoverished from the most desperate conditions. Although our social programs fall far behind those of our Western European counterparts (we are the only advanced capitalist democracy without a comprehensive health care plan, for example), there is little doubt that the implementation of these programs increased the standard of living for millions of Americans.

Despite the relative success of these programs (and this chapter has only mentioned a very few of them), just as the accord between labor and business unraveled, so too did the accord between the poor and the government. The sundering of that contract is linked to tensions between market and citizenship rights as well as to moral conflicts that have arisen in the past couple of decades.

Market Freedom Versus Citizen Rights Of all the sources of tension undermining government commitment to helping the disadvantaged, perhaps the tension between market and citizen rights is the most central. One of the consequences of adopting the concept of the citizen wage was that individuals acquired an alternative to participating in the labor market. In other words, in the absence of the citizen wage, an individual would have to take any job available, no matter how odious the conditions of labor or how low the pay. With an alternative source of income available from the government an individual could choose not to work (Piven and Cloward, 1982).

Although not working might mean living in poverty with the stigma of receiving a handout, it was often more attractive than the alternative. A young unmarried mother who chooses a minimum-wage job over AFDC would have to give up the food stamps and medicaid that provide health care and food for her and her children. She would have to pay for transportation, clothing, and so forth to allow her to maintain her job. She would have to either pay for or forego child care. Finally, a minimum wage would fail to keep her out of poverty. In effect, to accept a minimum-wage job would end up costing her money and depriving her family of what it needed. This trade-off is economically irrational.

This aspect of the welfare state, more than any other, became anathema to many people, particularly those who were working at low-income jobs and did not have the benefit of social insurance or public assistance to raise their standard of living. For all kinds of people, the image of a lazy woman bearing children as a way out of work became a symbol for all that was unfair about their own economic difficulties. She became the symbol on which anti-welfare-state politicians fixed.

The real threat was not this woman, however. Rather it was an empowered working class. Remember that the labor–capital accord strengthened the position of working people by institutionalizing unions. The citizen wage also strengthened workers by offering some protections to those who were nonunionized. By having a source of income in the absence of a job, workers had more power to make demands on employers for safer workplaces, nonwage benefits (such as health benefits), and decent working conditions. But as corporations faced increasingly unprofitable conditions in the 1970s and 1980s, some realized that one way to minimize labor problems was to once again make workers more compliant. Making them more economically vulnerable would accomplish this end.

The election of President Ronald Reagan unleashed a wholesale attack on the welfare state (though it had begun earlier). Reagan's reforms sought to revoke the citizen wage and redefine citizen rights as privileges accruing from active participation in the market. Within a year of his election, Ronald Reagan slashed $140 billion from social insurance and public assistance expenditures. Though he originally included social security in the potential cuts, the increased political clout of the elderly stopped him. His attacks fell, then, on the most vulnerable, the poor. AFDC payments decreased from about $403 in 1970 to $260 in 1985 (Devine and Wright, 1993, p. 143). Similarly, Reagan initiated decreases in expenditures for food stamps, health care, school lunch programs, job training, and other social programs (Piven and Cloward, 1982, 1993).

The Reagan policy toward housing also had dramatic consequences (Rubin, Wright, and Devine, 1992). A period of increased economic instability, industrial restructuring, worker displacement, and joblessness increased the ranks of poor and low-income people and decreased the supply of low-income housing. Tax policies that favored the gentrification of inner cities (tearing down old apartments and putting up expensive condominiums) removed many traditional sources of low-income housing such as flophouses and government-built low-rent housing. The Reagan–Bush agenda of deregulation and privatization removed government from the business of providing low-income housing and turned that responsibility over to private business. It is, however, more profitable to build and sell upscale housing than low-income housing. Thus, for example, in Louisiana, there was a 45.5% gap between the number of low-income households and the number of low-income housing units. In New York there was a 137.6% gap (Rubin, Wright, and Devine, 1993, p. 128). The result was a surge in homelessness.

In sum, the Reagan administration aggressively, and the Bush administration less so, pursued policies that once again elevated market and property rights over citizenship rights. Rather than seeing the role of government as one of protecting citizens from failures in market policy, these administrations viewed the role of government as strengthening markets and businesses. The assumption was that if businesses could act relatively free from regulation and demands by an empowered working class, profits would increase—and those profits would trickle down to the rest of society. As I discussed in chapter 2, profits did not trickle down (see also Treas, 1983).

Moral Conflicts Another tension that the welfare state generated existed between religious fundamentalists and secular liberals. Many conservative politicians and members of the religious right, led by Jerry Falwell's Moral Majority, now reconfigured as the Christian Coalition, believe that the welfare state encourages illegitimacy, cohabitation among unmarried youth, and a general abandonment of traditional values. Beginning in the 1970s, the religious right increasingly supported and was represented in the right wing of the Republican party. They sought to make values, particularly family values, the center of policy initiatives.

Popular support for the Moral Majority and later for the family values platform undoubtedly stemmed from the anxiety caused by many of the economic changes discussed in the earlier chapters.

Increased economic pressure and declining economic security created pressures on families for both adults to work (see chapter 4). Traditional gender roles were threatened, family stability appeared threatened, and children were increasingly unparented.

Given this range of pressures on families and other unsettling changes, the call for a return to family values was enormously appealing to many people. And what better to symbolize the failure of family values than a young, unwed welfare mother, having ever more and more babies to increase her welfare check? Although there is little evidence of such behavior, these fictitious "welfare queens" (Devine and Wright, 1993) were useful ideological tools to those who sought to dismantle the welfare programs that cost business and taxpayers money.

While the beginning of the post–World War II period was characterized by a growing economy and a redefinition and expansion of the government's role, the opposite conditions prevailed roughly 40 years later. The decade of the 1980s was characterized by a general willingness to chastise the poor and celebrate the rich. Haute couture, condominiums, yuppies, and "Beamers" (BMWs) came to symbolize the decade. Not only did society actively reject involvement in providing for the disadvantaged, but it celebrated the ability of business, not government, to solve all of the country's problems.

THE DISTRACTED STATE

Government's involvement in providing for the disadvantaged has diminished to some extent because of its increasing inability to maintain this role. The end of the cold war, the fall of the Berlin Wall, and the breakup of the Soviet Union, in conjunction with the increasingly globalized economy, have created a new set of tensions and demands on the government. Fiscal crisis, technological developments, and the emergence of new social movements have also made it more difficult for government to focus on the social problems and demands that the policies of the Reagan/Bush administrations either ignored or exacerbated. The result is an orientation more accurately described as *distracted* than as uninvolved.

Among the many signs of the distracted state was President Clinton's difficulty in formulating and selling a universal health care plan to Congress and the public. One disagreement is over the best mechanisms for providing such care. Those who had a sense, because of the post–World War II government involvement, that government policy could solve problems, favored government-guaranteed universal coverage. Others favored the market as the source of health care. The dispute is complicated by tight federal budgets and continuing moral conflict. Thus the Clinton administration's ability to resolve these issues was confounded by the complexity of the era in which they were occurring.

Government in the 1990s is highly distracted by a range of problems and concerns. The remainder of this chapter focuses on four major characteristics of the current era that pose a challenge to government involvement in society: specifically, globalization of the economy, fiscal crises, technological distractions, and the emergence of new social movements. What is the nature of the social contract that is being written by government and citizenry in this era of dramatic institutional transformation? The answers are still far from clear.

Globalization of the Economy

The end of the cold war destabilized the international balance of power that had dominated the world system for four decades. That shift has had and will continue to have enormous implications for the role of the government in the United States. Many argue that the end of the Soviet threat means that the United States need no longer police the world to halt the spread of communism. In addition, they argue, the government can decrease the military budget and turn those resources to problems at home (e.g., building schools and low-income housing, providing health coverage for the poor, etc.). The prospects of such a "peace dividend" are uncertain, however.

One impediment to making that budgetary shift is the huge deficit in government funds. Basically, the government has borrowed several trillion dollars to finance many its activities. Thus, just as with any loan (auto, mortgage, and credit cards), when the debt is high enough, most if not all of the payments against it simply are payments on the interest and don't even touch the principal. As a result, it takes years and years to eradicate the built-up debt. Even if the entire military budget were directed toward the deficit, there would be no surplus to direct toward other domestic needs.

Observers point out that there are now new conflicts to which the government must turn its attention. These are increasingly economic rather than military (Kennedy, 1993). Probably the most important of these entail trying to stabilize, both socially and economically, the countries of the old Soviet bloc.

As recent conflicts in Somalia, Bosnia-Herzegovnia, Iraq, and elsewhere make clear, the end of the cold war has not meant the beginning of international peace. During this period of international political and economic transformation, battles between different visions of how to reorganize the world community take center stage. Will societies organize around fundamental religious principles? economic freedom? political democracy? ethnic purity? All are possible political worlds; none is preordained.

These situations create an unstable environment for those influential economic actors such as Coca Cola and IBM who increasingly operate in a global rather than a national context. Although they operate independently of nation-state boundaries, governments do not. This contrast creates one of the greatest challenges to government and results in what many call a shrunken state; that is, a state with diminished power and jurisdiction (see, e.g., Beck, 1992; Crook, Pukulski, and Waters, 1992; Lash and Urry, 1987; Kennedy, 1993).

Given the gap between the arena of economic activity and the arena of political jurisdiction, how can the nation-state assure global economic and political stability? The U.S. government has far less freedom now than before World War II to intervene militarily when trade is threatened. Since the Vietnam War, there have been two major changes that have curtailed that freedom. First, the American people are far less likely to support military intervention and the resultant loss of life in the absence of a clear and unambiguous threat to national interest. Second, many countries that had U.S.-backed rulers are now ruled by leadership that is hostile to United States intervention. The international political climate is much less favorable to economically motivated military intervention than it was during earlier periods. The government's involvement has diminished in other ways too. Many of the concerns of government policy (e.g., negotiating economic and trade policies) have been taken over by other institutions such as corporations, industrial federations, and specialized agencies (Crook, Pukulski, and Waters, 1992, p. 80).

On a completely different level, the internationalization of markets puts them outside the control of any one country's government. Globalized economic activity makes it difficult to stabilize a given nation's wages or solve its unemployment problem because governments do not make the decisions that put people to work or stabilize prices. Instead, private actors make investment decisions that affect employment rates and prices. If Corporation X decides that it doesn't want to pay higher taxes or pay to clean up the waste it has dumped into the water or air, it can relocate to some business-friendly location that does not put those demands on business. When that corporation relocates, employment in the city or state or country of origin decreases, and so does the political popularity of whomever the voting public holds responsible for the downturn. Politicians who promise to address problems like unemployment have only limited ability to deliver on those promises. While this constraint has always existed, globalization makes governments even more constrained.

The consequences of these failures are particularly dramatic in the former command economies that seek to become market economies (e.g., the former East Germany, Russia, and other former Soviet bloc countries). But it is also true for the United States. For example, in response to economic hardship in the mid-1990s, the Clinton administration pursued policies to stimulate corporate investment (which creates jobs). Encouraging those policies, however, cannot ensure that corporations invest in the United States rather than in third world countries, where they can avail themselves of nonunionized, low-wage work forces in unregulated environments.

The various economic agreements, such as the North American Free Trade Agreement and GATT, represent efforts on the part of governments to overcome some of these limitations by creating global policies and protocols for business and industry. Another example of such protocols is an effort to develop rules about how to distribute the potential mineral rights associated with the ocean floor. An article in the *New York Times* (1994) indicated that such policies are roughly 10 years away. This type of organization was foreshadowed in the television show *Seaquest DSV*. There, the UEO (United Earth Organization) serves as a supranational organization policing the international use of the oceans' resources. But that is television.

The reality is that national governments within a global economy are simply unable, on their own, to play the historical role that governments play: regulating the economy and maintaining social stability. Governments tried to respond to this challenge by returning to earlier forms of minimal involvement, through deregulation and privatization, but the failure of those responses was unambiguously indicated, for example, by the increased homelessness caused by Reagan–Bush policies.

Fiscal Crisis

The problem of diminished government jurisdiction contributes to another major distraction to the government: The ability to respond to economic problems is hampered by the inadequate resources the current economy generates. One of the most basic characteristics of the involved state was its role in expanding the definition and protection of citizenship rights—for example, the right to income even when unemployed—and providing the associated citizen wage (e.g., unemployment insurance). The ability to provide that wage and ensure those rights rested, however, on a sufficient tax base and a relatively affluent work force.

For the government to pay social security benefits, unemployment benefits, disability benefits, and AFDC payments, to build schools and repair roads, and to do all the other things that the citizenry requires and expects of its government, it must have the revenue provided by taxes. However, taxes are (with the exceptions that loopholes provide) a function of income. Part-time, unskilled, contingent, and otherwise "flexible" workers tend to have low incomes and thus are unable to contribute significantly to the tax base. Unfortunately, low-income workers are becoming more prevalent in the current economy of globalized corporations. The result is a deepening of the fiscal crisis that has plagued the government for roughly two decades. **Fiscal crisis**, a term made popular by James O'Connor in his book *Fiscal Crisis of the State* (1973), refers to the increasing gap between necessary funds and necessary expenditures.

The growth of a contingent work force also creates a whole new set of demands on government (duRivage, 1992). As chapter 3 demonstrated, contingent work is characterized by, among other things, economic instability. However, pension and health care programs, as structured during the Accord years, are tied to long-term, stable contributions on the part of wage earners. Workers whose careers are characterized by multiple employers and spells of unemployment will find themselves with inadequate health care and retirement benefits under the current system. My mother's experience is a case in point. Since she had only started working in her 40s and had worked in several jobs (the last of which was part-time), had she lived to age 65, her monthly social security payments would only have provided around $200 a month on which to live. Contrast her situation with a white, male breadwinner with a lifetime of stable employment and a traditional breadwinner–homemaker family. On average that family would have a monthly payment of $567 (in 1989). Since the *Statistical Abstract* provides only an *average* monthly payment, we know that some retired couples receive far more. In addition, they would receive the private retirement benefits associated with the breadwinner's job. Not surprisingly, the poverty rate for elderly women living alone in 1990 (few of whom would have made more than minimal payments into the system) was 15.4 %, while for white males in families it was 4.5% (Wright and Devine, 1994; recall Figure 4.2).

Retiring contingent workers will create a whole new set of demands on government, but if everything stays as it is the government will not have the resources to meet these demands. The result would be massive poverty and anguish for the nation's ill, injured, and elderly.

Many welfare programs, particularly social security, are entitlement programs and have therefore been politically untouchable. Yet, sheer demographics threaten to undermine social security. For the first time, Congress in the 1980s began talking about the necessity of taxing, limiting, or somehow altering entitlement programs as a way to save them. However, poverty is not increasing because social security payments are going to the well-off elderly. The problem is linked more directly to the increased percentage of the young who live in poverty (see Figure 4.3) because of the increase in low-wage and contingent jobs (Wright and Devine, 1994; Rubin, 1995).

There are many other ways in which the transformation of the economy and work force creates new demands on the government, but not the funds to address those demands. In chapter 4 I wrote about the increasing pressures on all family members to participate in paid employment and the resultant difficulties for parenting. Thus, one of the new demands on the government is for the provision, or at least regulation, of child care centers. Unfortunately, government-funded social service agencies are hopelessly understaffed, under-budgeted, and overburdened. While states may pass laws requiring certain day care standards, there are few resources available to enforce those standards. When then-Governor Clinton became President Clinton, state governors were thrilled—thinking that now there would be a president in the White House who recognized the difficulties of addressing the problems of crime, school systems, poverty, housing, and all the other things with which local governments must deal. In fact, they have been sorely disappointed. No funds have poured into local governments, and those governments—like the federal government—still face increasing demands with decreasing funds.

The ability of the government to accomplish its role has always rested on its ability to finance its activities by taxing and borrowing. Continued borrowing has created a huge and politically unpalatable federal budget deficit. The flexible economy has yet to create sufficiently high-income and stable jobs for the mass of citizens to provide revenue through taxes. At the same time, the government has yet to develop a tax system that derives much tax revenue from global corporations. Both flexible work and the global economy create, however, a range of needs to which the government must respond, and therefore the fiscal crisis deepens.

Technological Distractions

Television creates an additional distraction for governments. Without doubt, television has created a global village of shared images. Golden arches and Coke signs are recognized from Red Square to Times Square, from Nigeria to Vanuata. Chapter 6 discusses the cultural implications of these pervasive media-disseminated images. The point here is that television presents these images to everyone. This shared imagery changes politics both globally and domestically.

A *Los Angeles Times* article (October 20, 1992) reported that there are now more than 1 billion television sets. Similarly, more than 300 satellites deliver services over the airwaves. Like many economic actors, TV has no national boundaries. It brings images of unbelievable affluence to communities living in unrelenting poverty. Moreover, governments are essentially unable to control the images the airwaves spread. Governments around the world increasingly try to harness the ideological power of television to promote the ideas that they prefer, but they have been far from successful.

The consequences of this pervasive force are the subject of considerable debate. On the one hand, the scope of TV's influence means that ideas about democracy and freedom are available to countries that may have limited experience with such ideas. On the other hand, television shows are owned by corporations seeking profits. While they may indeed circulate ideas of democracy, they also seek to create new markets for the products of their advertisers. The images of democracy are clearly less important than the images of consumers. Thus, some argue that instead of helping countries move toward more productive, open, and democratic societies, television serves the purpose of creating new material wants. Rather than working for freedom, viewers will work for the most stylish blue jeans (or sneakers, or whatever commodity corporations are pushing).

Global television is only one of the ways in which technology has outstripped government's ability to use or regulate outcomes. Another, far more pernicious technological distraction than television is pollution. Pollution and environmental degradation also are not confined within the national boundaries that create them. Slash-and-burn deforestation in the Amazon affects the ozone layer covering the entire globe; industrial pollutants in the United States cause acid rain to fall on Canada; illegal dumping of industrial waste in Russia deforms the ocean's ecosystem and thus affects South American fisheries. There are no countries that have not contributed to the problems facing the environment. Since the problem is global, so must be the solutions. There is, however, no real supranational entity to date that can tackle this problem.

Nation-states are in a difficult situation, in which the technological problems they face and the public's awareness of them outstrip their jurisdictions. Pollution knows no boundaries; neither does television. National laws, however, do.

New Social Movements

Contributing to the difficulty of responding to the problems confronting the shrunken state is the decline of traditional political constituencies. A new set of concerns and movements has generated challenges to existing political coalitions and has made traditional political answers unacceptable.

For most of the Accord era, electoral politics and competition between the Democratic and Republican parties were organized loosely around class lines. The upper class (those who live off profits and dividends in addition to other sources of wealth) and upper middle class (professionals, technicians, and managers) tended to support the Republican party. The traditional industrial working class, minorities, and semiprofessionals (e.g., teachers, social workers) tended to support the Democratic party. The Republican party developed policies addressing the needs of big business and the military. The Democratic party mobilized around the citizen wage and civil rights. Though class voting has never been as clear-cut nor as consistent as it was in Western

Europe (where there are labor and Socialist parties representing the interests of workers directly opposed to those of business), these broad coalitions allowed policy efforts to cluster broadly around either business or worker concerns.

The end of the labor–capital accord was associated with the decline of party alignment. Now the array of political demands is as fragmented as political parties. Southern Democrats, once firmly locked into and shaping Democratic party platforms, increasingly vote with Republicans. Republicans may be fragmented by the Christian right, which pushes a far more socially conservative agenda than that supported by much of the Republican party. While issues of civil rights and economics are still present, they no longer fall into the neat political packages that they did in earlier eras.

What has emerged in the place of politics organized around traditional Republican or Democratic agendas is politics organized around issues of identity. *Identity politics* emerge out of peoples' efforts to protect and expand rights associated with group identities such as race, gender, and sexuality. For example, the gay rights movement has been sufficiently organized and vocal to pressure for the end to policies forcing gays out of the military. Similarly, women have organized around gender issues to such an extent that in 1994 they were able to dramatically increase the number of women in Congress. Blacks increasingly organize as a community (using the label *African-American*) that strives for success independent of larger government involvement and that celebrates African heritage. All these phenomena reflect social movements centered on identities other than class.

Political mobilization also focuses on quality-of-life issues. Perhaps the most important of these is the environmental or green movement. Like the other new social movements, the environmental movement is clearly global in scope because the problem of environmental degradation is global. Moreover, its concerns transcend traditional party boundaries and make new coalitions not only possible but necessary.

Many of these new social movements differ dramatically from prior political movements. They are often, for example, antigovernment. They seek social change but view the government with distrust. Thus, participants in the new social movements may eschew electoral participation. This reluctance to participate in institutionalized politics, including voting and lobbying, is a key change. The civil rights movement of an earlier era, for example, had a more radical wing but sought power through representation within government (Cohen, 1985; Melucci, 1985; Gamson, 1992; Crook, Pukulski, and Waters, 1992).

In addition, many of the new social movements are heavily dependent on television and the distribution and manipulation of symbols. ACT-UP, the AIDS Coalition to Unleash Power, is a case in point. It is a single-issue movement geared toward pressuring the government to devote more resources to finding a cure for the AIDS virus. Its main form of political action has been to use disruption, propaganda, and theatrical protest rather than voting, lobbying, and other more conventional forms of political action. Its use of graphics, beginning with the powerful SILENCE = DEATH logo superimposed on a pink triangle (the symbol gays had to wear during the Nazi reign of terror), was an instantly successful ideological tool. ACT-UP has been particularly creative in its acts of civil disobedience. Early on in the movement, ACT-UP targeted the Food and Drug Administration (FDA) for its sluggish response to HIV. Before one demonstration, they contacted the media and presented them with all the information. Members of ACT-UP appeared on talk shows, gave interviews to reporters, and "sold" the demonstration in advance. By the time the media came to cover it, they knew what they were going to cover and why (Crimp and Rolston, 1990). The demonstrators showed up in costumes and used props. To a great extent they were successful in getting the FDA to begin to take AIDS seriously (for an excellent depiction, see *AIDS Demographics* by Douglas Crimp and Adam Rolston, Bay Press, 1990).

Politics is the struggle over who gets what, how they get it, and when they get it. In the United States during the Accord period, politics was loosely organized by the Democratic and Republican parties. Membership in either of these parties connoted a set of beliefs and political preferences politicians could draw on to develop policies and garner support for them. New social movements make the process of "doing politics" much more complex for politicians. The old clustering is less and less applicable. Last semester, one of my most conservative students, one of the officers of the campus Young Republican organization, let people know that he was gay. He wrote a letter to the student paper that explained why he "came out." In part, he said, he was motivated by people's assumptions that because he was a Republican and economically conservative that he was homophobic. He is an example of how identity politics complicates traditional ways of doing politics. Identity politics distracts politicians from successfully engaging in politics as usual.

CONCLUSIONS

This chapter has covered the transformation of the relationship between the government and the rest of society from the pre–World War II era to the end of the twentieth century. For most of the pre–World War II years, government policy was narrowly focused on accomplishing its major goals of ensuring the security and stability of the nation. At that time, that focus meant maximizing the interests of the business community over those of any other sector of society. The government in those early years was uninvolved in protecting the citizenry from some of the harshest consequences of a growing economy. It concentrated on helping the economy grow through its use of military force, creation of the infrastructure, minimal regulation of business, and maximal regulation of labor.

The Great Depression and World War II were a historical watershed. In response to the social, political, and economic crises of those periods the government expanded its role. It developed a set of policies that were a major part of the labor–capital accord. These policies assisted many of those in economic need such as the poor, the elderly, and disabled veterans. This welfare state came under attack as the Accord declined.

At the end of the twentieth century, the government is again making a transition, trying to develop policies that allow it to perform its historical role of protecting the nation and ensuring internal economic and social stability in a changed international context. The globalization of the economy and technology, the changing structure of the work force, fiscal crisis, and new social movements have created new challenges that make old ways of governing unmanageable.

One of the greatest challenges to the government is its diminished jurisdiction and ability to manage social problems. The 1990s are a decade of social and political exploration. The problems of poverty, crime, violence, and homelessness that have plagued major cities (though they are not confined there) stem from many of the social changes I have discussed. For some people, the fear with which they are living promotes support for an authoritarian state that restricts civil rights in exchange for guaranteeing protection. For others, the response to these and other social problems requires a government newly committed to a reformed welfare state that is inclusive and nonpunitive. Globalization of business and the work force, increased immigration, decreased state jurisdiction, and the aging of the population might well lead to increased conflict between those who support policies based on entitlement (such as social security) and those based on welfare.

Technological developments can create new economic, political, and cultural linkages within and between countries. Creating these may require new supranational organizations. The decline of old blocs makes such transnational alliances possible to a greater extent than ever before. However, the resurgence of ethnically based, tribal warfare inhibits such progress.

Periods of dramatic social change such as the current one create new forms of government and politics. After World War II, the role and form of the state changed dramatically. We are once again in a period in which such major changes are likely. Then, as now, the direction that change takes depends on the extent and form of popular involvement. That involvement will result in a new social contract.

The social spheres of power, government, and politics, perhaps more than any other sphere of social life exemplify the social contractual nature of relationships. After all, as Jean-Jacques Rousseau and other early political theorists recognized, a fundamental basis of democracy is government's *right* to rule and to monopolize the means of destruction. That legitimacy rests on a social contract that exchanges power and rule for representation of the social will (Blau, 1993). In periods of social transformation such as the late twentieth century, that social will is less cohesive and less discernible than ever. Uncovering that social will and overcoming the forces of fragmentation are crucial; however, failure to do so will result in a social contract for the few—the antithesis of a democracy.

CULTURE IN A CHANGING WORLD

New Orleans has an annual jazz festival where musicians of all sorts perform for days. During one of the days I attended, the Allman Brothers played. As I stood in the sun enjoying the music I noticed one of my undergraduate seminar students several yards away enjoying the same music. At that moment, the Allman Brothers were playing a cut from an album that had been extremely popular during my first semester of college, more than 20 years ago. I was struck by the irony that the student and, in fact, much of the audience, hadn't been born when I first enjoyed the song. In class the next day I mentioned our shared experience to the student and the rest of the seminar, and we began to talk about the differences between the **culture** in which I had enjoyed that music and the culture in which they enjoyed the identical music. Our discussion centered on the manifestations and consequences of the economic, political, and social changes that have been the focus of this book. The decline of long-term, stable relationships as the basis of social institutions has been accompanied by many cultural changes.

This chapter begins with a discussion of what I mean by **culture**. Then, I turn to several of the major cultural changes occurring with the transition to globalized, flexible capitalism. Within that context, I look at the emergence of religious fundamentalism that is directly related to the other structural changes on which I have focused. The chapter then turns to some of the ways in which immigration and technology, two important components of globalization, are affecting American culture. While the topic of culture could include almost any aspect of social life, I focus on these two because I think they exemplify some of the most dramatic, contradictory, and important ways in which current social changes are creating deep divisions within the culture. These major cultural shifts result in a multiplicity of meanings that people must negotiate to make sense of their day-to-day lives.

CULTURE: THE CREATION OF MEANING

Humanists often use the word *culture* to refer to the best that societies produce, as in the term *high culture* (Griswold, 1994). High culture includes art, operas, symphonies, poetry, and literature. In bookstores, for example, books are often differentiated as "popular fiction" or "literature." Literature connotes high culture. Popular fiction connotes popular culture; that is, culture for "the masses." Television situation comedies, or sitcoms, are an example of "mass culture." Academicians in the humanities are often interested in the differences and relationships between "high culture" and "mass culture."

Anthropologists use the term *culture* to refer to people's ways of life, a definition that, as Griswold (1994) notes, is overly broad. The anthropological definition of culture includes law, politics, and economics—all the aspects of society that sociologists examine as distinct structural components of society. The anthropological definition does not allow specific analysis of the parts of a society that are of sociological interest.

Neither the humanistic nor the anthropological definition of culture will suit our purposes because neither takes into account the *socially constructed* nature of culture. Culture is not a given; it is a product of the society and thus changes with time and place. Thus in the discussion of culture to follow, I am going to focus on the *sociological* definition of culture: the creation of meaning within social contexts. The meaning of objects or actions is not embedded in the thing or action, but rather is a construct of a specific society. Consider, for example, the same behavior in two different societies, each with its own culture. In each instance, two young, attractive men are walking toward each other on a city street. When they meet, they greet and kiss (on the cheeks). In the first case, the street is in San Francisco, where there is a large homosexual population. There, an observer would probably assume that the two men were gay and, perhaps, lovers. In the second instance, the two men are in Budapest, Hungary. There, the assumption of homosexuality would be entirely incorrect. In Hungary, when two male acquaintances meet, they kiss on each cheek, rather than shaking hands by way of a greeting. In this example, the meaning of kissing varies considerably depending on the social context. Culture incorporates the meanings associated with actions and objects in a given society.

Culture Versus Social Structure

Throughout this book I have been writing about the institutions that constitute the **social structure:** the economy, work, family, government, and the relationships between and among them. In our day-to-day interactions and behavior within these institutions, we engage in material behavior (e.g., moving desks and chairs around) and instrumental behavior (e.g., taking notes to increase the likelihood of getting a good test score). But when we think about social life and our participation in it, we think about far more than these institutions and our material and instrumental behavior. We also engage in symbolic and expressive behavior. The *way* we engage in that material and instrumental behavior (that is, how we express those actions and use those objects) reflects the cultural component of life.

Consider differences in child rearing. All societies must nurture their children. Nurturing children includes material components (child, food, parent, shelter, etc.) and instrumental components (reproduction of the population and so forth). The form of nurturing varies considerably across cultures, however. Compare, for example, the image of an affluent women pushing her infant child in a jogging stroller to that of a Mexican Indian woman working in the field with her child wrapped in a rebozo. In both cases, the mother is keeping the child close to her while she is engaging in the behaviors that occupy her time. The way in which the material and instrumental behavior is expressed varies with the culture in which it occurs. In other words, we participate as *cultural* as well as social actors.

Take the classroom, for another example. The material base of the classroom is the building, which has walls, a floor, a ceiling, tables or desks, and chairs. Perhaps it also has a blackboard, an overhead projector, and a podium, behind which a teacher stands. Those objects represent the material components of the classroom. The classroom is also part of an educational institution, a social structure. The grades, credits, and knowledge are resources that one set of participants (the students) seek from another participant (the teacher) who has the power to reward and punish students. The students need these resources and have to comply with the requirements of the specific class to get these resources from the teacher. The instrumental component of the classroom is, then, the transmission of knowledge and information and the behavior necessary to receive that knowledge.

Also important to a class are the expressive and symbolic components. When you ask one of your friends about a class, you are looking for more information than how many tests there are (though you certainly want to know that, too). You are often asking about the culture of the classroom. Is it relaxed? Is it competitive? Is it interesting? Is the teacher nice? You want to know how the particular teacher and the students play their roles.

Roles are the expected behaviors associated with certain positions, and they are structured by certain *norms,* or rules of behavior. For example, when students go into a classroom for the first time, I can predict what they will do. They will find a place to sit and probably pull a notebook out of a backpack or bag and wait for the instructor to get started. How the seats are arranged also symbolizes something about the power relations in a classroom. Consider the difference between a classroom with seats arranged in a circle rather than in rows. Most teachers will observe certain norms, too; they will come in and hand out a syllabus, introduce themselves, and describe the course. Students will observe each teacher's style of dress as a cue to the type of teacher he or she will be. A teacher in blue jeans communicates something different about the formality of the classroom than does a teacher wearing a suit.

Classroom culture embraces more than roles and norms. For example, my classes tend to be relatively informal. I encourage lots of debate, questions, and discussion. I try to vary the daily activities, and I give students considerable input into the form of their tests and assignments. The informal language, the feeling, the norms of behavior that I encourage are all part of the culture of the classroom. Contrast that with a classroom in which the teacher always lectures for 50 minutes. He asks no questions and calls on students infrequently. Note that the same material objects compose both classrooms. The classroom is structured by the same relationships of power between teacher and student and the same effort to obtain and distribute resources. However, there is a big difference in what both teachers spend class time doing. Whereas some teachers emphasize the *process* of learning and view themselves as guides, others emphasize the *content.* They want to impart their truth, their knowledge, their answers. Teaching *means* something different to each of type of teacher (such as myself and my colleague). Our behavior, values, beliefs, and standards of success in relation to teaching differ considerably. We each create very different classroom cultures.

Part of the sociological study of culture deals with the question of causality. For some sociologists, culture merely *reflects* social structure. Griswold (1994) explains this approach using the example of media violence. The excessive violence on television reflects the excessive violence in society. For other sociologists, cultural change *causes* structural change. For example, critics of television violence claim that it causes social violence and that banning violent television programs would reduce the incidence of violence in society at large. For example, in Oslo, Norway, two young boys stripped a younger girl, beat her, and left her outside to freeze to death. Many people, including the victim's parents, blamed the boys' behavior on a popular children's television show. The program was pulled from the airwaves in response to public outrage (*Times-Picayune*, October 19, 1994). Similarly, the effort to label certain records for their violent and sexual content is based on the assumption that these cultural objects *create* social change—specifically, social violence or violence against women.

I will neither assess nor adjudicate these debates. My own viewpoint is that at different times and in different places, the causal relationship between culture and social structure changes. Culture both reflects and affects social structure. The focus of this chapter is on the ways in which the structural changes described in previous chapters are changing the culture. However, cultural changes, in turn, can affect social structure.

The Social Contract as Cultural Metaphor

The symbolic expression of day-to-day existence is a major part of any culture. That symbolic expression includes dress, such as the uniform of a successful businessperson or the shaved head and pierced nose of a disaffected adolescent. Symbolic expression also includes such things as the graffiti on walls that identify the turf of "gangbangers" and the codes of electronic bulletin board users, such as :-) to represent a smile. In addition, language is a very important set of symbols.

In language, words can be culturally important as **metaphors**. A metaphor is a word that stands for something else. Just as there are metaphors in literature, so there are metaphors in the culture. In the chapter on the economy, for example, I used the term *market* quite a lot. We refer to America as being a *free market society*. One literal interpretation of that would suggest some sort of place in which goods and services were exchanged free of any cost. *Free market*, however, stands as a metaphor for noncommunist, democratic, meritocratic (position based on merit, not birth), and economically rational. There is an entire package of meanings crammed into the phrase *free market society.*

The social contract, an organizing principle of this book, is also a cultural metaphor. I have used the concept of social contract to stand for the shared understandings that characterized the Accord era. The dominant system of beliefs was premised on the implicit exchange between workers and employers: a long-term, stable job in exchange for stable, reliable production. Moreover, that job provided sufficient income to allow maintenance of a breadwinner–homemaker household, high levels of consumption, and a secure retirement. Improving one's education was worth foregoing immediate income because that education would lead to future economic returns (higher wages). Additionally, individuals had the right to maximize their individual well-being free from the constraints of tradition or social obligation (Bell, 1992, p. 319). The government would intervene to ward off economic crises and would provide some sort of protection in old age (see chapter 5). A strong economy, an expanded welfare state, and gender relations based on segregated gender roles created a package of meaning that structured people's lives. With the breakdown of the Accord, the understandings people have about their lives have become inconsistent with the social context. This disjunction creates the need to search for new ways to understand people's lives.

The transition to flexible capitalism (which is based on short-term, temporary employment relationships to a greater extent than in earlier periods), the rapid transmission of information and capital, and a more globalized, electronically mediated economy render much of the prior social contract invalid.

I have used the social contract as a cultural metaphor throughout this book. Each chapter has used the concept of the social contract to represent the meanings that surround the changing structural relationships within that institutional sphere. In what follows, I discuss more directly some of the ways in which the decline of that social contract and these structural changes are affecting the culture.

FORCES OF CULTURAL CHANGE

In talking with my students about the Allman Brothers, we agreed that the culture in which I had first listened to their music differed remarkably from the culture in which they were listening to the same music. Several issues emerged over and over throughout that discussion. Here are some of the things the students said: "Our future is bleak compared to what yours was." "We listen to the music of the sixties and the seventies as a symbol of a more idyllic period in which to be young." I asked them why they viewed the 1960s and 1970s as more idyllic periods. One young woman said, "My generation missed a good time to be young; we have to worry about AIDs, the environment, urban decay, an unfathomable national debt, and no good jobs." Another young man chimed in, "Yeah, it's too much to deal with, it's too scary to explore, it's too dangerous," and the first young woman added, "People are afraid to get close. It's too dangerous to trust anyone." My students shared a sense of anxiety about the future and were angry about having those anxieties.

In discussing how they dealt with those anxieties, my students talked about the difficulties of forming relationships, friendships, and community. One young woman made a statement that most of the class agreed represented their feelings. She talked about going to her grandmother's funeral and about her amazement at the number of people who were there, who had known her grandmother for decades. Then she talked of how few people she knew and how few she anticipated being able to get to know (given the likelihood of having to move in order to get and keep a job and the problems associated with keeping and succeeding in a good job). "Who," she asked, "will come to my funeral?"

While many of the anxieties these students expressed are a function of age, others are a function of the age in which they are living. Their concerns with the difficulty of finding and maintaining stable and permanent relationships, with forming and living in communities, and with finding stability and permanence in work and family relationships make sense in light of the social changes I have been discussing throughout this book. My students' comments grow out of their perceptions, like those of many others, that society is changing in unpredictable and, for many, disturbing ways. They lament the decline of the old social contract and debate the shape of new social contracts. They are searching for new ways to understand the world in which they live because the old ways seem to be inadequate guides.

For many in that position, religion is once again becoming an answer. Others are using television as a window on the world or launching themselves full speed on the information highway, using computers to create new worlds of knowledge, interaction, and meaning.

Religion and technology are two very different answers, but both enable sharing and convergence across culturally diverse groups *and* create new lines of difference. Let's turn first to the role of religion and particularly the emergence of fundamentalism in contemporary society as one of the major cultural ways in which people have responded to the anxieties my students expressed.

Faith, Hope, and Culture

Religion, historically, has been one of the major ways in which people create meaning and one of the foundations of Western culture. However, one of the defining characteristics of the transition from traditional society to modern society was the shift away from religion and toward science as the source of explanation for people's day-to-day experience. The shift from a belief system based on the sacred (or extraordinary and otherworldly) to a belief system based on the profane (or ordinary, rational, and internal) is called **secularization** (see Chaves, 1994). The modern era, as distinct from the traditional era, has been characterized by belief in the rational pursuit of self-interest and in the power of science, technology, and the state—rather than God—to solve social problems and guide people's lives.

As we approach the end of a century, religion has once again emerged as a powerful social force. Think, for example, of the debate about abortion, which is one of the most contentious political debates of recent decades. A wide range of issues is involved. For those to whom abortion represents women having control over their bodies, the debate is about women's rights. For those who consider abortion to be the murder of an unborn child, the debate is a moral one. To a great extent, the basic disagreement is over where decision-making authority resides. Those who oppose abortion tend to believe that only God can make decisions about life and death. Those who support abortion rights tend to believe that the decision about terminating a pregnancy should lie only with the woman who is pregnant, not with some external actor.

Another example of the renewed vigor of religion is the case of Dr. Kevorkian. He is the Michigan doctor who committed himself to helping people who are terminally ill or living with incurable disease to die with dignity. He has assisted in a number of suicides and has been tried and acquitted for murder. For those who believe in following God's will, his assistance is murder; for others it is a humanistic act of mercy. Debates about his actions are debates about some of the most fundamental realities with which people must cope: when to die and who has the right to make that determination.

Other debates about life and death fill the news. Does life begin at conception? Should surrogate motherhood (bearing someone else's fetus) be legal? When is a person legally dead? How long should a brain-dead pregnant woman be on life support? These debates about life and death have never before been so public. Moreover, people are looking to religion for answers that secular society has not been able to provide, in part because many questions being raised today were never before possible to ask. There are also movements toward increasing religiosity in some unexpected places. A *New York Times* article about contemporary rock and roll points to "the spiritual slant in today's music." Whether in rap (Arrested Development, Snoop Doggy Dog), hard rock (Concrete Blonde), folk rock (Rickie Lee Jones), or grunge rock (Pearl Jam and Nirvana)—in all these, God, angels, the Disciples, Scripture, and the search for divine answers are ongoing themes. The reason? The reporter stated that, given "the increasingly ephemeral nature of modern life . . . the timeless verities of good and evil speak with new authority" (Guy Garcia, *New York Times,* January 2, 1994).

The application of religious terms like *God, good,* and *evil* to secular political matters runs directly counter to the long-term modern trend of separating the state from religion, particularly in political conflicts over rights. In fact, this separation of religion from political action is a defining characteristic of secularization. Religion is now playing a greater role in contemporary political life, however. Most dramatic was the role of the Christian right of the Republican party in the election of Ronald Reagan in 1980. Certainly at no time in late twentieth-century American politics has organized religion played such an overt role in electing a president and shaping his political agenda. Jerry Falwell and his Moral Majority, an organization of conservative Christians, used television and sophisticated marketing techniques to mobilize thousands of dollars and voters. Their support for the Reagan candidacy gave the Moral Majority a voice in subsequent policy formation.

The emergence of religion as a social force during a largely secular era creates a sociologically interesting question: Has the general secularization of society come to an end? If so, why? Durkheim (1897/1966, 1915/1965) argued that rapid social change can create a state of normlessness that he called **anomie**. The shift to modern society has undermined the social sources of support and the social regulation of individuals. Durkheim argued that modern society, based on science and rational skepticism, deprives people of a sense of higher meaning and that the rapidity of the transition undercut their social moorings. Certainly, the social structural changes with which this book has been concerned have been disruptive to the patterns of people's lives. The turn to religion is one response to the resulting anomie (Robertson, 1992). In the rejection of modernism, the emphasis on religious values, and the effort to reorganize all spheres of life around these values, some people seek to understand the changing world. Perhaps the increased uncertainty that has accompanied structural change explains the rise of fundamentalism, which is the most extreme and striking form that this trend toward religion takes.

Fundamentalism and Social Change

Fundamentalism is a conservative religious doctrine that emphasizes a literal interpretation of Scripture, the personal experience of otherworldly forces, the defense of traditional beliefs, and a rejection of religious pluralism (tolerance for other religions). For fundamentalists, there is only one truth, and all other claims to truth are a threat to God-given ways of life. Fundamentalists may use distinctive forms of dress, such as the payes of Orthodox Jews, as a way of indicating shared group membership and distinguishing members from outsiders. While there are certainly differences among fundamentalist religions, they tend to share these features (Ellison and Musick, 1993).

By and large, in the United States, the term *fundamentalists* refers to evangelical Protestants. However, they exist in other denominations and countries. Hasidic Jews and the Islamic revolutionaries in Iran are fundamentalists. Catholics also have a fundamentalist wing that accounted for about 30% of the Moral Majority in 1980 (Hunter and Rice, 1991).

Because fundamentalists view Scripture as the only necessary guide for behavior, they are particularly resistant to what they call "secular humanism." Secular humanism is the view that decisions about good and evil, right and wrong, responsibility and moral choice come from an individual's rational and logical understandings. Secular humanism also respects the differences that people from different cultures and religions have in their belief systems. Note that secular humanists need not be antireligious. For example, one of my cousins, who is Jewish, married a woman who is Catholic. During December, they celebrate both Christmas and Hanukkah and explain the significance of the rituals and traditions of both holidays to their daughter. Their assumption is that when their daughter grows up, she will decide which traditions to follow. From a fundamentalist perspective, whether fundamentalist Catholic or Orthodox Jew, such choice would be unthinkable. God, not the individual, determines the appropriate rules of worship to follow.

Scholars debate the causes of the recent upsurge in fundamentalist religions both in the United States and abroad (Robertson, 1992; Kosmin and Lachman, 1993). The overthrow of the Shah of Iran in 1978, the militancy of West Bank Jewish settlers, the political activism of the Moral Majority—all these reflect the growing presence of religious fundamentalism in modern society. However, sociological research suggests that at least three major structural changes are associated with the rise of fundamentalism. These are changing family and gender relations, the changing meaning of work, and globalization.

The transformation of the economy and changes in the workplace have created pressures that made the breadwinner–homemaker Accord family economically untenable (see chapter 4). Similarly, workplace relationships, increasingly based on short-term contracts, create a sense of instability. As people are forced to be geographically mobile in search of jobs, as plants close or relocate, or as corporations internationalize, the meaning of workplace relationships becomes more ephemeral. Meanwhile, transition to a global system characterized by flows of people creates a diversity of belief systems. These changes combine to destabilize the ways in which people understand the world in which they live; for some, the response is the search for clear-cut fundamental truths.

Family and Gender Relations Changes in the family, including changes in traditional gender roles, create new dilemmas about this fundamental social institution. Early twentieth-century American culture had very clearly defined roles for men and women. The family was the major source of socialization and the way in which children learned morals and values. Young men and women could count on forming relationships and getting married. The husband would go to that stable, economically secure job, and the wife would stay home and raise 2.5 children. Their lives would be better than those of their parents. As we saw in chapter 4, this stability is gone.

Now, young men and women are faced with a range of family forms and choices, some of them voluntary, some not so voluntary. Notably, First Lady Hillary Clinton told an audience of recent college graduates that they needed to form a new community and be family to one another because "instead of families looking like the Cleavers on 'Leave It to Beaver,' we have families that include test-tube babies and surrogate moms" (*Times-Picayune*, May 9, 1994).

Notions of masculinity and femininity have also changed. Traditional male characteristics included being strong, aggressive, competitive, and unemotional, compared to female characteristics of being fragile, passive, compliant, and emotional. But today American culture no longer defines men as the protectors of the "gentle sex." Instead, men are urged to be more nurturing and supportive and to participate in parenting. Women are less often sanctioned for being aggressive, competitive, and strong. Whereas the image of women was once exemplified by the sexy, soft, and weak Marilyn Monroe, now Janet Reno (attorney general), Ruth Bader Ginsberg (supreme court justice), Jacqueline Joyner-Kersee (Olympian), and others present a far different image of femininity (see Kimmel, 1987a, 1987b, on changing gender roles).

Along with those changed images of the masculine and the feminine are prescriptions for behavior. Women compete and work with men in the corporation and on the construction site. Though some stay home as full-time homemakers, most participate in paid labor. As chapter 4 indicated, these changes undermine traditional families and, for some, the moral base of society.

The debate about family values is a reaction to these changes in family structure and gender roles. The multiple forms of family—female-headed, same-sex, unmarried parents, and families extended by divorce rather than blood—all challenge the *cultural meaning* of family. Families are basic social institutions; it is not surprising that their alteration is viewed by some as a threat to society. The charge to return to "family values," however, is really about returning to a family structure that no longer predominates and about rebuilding the foundation of society. Those who make this claim see the transformation of the family—not of the economy, polity, or workplace—as the source of major social problems.

Meaning of Work   Growing fundamentalism is also a response to the lack of stability and constancy in the workplace. Workplace relationships increasingly seem transitory and ephemeral, and the pace of change seems unfathomably rapid. My students' concerns are a direct response to these changes. Their concern about having to be geographically mobile and rootless and their concerns with the speed with which jobs come and go are symptomatic of an economic world in which the short-term contract increasingly replaces the long-term contract.

Much of the new economic flexibility results from the technologically induced compression of time and space (Harvey, 1989). The ability to rapidly disperse new images, resources, and ideas affects more than the economy; it also challenges people's existing definitions of self, place, and society. If a computer network lets people commute to an office in Taiwan via their modems in New York, or if stock prices in Hong Kong affect the stock market on Wall Street, what is the meaning of either time or space? The search for fundamental truths in things that are not subject to rapid change, such as religion, is one response to this disruption of people's understanding of their world.

Globalization   Globalization also drives many to the search for fundamentals (Robertson, 1992). Technological and economic developments increase the diversity of perspectives available to members of society. Culturally diverse concepts of God, life, death, truth, and beauty increase discourse about fundamentals. Television and international travel confront different groups with new ways of expressing themselves to themselves. The French, for example, are so concerned about the impact of English on the French language that they seek to render the use of English illegal in advertising and in many official venues. The French premier presented these actions as "an act of faith in the future of the country" (*New York Times,* March 15, 1994). For proponents of this law, the very heart and soul of French culture are imperiled by the creeping anglicization of the language (e.g., *le hit parade*).

Similarly, as television and international travel confront people from very different cultures with different perspectives on gender roles, the result can be deadly as traditional cultures react to change with violence. In Algeria, for example, Muslim women who attempted to move through the streets unveiled were stoned to death. As the number of perspectives multiplies, so too do the challenges to traditional beliefs (Robertson, 1992; Kennedy, 1993). Some adjust their belief systems to accommodate diversity; others cope by renewing their commitment to tradition and discounting the "nonbelievers."

Religion and the Emerging Social Contract

The search for fundamentals emerges when there is no longer consensus about life, sex roles, work, death, and other basic issues. The post-Accord, global era has put all of these up for grabs. As Fred Block writes, "This is a strange period in the history of the United States [and the world] because people lack a shared understanding of the kind of society in which we live" (1990, p. 1). Not all have turned to fundamentalism as a way of answering questions about social meanings in the context of rapid social change, but many do turn to religion and religious organizations. The growth of fundamentalism has created new schisms and alliances within religious organizations. The political mobilization of fundamentalists has illuminated the differences between them and other religious groups. In fact, the differences between fundamentalist and progressive organizations within religions have, according to some research, become more important than the differences among denominations. In their attitudes about women's participation in the clergy, birth control and abortion, civil rights, gun control, capital punishment, and other issues, progressive Protestants and Catholics and Reform Jews are more similar than, say, Reform and Orthodox Jews. More than at any other time in our history, orthodoxy and progressivism are more important than denomination in predicting political, social, and economic attitudes (Hunter and Rice, 1991, p. 325).

Interestingly, just as people are turning to organized religion, organized religion is reorganizing along different axes. The result is a new array of cross-denominational groups that are increasingly visible as *social* actors. In New Orleans, for example, a multidenominational group called All Congregations Together (ACT) has mobilized to fight drug use, poverty, and an inadequate local education system. They meet regularly, have membership in the hundreds, and are politically active. They tend to use the tactics of civil disobedience and protest. They have stormed city hall, held rallies, and often embarrassed city officials into responding to their demands. Their mobilization has effectively forced accountability and action from an often recalcitrant city hall. Other groups have mobilized to respond to the legalization of abortion, pornography, apartheid, and other social issues. What is perhaps most interesting about these groups is not simply their social activism but the nature of these alliances.

These cross-denominational alliances represent a major cultural transformation. The strengthened role of religion in contemporary social debates and the emergence of fundamentalism have created passionate cultural divisions, what sociologist James Davison Hunter (1991) calls "culture wars." However, reorganization of alliances along fundamentalist or progressive lines demonstrates some of the ways in which new divisions also create new connections. Both of these changes accompany a period of social transformation in which people search for a new contract around which to center and understand their lives.

GLOBALIZATION AND CULTURAL CHANGE

The global flow of people, ideas, and images has created major challenges to the culture. When people migrate from one country to another, they cannot help transporting at least some of their native culture as well. Ideas, values, languages, styles, and cuisines all cross national boundaries. This process may confront the self-definitions of both the newcomers and the members of the host culture.

Similarly, the technological dissemination of ideas and images across national boundaries also challenges people's understanding of who they are and what they believe. Television and computers are therefore major factors in cultural change.

The Impact of Immigration

In the immediate post–World War II period, America's self-image was pretty clear. We were white, middle class (this group constituted the majority of the producers and consumers of culture), and happily ensconced in good jobs. We were largely Christian and of European descent.

At the end of the century much of that description sounds incredibly off base, especially the parts about race, ethnicity, and cultural heritage. According to *US News and World Report* (October 4, 1993), 8.6 million people from Asia, Latin America, and the Caribbean immigrated to the United States in the 1980s. Two thirds of them went to California, New York, Texas, Florida, and New Jersey. One quarter of these immigrants is Mexican. The "face" of the nation is changing. California is about to become the first state in the country in which the majority of the population is "minority"; the combination of higher birth rates among Hispanics and continued immigration has led demographers to predict that by 2030, one half of all California children will be Hispanic (Kennedy, 1993, p. 313).

The American Immigrant The United States has always been a nation of immigrants, ever since Native Americans were displaced by militarily aggressive and technologically advanced European immigrants in the 1600s. Perhaps because of common European descent and shared membership in the larger cultural group, most immigrants during the first three centuries were able to integrate relatively easily, especially during periods of economic expansion. Their sons and daughters became relatively affluent members of the mainstream.

The exceptions to this optimistic picture are, of course, African-Americans, who immigrated largely through the force of the slave trade. Given this beginning and their obvious differences from the majority, they have been less able to move up the economic ladder. When they left the South, it was often to move to central cities that more privileged groups had abandoned for the suburbs.

In the past 20 years, a new wave of immigrants has begun changing the face of America. The new immigration dates to the 1965 liberalization of immigration policy that opened the door to more Asians and Latin Americans than ever before. Not only are many of these immigrants people of color, they also have cultural traditions quite different from those of the earlier European immigrants.

In many ways, however, the new immigrants are like earlier waves of immigrants. They come from a mix of occupational backgrounds, some impoverished and poorly educated, but many from professional, managerial, or executive backgrounds with high levels of education and comfortable monetary resources. These resources, by the way, are a better predictor of economic success than is the ability to rely on an ethnically homogeneous urban enclave (Rumbaut, 1992; Bates, 1994). Similarly, like immigrants of the past, the new immigrants tend to work extremely hard, often taking jobs that native-born Americans refuse. In fact, in general, immigrants are highly motivated, have above-average educational and occupational skills, and are seeking opportunity and advancement beyond what their homelands offer (Rumbaut, 1992, p. 229). Thus, if one thinks of the cultural metaphor of the American Dream—work hard, get an education, and anyone can make it—then clearly, many of the new immigrants have norms, values, and behaviors that are highly compatible with those of the dominant culture. Despite these facts, the new immigration has intensified the debate about how society can accommodate multiple cultures.

The Challenge of Multiculturalism

Surges of immigration have never been easy. Whoever is native-born at the time (and, obviously, that is a historically specific term) resists the impact of the new entrants. A relatively benign form of resistance is to assimilate the newcomers into the dominant culture, making them indistinguishable from the native-born. Many immigrants, then and now, share the goal of assimilation.

Assimilation was relatively easy when most immigrants were from Europe. While there was often a great deal of conflict among these groups, by and large most were rapidly stirred into the "melting pot." Today, however, the increasingly diverse and non-European character of immigrants is calling assimilation into question. An increasingly popular alternative is multiculturalism, which calls for acceptance of and respect for cultural diversity.

Some see cultural pluralism as a threat; others see it as a necessary step in overcoming the privileged position of those from white European descent. These are not easy issues to unravel. How many cultures should a multicultural society include? How minute are the groups? What is lost in the emphasis on difference rather than shared membership in a single society? Fears about the "browning" of America are also a factor (Kennedy, 1993), as are concerns about the impact of unassimilated immigrants on welfare systems, labor markets, and education. Many of these concerns are based on stereotypes rather than fact. Most immigrants do not rely on welfare; a majority have at least a high school diploma; and most share the political attitudes of native-born Americans.

Nonetheless, anti-immigrant sentiment has increased. As immigrants concentrate in more cities, they gain political power. Some immigrant groups assert the right to maintain their languages and their cultures. These are the ingredients for cultural conflict. More and more, politicians are calling for get-tough policies in response to their constituents' concerns with the effect of immigration on the economy and culture (*New York Times,* March 8, 1994).

During the midterm elections of 1994, for example, voters in California approved Proposition 187, which denies the use of public monies for illegal immigrants. Specifically, Proposition 187 stipulated that education and health care practitioners were not only to deny services to illegal immigrants but that they were to report those immigrants to the appropriate authorities; this is a clear example of an anti-illegal-immigrant policy.

Though there are very real cultural differences between some immigrants and the mainstream, many would argue that they enrich rather than diminish extant American culture. Take cuisine, for example. In the early 1960s, when I moved with my parents to the Maryland suburbs of Washington, D.C., I remember my parents complaining about the lack of interesting restaurants. They missed the cannoli of Little Italy in New York City, the smoked whitefish from Zabars, and the Lo Mein from Hung Fat's in Chinatown. But in the last 10 years or so, Washington has become a fabulous food city. The hip Adams Morgan section, for instance, sports Ethiopian, Spanish, Mid-Eastern, Chinese, Vietnamese, Mexican, French, Thai, and Japanese restaurants, to name just a few. Such culinary diversity is not confined to big cities. The cuisines of beltway communities now routinely offer what were once exotic and rare cuisines. In North Raleigh, North Carolina, where I recently attended a conference, in a single day I ate Southern-style ribs for lunch and Thai food for dinner. Such cultural diversity certainly enhances contemporary culture.

Admittedly, however, cultural diversity also creates substantial challenges. Perhaps one of the most pressing challenges is to the education system. Education, as chapter 3 indicated, is crucial for preparing people for their future roles in the labor market. Just as important, however, is the transmission of rules, norms, and values of a society. Immigration from cultures that are very different from the host culture complicates this task.

Consider the issue of language. Schools are faced with growing numbers of students for whom English is a second language. In the late 1980s, a third of California's 4.6 million students in elementary school through high school spoke a language other than English at home. Moreover, while 70% of them spoke Spanish, the rest of those non-English-speaking students spoke 100 different languages (Rumbaut, 1992, p. 239)! Offering bilingual education, given the wealth of languages represented in the student body, would be exceedingly difficult. However, not offering bilingual education may make it harder for immigrant students to learn and become part of the dominant culture. Ironically, the preference of immigrant children is to learn English. Given the social pressure for assimilation and the overarching presence (or hegemony) of English as the international language of politics, finance, technology, and mass culture, some argue that it is not American culture that is threatened. Rather, the unique cultural symbols, languages, and styles of diverse immigrant groups are more threatened.

Schools also teach "American" values and culture. What that means is becoming increasingly difficult to determine. Whose history constitutes American history? And from what vantage point? Teaching American history from the perspective of the Navajo Nation presents a very different view from that of a European perspective, for example. Multicultural education teaches respect for racial and ethnic subgroups; it reinforces cultural pluralism and attempts to look at noncore cultures in their own terms. These demands have created conflict throughout the country's school systems.

Another challenge attending multiculturalism is that the cultural meaning of race and ethnicity is not all that straightforward. Race and ethnicity are culturally created and culturally altered. For example, one semester when I was talking about the distribution of income by race, I presented the class with data on white, black, and Hispanic Americans. One of my students, who had what sounded like a Hispanic last name, became irate at a classification that labeled him nonwhite.

He said that he was creole and the child of European elites. One side of his family is French, the other Spanish. Clearly this lineage is European and white. Yet, the racial and ethnic categories I presented had forced people to identify themselves as either Hispanic or white. The census now allows for more complexity; one can check Black-Hispanic or Caucasian-Hispanic. Such census categories still fail to capture the ethnic complexity of many people. One consequence of the Vietnam War, for example, was the birth of children who are half white and half Vietnamese, or half black and half Vietnamese. Some of these are also Jewish (as was one of my students). Often, these young people (since those children are now college age or older) do not even attempt to identify themselves by exact categories until some form (e.g., college applications) forces the issue.

But even a label such as *Hispanic* is a cultural creation that obscures a highly diverse group. It lumps together people of differing ethnic backgrounds (some are Caucasian, some are not) and cultures (such as Mexicans, Guatemalans, Puerto Ricans, Indians). Such complexity is present for other groups as well (Leiberson, 1980).

The population of New Orleans presents another example of the ambiguity of these definitions. New Orleans recently had a mayoral election that made the national news because of the racial nature of the politics. One candidate was Jewish and Caucasian; the other was, according to the media, black. Within the New Orleans black community, however, one was Jewish and the other was creole (a mixture of black, Spanish, and French in this case). An African-American friend of mine explained that some members of the black community did not support the creole candidate because they thought he was racist— against blacks. This complex relationship among different groups in New Orleans exemplifies the claim that different people create different meanings for race and ethnicity. To the white community, the term *black* includes both African-American and creole. But what white New Orleanians see as a single black community is in reality complex, stratified, and differentiated. A recent article began with "Within 20 years the Morris family went from being black to mulatto to white" (*Times-Picayune,* March 5, 1995) and then continued to recount the complexities and changing definitions of race in New Orleans. According to sociologist E. Reginald Daniel (as cited in the same article), "In terms of ancestry, the entire planet is racially mixed." The article concludes with the claim that in the United States, not just in New Orleans, these issues remain difficult, because class and race are tied to skin color.

Immigration, race, and the meanings of ethnic diversity create problems and challenges to understandings of "us" versus "them" throughout American society and the world. At bottom, that is what multicultural debates are about. These difficulties in creating a community of shared meaning pose one of the greatest tests to American culture.

The Impact of Technology

Our awareness of multicultural issues and many others comes not only through our participation in day-to-day life, but through our experience of the media. Television is often accused of highlighting differences and conflicts among people, but it also creates images that are shared by very different people. And computers not only have changed the experience of work for many people but also have made it easier for people from different cultures to communicate.

Two major metaphors that have become part of the culture are *global village* and *information highway.* Both refer to the tremendous impact that technology has had on contemporary culture. Marshall McLuhan coined the term *global village* in 1964. In his influential book *Understanding Media: The Extensions of Man*, McLuhan explored the role of television in creating a community of culture throughout the world (Robertson, 1992). While that has yet to happen, there is no doubt that television is more globally pervasive than it has ever been. The frequent use of the term *information highway*, coined by Vice President Al Gore, is a recognition that computers and the connections they create allow people access to knowledge, information, and opportunity unique in history. Highways have always been associated with opening up America; the image of the information highway conveys that optimism.

Television At the end of the twentieth century, television's universal appeal cannot be denied. In 1992, the *Los Angeles Times* reported that more Japanese had television sets than had flush toilets. Similarly, the same article reported that virtually all households in Mexico had televisions and that Thais were more likely to buy televisions than they were to buy fans or refrigerators. This fact is pretty dramatic given the climate of Thailand, which in January has temperatures in the 90s and humidity to match (*Los Angeles Times,* October 20, 1992). More and more television shows are being disseminated across national boundaries. Although a few shows (mostly British) are imported into this country, we have become masterful exporters of television entertainment. "Wheel of Fortune," for example, plays in some variant in Italy, Turkey, and France.

Much is made of the political and cultural importance of television. It is interesting to speculate on the political effect, for example, of televised images of the fall of the Berlin Wall. To what extent did they inspire and embolden anticommunists throughout Eastern Europe? Television is also a cultural mirror, reflecting the values and customs of the country where a program is produced. Around the world, many people think of the United States as having a violent culture, in large part because they have been watching American action shows on television. The nighttime soap opera "Dallas," which was internationally popular, convinced many overseas that Americans are rich, materialistic, superficial, and manipulative. Unfortunately, television often distorts and caricatures the culture it depicts.

But 30 years of research have not shown definitively that television is efficient at creating culture. Despite some signs that it is—after a spate of American Christmas shows in Ethiopia, Ethiopians rushed out to get Christmas trees!—there are many other signs that viewers resist cultural messages that are too foreign. In fact, television images that are alien to the viewing culture are often blocked by officials. Steamy soap operas don't play well in countries like Iran, which do not allow women to be shown with their heads uncovered, much less their arms and legs. Similarly, it is hard to imagine "NYPD Blue," a somewhat risqué cop show, playing in Singapore, where obscene matter and vulgar language are forbidden.

Nevertheless, television is important globally in three ways. First, television is the major marketing tool of flexible capitalism, which is characterized in part by rapidly shifting patterns of consumption. Television speeds up the process by which items become trendy and are marketed and sold, and it expands the size of the available market (Harvey, 1989). To sell Levi's blue jeans in France, Mexico, and Thailand, potential consumers in these countries must learn to *value* blue jeans, the attire of laborers. In presenting Levi's in ways that are appealing and attractive, television advertising can make them valuable to new consumers. In the process, the advertising also affects the culture. I find disconcerting, however, pictures of people in relatively low-technology, isolated places (e.g., the rain forests of Brazil) wearing T-shirts and Levi's instead of clothing indigenous to their culture.

Second, television brings universal access to certain ideas, images, values, and events. The consequences of so doing are contradictory. For example, in the winter of 1994 despite peace negotiations in the Middle East, war in Bosnia-Herzegovina, and relief efforts in Somalia, people throughout the world were caught up in the Olympic soap-opera competition between two figure skaters, Nancy Kerrigan and Tonya Harding. When Michael Jackson was accused of molesting a young boy, adolescents all over the world watched the tarnishing of a shared cultural hero. (Note that television enabled a shared cultural hero to exist in the first place.) On a less trivial note, television images of democracy, gender equality (at least relative to some places), and mass participation can have enormous political consequences. In Mexico in 1994, for the first time in history, the presidential candidates had a nationally televised debate like the ones they had perhaps seen televised by their North American neighbor. Some observers fear, however, that television may trivialize important occurrences. When the marines invaded Kuwait to stop Saddam Hussein, they complained about the lights, cameras, and reporters that reached the beach before they did. What should have been a military action occurring at night became a media circus. Similarly, some fear that television's consistent images of war, violence, and death will make people bored and insensitive to the reality of human tragedy.

A third way television affects the culture is in reinforcing and reflecting the short-term, ephemeral nature of contemporary life. Channel surfing through 500 channels not only presents a collage of images from all walks of life and all parts of the world, it adds to the sense that little is real, stable, and of consequence (see Harvey, 1989, for an extended discussion of these cultural changes).

Computer Networks Globalization required and was fostered by the development of new information technologies, especially computers. With the microchip came the ability to transfer capital, products, and knowledge almost anywhere in the world almost instantaneously. Computers have permitted more, however, than merely new ways of doing business. Computers also connect people to libraries, schools, politicians, and clubs all over the world. In fact, the President of the United States has an e-mail address, providing instantaneous ability to communicate with his office. In this way, computers seem to open up the culture, to bring people together regardless of race, class, or location.

At a party I attended, a group of people began talking about the various computer networks in which they participated. Some spent several hours a day communicating with an international group concerned with the destruction of the Amazonian rain forest. Another was a member of a hard science fiction bulletin board in which the participants discussed speculative science and devised potential societies by extrapolating from current scientific innovations.

Computer network participants can be anywhere in the world and may never meet. Some participants develop false personas, personalities with fictitious names and biographies. More important, no participant's race, gender, physical abilities, or sexual preference has to be part of the interaction. Just as the speed of transmission seems to break down barriers, so does the facelessness of communication.

The freedom from the constraints of space allows participants in computer networks to form new types of communities that are a very real and important part of their lives. For example, when a 42-year-old computer programmer, father of two and husband, was killed in New York City, a cyberspace community mourned him for weeks. Moreover, when those cyberspace friends learned that he had no insurance and thus his family was left destitute, they compiled a cyberspace cookbook, the sale of which provided the base of a trust fund for his family (Peter Lewis, *New York Times,* March 8, 1994). Other cyberspace communities have provided emotional, economic, medical, and intellectual support for their members.

It is increasingly clear that these networks represent more than channels of information; they are also channels of interpersonal connection. In a world characterized by short-term relationships, rapid flows of people, and instability, computer networks could well become the twenty-first century's "ties that bind."

There is a darker side to this web of connections, however. In chapter 3, I discussed the impact of computer technology on the workplace. One of the less advantageous effects, at least from a worker's point of view, was the enhanced ability for employers to monitor their workers. Similarly, the interconnection of computer networks creates a fear of inappropriate surveillance and monitoring of citizens by faceless but computer-literate bureaucrats. As the linkage between computers and television becomes even closer (as with interactive television), the Orwellian image of a Big Brother able to monitor and assess everyone becomes more reality than fiction. The global village is connected by the information highway; together they create the new map of the twenty-first century. As more and more people travel in cyberspace, however, they will need to create new norms, rules, and protocols to protect their rights and their privacy.

As with the other cultural changes that I have discussed in this chapter, the connections between people that computer networks create have both limiting and liberating potential. The weaker the social contract, the more likely that computers will be used to manipulate and control people. The stronger the social contract, the more computers will be tools in creating ties and in empowering people.

CONCLUSIONS

This chapter has focused on some of the ways in which individuals' search for meaning—when the "old way" no longer suffices—leads to contradictory processes of cohesion and fragmentation. Periods of dramatic social change undermine the meanings that structure how individuals experience the world they live in and that represent those experiences. At the same time, flexible capitalism and globalization create new connections among people who were once unconnected, unaware of, and invisible to one another. In forging these connections, however, these forces create new cultural divisions. Having so much exposure to "them" creates concern about who is "us."

The growth of fundamentalism and the increasing religious conflicts in society are about understanding and defining who and what provides the moral authority for social behavior. The search for fundamental truths is a response to the upsetting of extant truths. Similarly, waves of immigration and technological advances that spread cultural icons, images, and information across the information highway create cultural debates over the following: What history is "my" history? What history is "your" history? Whose truths are true? Whose culture is "best"?

Modern American culture is deep in the midst of these debates and concerns. The ferocity of the exchange can at times be numbing, if not actually fatal, to participants—as for some Branch Davidians in Waco, Texas; as with Drs. Gunn and Britton, murdered by antiabortion radicals; as in Rwanda, where ethnic conflicts became genocide; and as in Bosnia, where Muslims are victims of the genocidal policy of ethnic cleansing. But there is an enormously positive side to this debate. The culture now is characterized by multiple attempts to "write" new social contracts and renegotiate cultural understandings. That renegotiation is happening within and between countries. For some, the outcome is unsettling or even brutal. But out of these conflicts might well come such synergistic notions as *our* history, *our* music, *our* literature, *our* culture. A truly global village, united by common values, concerns, and challenges, could well emerge in the twenty-first century.

TRANSITION TO THE FUTURE

I began this book with images of disorder and argued that much of it is occurring as a consequence of global economic and political change. As America and other nations search for new solutions to the economic problems of production and distribution, people's lives are disrupted. This disruption takes the form of increased unemployment, crime, political conflict, and family discord, among other things.

Such periods of social changes are not unusual. The transition from traditional agricultural society to modern industrial capitalism in Europe and in the United States resulted in a rearranging of the institutions in which people lived their lives. The church, for example, is no longer the major political power in society. In the United States, in fact, there is strict separation between church and state. However, institutions change at different rates, and some never change at all. For instance, the 9-month school year emerged in response to an agricultural cycle of planting and harvesting. Though less than 3% of the work force is still in agriculture (and many of those people are not independent farmers), it still influences the scheduling of school.

Ironically, the problems facing each era are often the result of the previous era's solutions. For example, much of the welfare state as we know it grew in response to social disruption during the 1930s and again in the 1960s. During both periods, the state deepened its involvement in people's lives and sought to protect them from falling below some sort of minimum standard of living. Yet now, many would argue that welfare as it currently exists, particularly programs for families with dependent children, prevents many people from attaining a decent standard of living by penalizing them when they do get work, no matter how low paid it is.

Many of the social relations of modern industrial society were based on implicit or explicit social contracts that mirrored those in the economic world. That is, contractual relations based on some notion of a fair exchange and mutual responsibilities structured not only

economic, but political and familial relations as well. As those contracts no longer organize economic relations, I expect they will play
less of a role in other relations.

A major component of those exchanges was the structuring of
relations around long-term stability. Yet the types of structures that
create stability—such as bureaucratic organizations with rigid hierarchies; or long and complicated procedures codified in rules, hand-
books, and so on; or rigid production technologies—do not allow
rapid response to changing conditions. Thus, where once bureaucratic
organization created efficiency in business management, now it slows
the ability of an organization to respond to new products or markets
that may emerge. An international economy linked by computers and
television, which allow instantaneous creation of consumer demand
and transfer of ideas, products, and money, intensifies the speed with
which businesses have to respond if they want to survive. It is a truism
in a capitalist economy that the business world has to be flexible to be
viable.

Rigidity is a problem not only in the economic realm but in the
political realm as well. In the past, for example, conflicts were dealt
with within an implicit set of cold war relationships, in which decades
of established protocol structure determined the nature of intervention. In the new world order, in which the cold war no longer
structures international relations, the United States' diplomatic processes have to be constantly adapted to changing conditions. We have
yet to develop or revise our military and diplomatic protocols along
these lines.

Flexibility, however, is a double-edged sword. Earlier chapters
have shown that flexibility for one group may increase rigidity or
barriers for another group. As employers turn to high-tech, knowledge-intensive production and service-producing processes, breaking
into a viable job may become even more difficult for those who are
already disadvantaged. Inner-city children, without access to computers and the innovative learning techniques that upper-middle-class
children have, fall farther and farther behind. In such a case, flexibility
in the workplace may increase the rigidity of class barriers.

Thus, the creation of new types of social contracts associated with
new types of market society creates tensions in other aspects of life
because all aspects of life—whether cultural, familial, or political—are
in one way or another connected to and affected by the economy. In
the remainder of this chapter I summarize the major components of
the transition to flexible capitalism and suggest some of the social

possibilities that transition creates. The end of the twentieth century finds us at the cusp of a new society. There is little doubt that although massive social change has already occurred, the process is certainly not complete.

THE DECLINE OF THE POSTWAR SOCIAL CONTRACT, REVISITED

The labor–capital accord emerged in the unionized core of the economy, particularly in manufacturing industries, in the immediate postwar period. It coordinated the interests of workers and employers by restructuring their relationships around a new social contract. Hard work by reliable employees was rewarded with high wages and long-term, stable employment. Under these conditions, business profits grew enormously, and the American working class became the richest in the world. Moreover, access to this lifestyle often required only a high school education.

This economic growth also allowed the college-educated middle class (white-collar, professional, and technical workers) to grow as well. They too flourished in corporations, universities, and offices that fostered and rewarded long-term stability.

The economic well-being of both blue- and white-collar workers affected families as well. The normative family structure to which working-class as well as middle-class families aspired was organized around a male breadwinner and a female homemaker. This family structure was now possible for more families than ever before.

During a period of prosperity and economic mobility for millions of families, that some were excluded because of racial discrimination or poverty was increasingly seen as a social problem that needed correction. Thus, a second component of the post–World War II labor–capital accord was the expansion of the government's role in society. Not only did the government intervene through legislative initiatives in the relationships between workers and employers, but the government also established a welter of laws and programs geared toward solving the problems of poverty, unemployment, and discrimination. The New Deal and programs that subsequently emerged from the postwar Democratic agenda established protection for the elderly, the disabled, the unemployed, the impoverished, and veterans. Through social security, Aid to Families with Dependent Children, the GI Bill, and other programs, people for the first time in our history had systematic protection (though still incomplete compared to our European counterparts) from economic hardship.

For a period of time, then, Americans enjoyed a rare measure of economic, political, and social security—and wealth. But as these chapters have shown, that period was undermined by a wide range of factors. Particularly important was the decline, by the mid-1970s, of the American economy in relation to its increasingly successful global competitors. In the early 1970s, most of the conditions that fostered American economic expansion changed. Competition from our global competitors became more intense, and linkages among international global actors became more complex. The economies of the world became more connected, but America no longer orchestrated those connections.

A NEW ERA OF FLEXIBILITY

Increased competition on a global level made American businesses less able or willing to offer workers long-term employment and high wages—and therefore less willing to tolerate or accommodate unions. Thus, for the next decade, American businesses launched an effort to free themselves of union-imposed rigidities that had been part of the postwar accord.

In response to these new conditions, manufacturing and other core industry employers explored a number of strategies to bolster their economic position. They decreased (downsized) their work force and relocated to nonunion and generally less expensive environments, both domestically (the South) and overseas. Computers, robots, and automation replaced many of their workers. Some simply shifted their assets into service-producing industries. The result was a fracturing of the labor–capital accord.

Whereas the postwar economy and workplace had emphasized stability in the use of technology, workers, and resources, the new economy increasingly is based on employer flexibility in the use of workers, production processes, organizations, and markets. Rapidly changing market conditions compelled American business to explore ways of responding to those conditions much more quickly than in earlier periods. Through the use of computers, manufacturers reconfigured the production process so that they needed fewer workers and could adapt existing production techniques faster than ever before.

While these strategies improved corporate profits, they hurt workers by displacing them from once secure and well-paid jobs.

Many of these workers turned to the service sector for new jobs. But the jobs that they could get, given their skills and education, often provided much lower wages than they had formerly received. The better jobs in the service sector (such as those in engineering and systems analysis) require high levels of education and computer literacy, something most displaced industrial workers do not have. Service-sector jobs in secondary labor market settings (such as jobs in casinos, restaurants, guard work, and even many jobs in health care, such as nurse's aides and orderlies) are low-wage, unstable, and non-unionized, and they provide few avenues for mobility. Thus, the extent to which workers are educated and computer-literate appears crucial to their success in the new labor market.

A notable difference between work in the future and work during the Accord period is the shift away from long-term employment regardless of education or skill, what *Time* magazine (March 29, 1993) called "the temping of America." That same article cited a 250% increase in temporary employment since 1982. Employers have restructured the employment relationship around a small core of relatively permanent but geographically mobile workers and a much larger work force of part-time, temporary, and contract workers. In other words, many workers who were once permanent now work on a contingent basis. They work *contingent* to employers' needs. This change affects not only blue-collar, low-skilled wage workers as it did in the Accord era but also highly educated, skilled professional workers. Lawyers, doctors, college professors, and even top managers increasingly find themselves working on a part-time or temporary basis. Workers can no longer anticipate long-term employment with a single company or even within a single industry. The loss of many well-paid blue-collar jobs requiring only a high school education and the move to contingent work relations throughout the occupational hierarchy have resulted in increased personal and economic insecurity for workers.

More and more workers find themselves with inconsistent pay and without such benefits as paid vacations, retirement, and health insurance that workers have taken for granted since the 1940s. The entire relationship between workers and their jobs over the course of workers' lives has changed. Gone is the orderly progression from school to first job, promotion to better job, and eventually a secure livelihood. Now, workers just out of high school are likely to find only the most minimal jobs if anything at all. If they find a job (and this scenario is even applicable to some with college educations), they might have to hold more than one, none of which will provide benefits, to make ends meet. This is the reason many young adults are returning home to live with their parents rather than forming their own households. Even those with education and skills must constantly work to upgrade and increase those skills to maintain their employability.

Changes of this magnitude affect not only the immediate economic position of workers but also their families, politics, and the culture. In regard to the family, for instance, few can still afford the breadwinner–homemaker structure of the Accord era. Economic necessity has driven more and more women into the work force, and more and more families are dependent on female heads for their economic livelihood. The continued liberation of women from narrowly defined roles is one of the positive social changes of the past 40 or so years. Still, in the absence of work accommodation to parenting needs, negotiating work and family has become incredibly unwieldy.

With the challenge to the implicit gender contract that structures most marriages has come considerable social conflict, particularly over reproductive rights. Although Americans continue to marry, the marriage contract has been separated from procreation to a greater extent than in the past. Economic independence allows women to leave failed marriages; thus the divorce rate has risen considerably in recent years. Likewise, much of the stigma of bearing children out of wedlock has disappeared. The result of all this has been an increase of new family forms—single-headed, blended, dual-career, and even same-sex.

These changes in the family and workplace pose considerable challenges to a government that is also facing enormous reorganization of the international world order. The end of the cold war has shifted the international balance of power and created new sources of instability, as countries that were once dominated by or allied with the Soviet Union struggle to create new identities. They also put demands on the American government for intervention and stabilization. In addition, the internationalization of the economy has created real limitations on the power of government to intervene effectively in the economy. Businesses operating partially or completely overseas employ fewer American workers than they might otherwise. Current law gives the government little ability to alter that situation.

The internationalization of business impoverishes governments by decreasing the tax base. First, it decreases the number who are employed and who thus contribute income taxes. Second, it allows many companies to avoid paying corporate taxes. The declining tax base cripples government response to the increased need that part-time, contingent employment and underemployment create. Government commitment to protecting the needy has also been undermined by the decline of postwar political coalitions.

The insecurity these changes have engendered throughout society has undermined a fundamental component of American culture—the American Dream. The trajectory of education, job, promotion, and security for one's self and family simply no longer exists for as many as it once did. In his observation of the American workplace, Robert Reich claimed that "the social contract is beginning to fray" (*Time*, March 29, 1993, p. 44). It is not only the insecurity of jobs, it is the transformation of families, the decline of parenting, the withdrawal of government from protecting the disadvantaged; all these have frayed people's belief in the future. The social contracts that were the foundation of the post–World War II Accord society are, indeed, changing. But what might they change into? The answer is far from certain.

POSSIBLE WORLDS

Life may be unsettled for increasing numbers of people, but that does not mean that the country is in a crisis. Periods in which all of society's institutions are changing also create *dangerous opportunities*. Dangerous because when old ways of doing things break down, better ways of organizing social life become possible—but so, too, do worse ways.

It is important to remember that no matter how much I have emphasized structures (family structures, economic structures, etc.), society is created by individuals whose actions and inactions may either strengthen or weaken structures. For instance, mass refusal to vote weakens democratic systems; participation strengthens those systems. Civil disobedience, a form of social protest, undermines existing social structures but may lead to stronger new ones. For example, when young black men demanded service at Woolworth's lunch counters in the early 1960s, they undermined the structure of Jim Crow racial discrimination, which was, until 1964, a legal way of denying African-Americans entry into stores, businesses, jobs, or even houses. However, because of the actions of those young black men at Woolworth's and of many other individuals, such discrimination is no longer legal.

The point is, what we create by our actions, we can also change by our actions (or inactions). Things change, moreover, because of individuals acting in a social context. In the process, people change the social context. Thus, our actions during this time of transition will shape the world of the future. Let me suggest two very different possibilities, both of which merely extrapolate from the present.

A Pessimistic View of the Future

One possibility is that the economy continues to globalize, with powerful high-tech corporations accumulating more and more, further freeing them from any political or economic limits. The successful corporations, requiring smaller and smaller work forces, act with less and less accountability to any region in which they operate. Without responsibility to any place or people, and more or less without regulation, these corporations continue to pollute the environment. International inequality becomes extreme, with a small group of countries doing well but most of the world growing increasingly impoverished.

One segment of the internal economy would comprise small, highly computerized, automated, and flexible manufacturing firms manned by a core of highly skilled, educated, and rewarded engineers, technicians, and professionals. Low-wage, dead-end service-sector jobs would proliferate in the other segment. Female and minority workers would tend to fill jobs in the low-wage sector.

For the decreasing number of male core workers, work would be stimulating, challenging, and flexible. Even these workers, however, would experience continual pressure to upgrade and expand skills. To maintain their edge, they would work long hours and travel often. To facilitate this lifestyle, these workers would either remain single, or, if they formed families, would seldom see them. Competition for the very few lucrative and comfortable positions would make collegiality and friendship with coworkers nearly impossible. For most workers, however, work would be characterized by either technologically induced monotony or the drudgery of underpaid, undervalued, but often personally taxing service work.

The insecurities of the workplace would force even workers with college and postgraduate educations to scramble from job to job. In addition to the insecurity of unstable wages would be the insecurity of inadequate or absent health care, retirement, and disability benefits. Paid vacations would be as antiquated as butter churns.

As a result of increased competition for fewer and fewer good jobs, those who are already in a relatively advantaged labor market position (white males) would intensify their efforts to exclude women and minorities from access to those positions. Increased efforts to segregate the workplace would be aided by a renewed attempt to make family the dominant arena for women. The push to return to homes would be supported by men throughout the occupational structure because getting women out of the labor force would cut that labor force (and therefore competition) roughly in half.

As Margaret Atwood suggested in her brilliant dystopian novel, *The Handmaid's Tale* (1987), reproductive technologies and abortion, both of which give women more control over their bodies, would become illegal. Cultural changes that reinforced highly separate gender roles could once again put women in a subordinate and powerless position. Similarly, minorities would continue to face discrimination as government withdrew its commitment to expanding and enforcing civil rights legislation. These workers would find employment solely in those low-wage service jobs that would predominate.

These changes would have enormous consequences for families. On the one hand, women who were systematically excluded from the workplace and increasingly denied access to technologies that give them control over their own bodies might well relish the return to the satisfactions of child rearing and homemaking. On the other hand, more and more families would have to survive on diminished incomes and with greater insecurity, which would make additional children an economic liability. This might entail a reversion to earlier coping mechanisms so dominant in third world countries. Such coping mechanisms include participation in the informal economy and various forms of infanticide and homemade birth control and abortion techniques! To survive, families would become increasingly extended; thus lives would be increasingly crowded.

At the other extreme, deepened economic hardship throughout society would make family formation increasingly impossible. Girls, denied access to information and birth control, would continue to have children. Young men, unable to support their offspring, would continue to abandon their young partners to fend for themselves. Given their own youth, they would fail to parent their children, since they themselves need parenting. Young children without guidance or structure from their own parents would seek structure from their fellow youths. Gangs would continue to proliferate. Undersocialized and increasingly sociopathic gangs would roam cities, suburbs, and the countryside preying on the weak, defenseless, unguarded, and elderly—as anticipated in William Golding's *Lord of the Flies* (1954) and as depicted in Anthony Burgess's novel *A Clockwork Orange* (1962).

Economic impoverishment, instability, and family disarray would further weaken social order. Citizens would turn to the government to impose order. People in fear will give up civil rights if they think their lives are endangered. Since a greater percentage of the voting population would be over 65 years old, laws would particularly limit the mobility, behavior, and rights of the young. Thus, government involvement would increasingly take the form of authoritarian control. Even today, curfews for the young are becoming increasingly popular.

Our government, along with the governments of other advanced countries, would likely coordinate efforts to impose a certain amount of order on the international scene (massive disruption is not good for business). At the same time other countries would continue to devolve into ethnically based tribes with an agenda of genocidal superiority. As Thomas Hobbes warned in *Leviathan* (1651/1962), the world would indeed become one in which life was "nasty, brutish, and short," a "war of all against all."

Only a small, international, and invisible elite, with the world's wealth and technology at its disposal, would be free from this misery. The rest would live in a hostile, soulless world focused on little but survival. For many inner-city dwellers, this nightmare is already reality (see, for example, Kotlowitz, 1991).

An Optimistic View of the Future

This gloomy scenario is only one possible world. Another possible world is far more optimistic. On a global level, the economic, personnel, and technological resources of advanced nations might allow coordination among them for coherent, compassionate, and collaborative intervention in those countries that want economic and political assistance. Existing communication technology would allow creation of a genuinely international community that could begin to address some of the resource constraints that hold back countries that want to move forward. With the aid of computer networks and translation software, for example, the children of the entire world could participate in global schools in which the libraries of the world would be at their disposal.

Aid in education, health, and other basics would help halt the growing polarization of the world's populations. As a community, countries around the world would address the unchecked population growth in the poorest of nations. Similarly, they would turn their attention to investing in environmental cleanup and protection. Environmentally responsible global corporations would put thousands of people to work and continue to profit by putting their energies into creating new products and markets, exploring and colonizing both the ocean and space.

To nurture this global economy, the nation-states of the world could develop democratic organizations that transcended national boundaries. Countries would contribute delegates to supranational political bodies that would work to prevent tribalism by stressing the inclusion and participation of all, no matter how poor. New communities might develop along the information highway as people all over the world connected on the basis of shared concerns and interests. As education and the economy continued to globalize, immigration would become less problematic. Ethnic identity and conflict might become a thing of the past.

Domestically, the transformation in the economy need not diminish the lives of a majority of Americans. The possibility exists for quite the opposite. Computer-based, robotized factories could well free people from the drudgery of monotonous production work. Educating and retraining displaced workers (rather than letting them fend for themselves) would create a work force of experienced and empowered workers who could use that experience to further develop production facilities. Those with the entrepreneurial spirit could have greater freedom to devise new businesses and services. A growing, creative small-business sector, aided by easier access to colleges and universities, could free up much of the stymied creativity that has historically fueled economic growth.

Employers in America have been reluctant to incorporate telecommuting into the structure of work for fear that without supervision, worker productivity will decline. Future employers would learn, however (as some did after the Los Angeles earthquake of 1994), that workers freed from the constraints of commuting and juggling child care are often more productive than they are with those pressures. Telecommuting would then become a major component of the work "place" of the future, thus enabling a genuine integration of work and family life. Individuals would no longer have their major identity in their workplace because for many there would be no workplace. People's identities—worker, citizen, family member, friend—would become more fully developed and integrated. If affordable health care, insurance, and other nonwage benefits were available to all workers, then freedom from nine-to-five jobs, five days a week, could well be liberating rather than impoverishing.

Flexible work arrangements could be nonpunitive in another way as well. By creating policies that are genuinely supportive of families (such as caregiving or parental leave policies), it would be much easier for those who continue to seek a monogamous marriage to maintain it. Productive work would no longer require long hours away from family. Moreover, with truly enriching child care programs, staffed with well-paid, highly trained professionals, parents who worked outside the home would not do so at the expense of their children's well-being. The greater security parents would feel would undoubtedly make them much more productive as workers.

Finally, the workplace now, more than ever, has little that necessitates gendering. Heavy agricultural and industrial work may, at times, have required the greater strength that men on average have. But the postindustrial economy does not require greater strength. Thus, there is every reason to suggest that gender differences may no longer slot women into lower wage jobs. The result of computerizing work could therefore be a much more creative and productive work force, stronger families, and a richer society.

Revitalizing the economy and creating a worker-friendly workplace would also generate more social income through taxes, which would give the government more ability to finance social programs that would help the most disadvantaged and excluded. In addition, diminished military budgets (resulting from international collaboration) would allow government deficits to shrink and would free resources for civilian expenditures such as job creation and training programs. Government programs encouraging clean, safe, affordable housing, guaranteed education, and universal health care have improved the lives of millions of Americans. There is no reason that such cannot be the case again.

Government might also become more direct and participatory with advances in computer technology. Referenda could be conducted with each household via computer; debate could occur over the information superhighway; voting could be instantaneous. Of course, the democratization of higher education would facilitate the democratization of politics. The more educated and informed people are, the greater their enthusiasm for political participation and the greater the government's responsiveness to their views.

An economy that provides jobs to all who want them, jobs that pay enough to maintain a decent standard of living, goes far in restoring the social contract. Restoring the social contract means restoring people's hope for the future. This restoration is crucial for the young. The anomie, anger, and fear that have become a part of so many young people's lives stem from a sense of having nothing to live for. When one of my colleagues interviewed adolescents who were imprisoned, he asked them, "Why did you shoot the victim?" The answer, over and over and over, was, "Why not?" With no sense of future, these angry, inadequately socialized, improperly educated, and socially neglected young people grew up with no concern about the consequences of their actions.

The transformation to flexible capitalism could rob people of hope, but that need not necessarily be the case. Certainly there is much work to be done in the world and, globally, there are millions of people who need work to do. While the cost of putting people to work and creating the infrastructures and economies in places like Somalia and Eastern Europe—as well as East Los Angeles, the Bronx, and Mississippi—may be enormous, the costs of not doing so are even more astronomical.

CONCLUSIONS

The positive scenario may sound impossible. But think about the world of your great-grandparents. Many of them lived without indoor plumbing, electricity, and telephones; television, computers, freezers, and microwave ovens did not exist. Women routinely died in childbirth, and few ran businesses. Most men labored without much understanding of the national, much less the global, economy. Now think about how different your world is. There is little reason to think that your great-grandchildren's world won't be as remarkably different.

But how do we know which possible world will emerge? We don't. Moreover, are the unstable conditions I have written about the result of a period of transition? Or am I claiming that change and instability will be the norm? I wish I could provide definitive answers to these questions, but I cannot. I believe that people will strive toward stability of one form or another, one way or another. However, the point of this book was not to map out the answer. It was to show the processes that are affecting us all and to suggest the worlds that might emerge from these processes.

Each and every one of us shapes the possibilities in one way or another. Understanding the sources of change gives you much greater ability to remake society in the image you prefer. I also believe that sociology provides some of the tools that you can use to make decisions, to act, to create the world that is emerging. History, to paraphrase Karl Marx, is what men and women make it, within the constraints that they have created over time. Sociology helps us understand those constraints and, therefore, remove them if we wish.

REFERENCES

Ahlburg, D. A., & De Vita, C. J. (1992). New realities of the American family. *Population Bulletin, 47*(2). Washington, DC: Population Reference Bureau.

Allen, R. (March 9, 1994). World's women strike for rights. *Times-Picayune*, New Orleans.

Amenta, E., & Yllan, Y. (1991). Political opportunity, the new institutionalism, and the Townsend Movement. *American Sociological Review, 56*, 250–265.

Appelbaum, E., & Albin, P. (1990). Differential characteristics of employment growth in service industries. In E. Appelbaum & R. Schettkat (Eds.), *Labor market adjustment to structural change and technological progress* (pp. 36–53). New York: Praeger.

Appelbaum, E., & Batt, R. (1994). *The new American workplace*. Ithaca, NY: ILR Press.

Armstrong, P., Glyn, A., & Harrison, J. (1991). *Capitalism since 1945*. Cambridge, MA: Basil Blackwell.

Associated Press. (July 3, 1993). 7 punished in plot to kill teacher. *Times-Picayune*, New Orleans.

Associated Press. (August 11, 1993). Lesbians can adopt, New Jersey judge decides. *Times-Picayune*, New Orleans.

Associated Press. (March 7, 1994). Labor: Unemployment a global crisis. *Times-Picayune*, New Orleans.

Associated Press. (May 9, 1994). Mrs. Clinton to grads: Take care of each other. *Times-Picayune*, New Orleans.

Atwood, M. (1987). *The handmaid's tale*. New York: Ballantine Books.

Babcox, D., & Belkin, M. (1971). *Liberation now!* New York: Dell.

Barnow, E. (1970). *The image empire*. New York: Oxford Press.

Bates, T. (1994). Social resources generated by group support networks may not be beneficial to Asian immigrant-owned small businesses. *Social Forces, 72*(3), 671–690.

Baugher, J. E. (1994). *Risk, stress and restructuring in the U.S. petrochemical industry: A case study from Louisiana*. Unpublished master's thesis, Tulane University, New Orleans, Louisiana.

Beck, U. (1992). *Risk society*. London: Sage.

Bell, D. (1973). *The coming of post-industrial society*. New York: Basic Books.

———(1992). Modernism, postmodernism and the decline of moral order. In J. C. Alexander & S. Seidman (Eds.), *Culture and society* (pp. 319–329). Cambridge: Cambridge University Press.

Belous, R. (1989). *The contingent economy: The growth of the temporary, part-time, and subcontracted workforce.* Washington, DC: National Planning Association.

Bengston, V. L., & Achenbaum, W. A. (Eds.). (1993). *The changing contract across generations.* New York: Aldine de Gruyter.

Berger, J. (December 22, 1993). The pain of layoffs for ex-senior I.B.M. workers. *New York Times.*

Berk, S. F. (1988). Women's unpaid labor in home and community. In A. Stromberg & S. Harkess (Eds.), *Women working* (pp. 287–302). Mountain View, CA: Mayfield.

Berke, R. (1994). Politicians discovering an issue: Immigration. *New York Times.*

Blau, F., & Ferber, M. (1986). *The economics of women, men and work.* Englewood Cliffs, NJ: Prentice-Hall.

Blau, J. (1993). *Social contracts and economic markets.* New York: Plenum Press.

Blauner, R. (1964). *Alienation and freedom.* Chicago: University of Chicago Press.

Block, F. (1990). *Post-industrial possibilities.* Berkeley, CA: University of California Press.

Bluestone, B., & Harrison, B. (1982). *The deindustrialization of America.* New York: Basic Books.

Bonacich, E. (1976). Advanced capitalism and black/white race relations in the United States: A split labor market interpretation. *American Sociological Review 41,* 34–51.

Bouvier, L. F., & De Vita, C. J. (1991). The baby boom entering midlife. *Population Bulletin 46.* Washington, DC: Population Reference Bureau.

Bowles, J., & Gintis, H. (1976). *Schooling in capitalist America.* New York: Basic Books.

———(1982). The crisis of liberal democratic capitalism: The case of the United States. *Politics and Society 11,* 51–59.

Bowles, S., Gordon, D. M., & Weiskoph, T. E. (1983). *Beyond the wasteland: A democratic alternative to economic decline.* Garden City, NY: Anchor Press/ Doubleday.

Boyer, R. O., & Morais, H. M. (1955). *Labor's untold story.* New York: United Electrical, Radio, and Machine Workers of America.

Braun, D. D. (1991). *The rich get richer.* Chicago: Nelson-Hall.

Braverman, H. (1974). *Labor and monopoly capital.* New York: Monthly Review.

Bridges, W. P., & Villemez, W. J. (1991). Employment relations and the labor market: Integrating institutional and market perspectives. *American Sociological Review, 56*(6), 748–764.

Brittan, S. (1978). Inflation and democracy, chapter 7 in *The political economy of inflation*. F. Hirsch & J. H. Goldthorpe (Eds.). Cambridge, MA: Harvard University Press.

Bureau of Economic Analysis. (1977). *National income and production accounts of the United States, 1929–1974*. Washington, DC.

——*Survey of Current Business* (monthly publication, July 1976, July 1978, July 1983). Washington, DC.

Callaghan, P., & Hartmann, H. (1991). *Contingent work: A chartbook on part-time and temporary employment*. Washington, DC: Economic Policy Institute.

Capital Bureau. (April 29, 1993). Children may get parental divorce rights. *Times-Picayune*, New Orleans.

Chaves, M. (1994). Secularization as declining religious authority. *Social Forces, 72,* 749–774.

Christensen, K. (1988) *Women and home-based work: The unspoken contract*. New York: Henry Holt.

CITIBASE. (1978). *Citibank economic database, 1946–present*. New York: Citibank.

Cohen, J. L. (1985). Strategy or identity: New theoretical paradigms and contemporary social movements. *Social Research 52*, 663–716.

Colclough, G., & Tolbert, C. M., II. (1992). *Work in the fast lane*. Albany, NY: State University of New York Press.

Collins, R., & Coltrane, S. (1991). *Sociology of marriage and the family* (3rd ed.). Chicago: Nelson-Hall.

Coontz, S. (1988). *The social origins of private life: A history of American families, 1600–1900*. New York: Verso.

——(1992). *The way we never were: American families and the nostalgia trap*. New York: Basic Books.

Cornfield, D. B. (1985). Economic segmentation and the expression of labor unrest: Striking versus quitting in the manufacturing sector. *Social Science Quarterly, 66,* 247–265.

——(1986). Declining union membership in the post–World War II era: The United Furniture Workers of America, 1939–1982. *American Journal of Sociology, 91,* 1112–1153.

Coverman, S. (1983). Explaining husbands' participation in domestic labor. *Sociological Quarterly, 26,* 81–97.

Coverman, S., & Sheley, J. F. (1986). Change in men's housework and child-care time: 1965–1975. *Journal of Marriage and the Family, 48,* 413–422.

Coyne, T. (January 8, 1995). 2 die in shooting at Ford car plant. *Times-Picayune*, New Orleans.

Craypo, C., & Nissen, B. (1993). *Grand designs*. Ithaca, NY: ILR Press.

Crimp, D., & Ralston, A. (1990). *AIDS demographics.* San Francisco: Bay Press.

Crook, S., Pukulski, J., & Waters, M. (1992). *Postmodernization: Change in advanced society.* London: Sage.

DeParle, J. (October 9, 1994). Census report sees incomes in decline and more poverty. *New York Times.*

Devine, J., & Wright, J. D. (1993). *The greatest of evils.* New York: Aldine de Gruyter.

Dizard, J. E., & Gadlin, H. (1990). *The minimal family.* Amherst, MA: University of Massachusetts Press.

Doeringer, P. B. (1991). *Turbulence in the American workplace.* New York: Oxford University Press.

duRivage, V. (1992). *New policies for the part-time and contingent workforce.* Armonk, NY: M. E. Sharpe.

Durkheim, E. (1897/1966). *Suicide.* New York: Free Press.

Edwards, R. (1979). *Contested terrain.* New York: Basic Books.

Edwards, R., Garonna, P., & Tödling, F. (1986). *Unions in crisis and beyond.* Dover, MA: Auburn House.

Edwards, R., Reich, M., & Weisskoph, T. (1986). *The capitalist system* (3rd ed.). Englewood Cliffs, NJ: Prentice-Hall.

Ehrenreich, B. (1989). *Fear of falling.* New York: Harper/Perennial.

Ellison, D. G., & Musick, M. (1993). Southern intolerance: A fundamentalist effect? *Social Forces, 72*(2), 379–420.

Fordahl, M. (1994). Family seeks sense in pushing of boy from city high-rise. *Times-Picayune,* New Orleans.

Freeman, R., & Medoff, J. (1984). *What do unions do?* New York: Basic Books.

Friedan, B. (1983). *The feminine mystique.* New York: Norton.

Frobel, Folker, Heinrichs, J., & Kreye, O. (1980). *The new international division of labor: Structural unemployment in industrialized countries and industrialization in developing countries.* Cambridge: Cambridge University Press.

Gamson, W. A. (1992). The social psychology of collective action. In A. Morris & C. Mueller (Eds.), *Frontiers in social movement theory.* New Haven, CT: Yale University Press.

Garcia, G. (January 2, 1994). Rock finds religion again. *New York Times.*

Garson, B. (1988). *The electronic sweatshop.* New York: Penguin Books.

Gerson, K. (1991). Coping with commitment: Dilemmas and conflicts of family life. In A. Wolfe (Ed.), *America at century's end* (pp. 35–57). Berkeley, CA: University of California Press.

Goldberg, G. S., & Kremen, E. (1990). *The feminization of poverty.* New York: Greenwood Press.

Goldfield, M. (1987). *The decline of organized labor in the United States*. Chicago: University of Chicago Press.

Golding, W. (1962). *Lord of the flies*. New York: Coward-McCann.

Goodman, W. (June 19, 1994). Television, meet life. Life, meet TV. *New York Times*.

Gordon, D., Edwards, R., & Reich, M. (1982). *Segmented work, divided workers*. Cambridge: Cambridge University Press.

Greenberg, E. (1985). *Capitalism and the American political ideal*. New York: M. E. Sharpe.

Griffin, L., Devine, J., & Wallace, M. (1982). Monopoly capital, organized labor, and military expenditures in the United States, 1949–1976. In M. Burawoy & T. Skocpol (Eds.), *American Journal of Sociology, 88* (supplement). Chicago: University of Chicago Press.

Griffin, L., Wallace, M., & Rubin, B. A. (1986). Capitalist resistance to the organization of labor before the New Deal: How? Why? Success? *American Sociological Review, 51*, 147–167.

Griswold, W. (1994). *Cultures and societies in a changing world*. Thousand Oaks, CA: Pine Forge Press.

Hage, J., & Powers, C. H. (1992). *Post-industrial lives*. Newbury Park, CA: Sage.

Harrington, M. (1962). *The other America*. New York: Penguin Books.

Harvey, D. (1989). *The condition of postmodernity*. Cambridge: Basil Blackwell.

Hastings, D. (April 11, 1993). Child-abuse epidemic confounding authorities. *Times-Picayune*, New Orleans.

Heilbroner, R. (1968). *The making of economic society* (2nd ed.). Englewood Cliffs, NJ: Prentice-Hall.

———(1976). *Business civilization in decline*. New York: Norton.

Hill, M. (November 8, 1992). Violence at work: Incidents rise with layoffs. *Times-Picayune*, New Orleans.

Hobbes, T. (1962). *Leviathan*. New York: Collier Press. (Original work published 1651.)

Hodson, R. (1968). Labor in the monopoly, competitive, and state sectors of production. *Politics and Society, 8*, 429–480.

Horan, P. M., & Hargis, P. G. (1991). Children's work and schooling in the late nineteenth-century family economy. *American Sociological Review, 56*, 583–596.

Hunter, A. G., & Davis, J. E. (1992). Constructing gender—an exploration of Afro-American men's conceptualization of manhood. *Gender and Society, 6*, 464–479.

Hunter, J. D. (1991). *Culture wars: The struggle to define America*. New York: Basic Books.

Hunter, J. D., & Rice, J. S. (1991). Unlikely alliances. In A. Wolfe (Ed.), *America at century's end* (pp. 318–339). Berkeley, CA: University of California Press.

Jacoby, S. (1988). *Employing bureaucracy.* New York: Columbia University Press.

Joekes, S. P. (1987). *Women in the world economy: An INSTRAW study.* New York: Oxford University Press.

Johnson, K. (October 9, 1994). Downsizing, layoffs change character of office. *Times-Picayune,* New Orleans.

Jong, E. (1973). *Fear of flying.* New York: Holt, Rinehart & Winston.

Kadaba, L. S. (1994). Workforce runs for cover from violence. *Times-Picayune,* New Orleans.

Kain, E. (1990). *The myth of family decline.* Lexington, MA: Lexington Books.

Kalleberg, A. L., & Berg, I. (1987). *Work and industry.* New York: Plenum Press.

Kennedy, P. (1993). *Preparing for the twenty-first century.* New York: Random House.

Kessler-Harris, A. (1982). *Out to work.* Oxford: Oxford University Press.

Kimmel, M. S. (Ed.). (1987a). *Changing men: New directions in research on men and masculinity.* Newbury Park, CA: Sage.

Kimmel, M. S. (1987b). The contemporary "crisis" of masculinity in historical perspective. In H. Brod (Ed.), *The making of masculinities* (pp. 121–154). Boston: Allen & Unwin.

Kochan, T., McKessic, R., & Capelli, P. (1984). Strategic choices and industrial relations theory. *Industrial Relations, 23,* 5–28.

Kohn, M. (1977). *Class and conformity.* Chicago: University of Chicago Press.

Kohn, M., & Schooler, C. (1982). Job conditions and personality: A longitudinal assessment of their reciprocal effects. *American Journal of Sociology, 87,* 257– 286.

Kolko, G. (1963). *Railroads and regulation 1877–1916.* New York: Norton.

———(1967). *The triumph of conservatism.* Chicago: Quadrangle Books.

Kosmin, B. A., & Lachman, S. P. (1993). *One nation under God: Religion in contemporary American society.* New York: Hermany.

Kotlowitz, A. (1991). *There are no children here.* New York: Anchor Books.

Kozol, J. (1991). *Savage inequalities.* New York: Harper/Perennial.

Kutscher, R. E. (1990). Structural change in the United States, past and prospective: Its implication for skill and educational requirements. In E. Appelbaum and R. Schettkat (Eds.), *Labor market adjustments to structural change and technological progress* (chapter 4). New York: Praeger.

Lancaster, H. (November 29, 1994). A new social contract to benefit employer and employee. *Wall Street Journal.*

Lash, S., & Urry, J. (1987). *The end of organized capitalism.* Madison, WI: University of Wisconsin Press.

Laslett, P. (1977). *Family life and illicit love in earlier generations.* Cambridge: Cambridge University Press.

Lee, S. P., & Passell, P. (1979). *A new economic view of American history.* New York: Norton.

Leiberson, S. (1980). *A piece of the pie: Black and white immigrants since 1980.* Berkeley, CA: University of California Press.

Levitan, S. (1985). *Programs in aid of the poor* (5th ed.). Baltimore: Johns Hopkins University Press.

Lewis, P. H. (March 8, 1994). Strangers, not their computers, build a network in time of grief. *New York Times.*

Likens, T. (September 5, 1993). Violence is rising at work, study says. *Times-Picayune,* New Orleans.

Lippman, J. (October 20, 1992). The global village: How TV is transforming world culture and politics. *Los Angeles Times.*

Lorence, J. (1991). Growth in service sector employment and MSA gender earnings inequality: 1970–1980. *Social Forces, 69,* 763–783.

Luker, K. (1984). *Abortion and the politics of motherhood.* Berkeley, CA: University of California Press.

Lynd, S. (1973). *American labor radicalism.* New York: Wiley.

Matthaei, J. A. (1983). *An economic history of women in America: Women's work, the sexual division of labor and the development of capitalism.* New York: Schocken.

McCall's. (1963). *McCall's cookbook.* New York: Random House.

McCammon, H. J. (1990). Legal limits on labor militancy: U.S. labor law and the right to strike since the New Deal. *Social Problems, 37,* 206–229.

McLuhan, M. (1964). *Understanding media: The extensions of man.* New York: New American Library

Mellgren, D. (October 19, 1994). Cartoon is yanked after girl dies: Debate renewed over TV violence. *Times-Picayune,* New Orleans.

Melucci, A. (1985). The symbolic challenge of everyday life. *Social Research, 52,* 789–816.

Mills, C. W. (1959). *The sociological imagination.* New York: Grove Press.

Mingione, E. (1991). *Fragmented societies.* Oxford: Basil Blackwell.

Morrow, L. (March 29, 1993). The temping of America. *Time.*

O'Connor, J. (1973). *Fiscal crisis of the state.* New York: St. Martin's Press.

Pahl, R. E. (1988). *On work.* Oxford: Basil Blackwell.

Perrucci, C., Perrucci, R., Targ, D., & Targ, H. (1988). *Plant closings.* Boston: Aldine de Gruyter.

Perrucci, R. (1994). *Japanese auto transplants in the heartland.* Hawthorne, NY: Aldine de Gruyter.

Piore, M., & Sable, C. (1984). *The second industrial divide*. New York: Basic Books.

Piven, F. F., & Cloward, R. (1977). *Poor people's movements*. New York: Vintage Books.

———(1982). *The new class war*. New York: Pantheon Books.

———(1988). *Why Americans don't vote*. New York: Pantheon Books.

———(1993). *Regulating the poor* (3rd ed.). New York: Vintage Books.

Poponoe, D. (1993). American family decline, 1960–1990: A review and appraisal. *Journal of Marriage and the Family, 55*(3), 527–541.

Portes, A., Castells, M., & Benton, L. A. (Eds.). (1989). *The informal economy*. Baltimore: Johns Hopkins University Press.

Presser, H. (1994). Employment schedules among dual-earner spouses and the division of household labor by gender. *American Sociological Review, 59*, 348–364.

Quadagno, J. (1988). *The transformation of old age security*. Chicago: University of Chicago Press.

Reich, R. B. (October 20, 1994). Hire education. *Rolling Stone*.

Reskin, B., & Padavic, I. (1994). *Women and men at work*. Thousand Oaks, CA: Pine Forge.

Ritzer, G. (1989). The permanently new economy. *Work and occupations, 16*(3), 243–272.

Robertson, R. (1992). *Globalization*. London: Sage.

Rosenberg, R. A., & Kalleberg, A. L. (1990). A cross-national comparison of the gender gap in income. *American Journal of Sociology, 96*, 69–106.

Ross, R. J. S., & Trachte, K. C. (1990). *Global capitalism*. New York: State University of New York Press.

Rousseau, J.-J. (1947). *The social contract* (C. Frankel, Trans.). New York: Hafner. (Original work published 1762.)

Rubin, B. (1986a). Unions, strikes and wages: Class struggle American style. *American Sociological Review, 51*, 618–633.

———(1986b). Trade union organization, labor militancy and labor's share of national income in the United States, 1949–1978. *Research in Social Stratification and Mobility, 5*, 223–242.

———(1993). Limits to institutionalization? A sectoral analysis of strike settlement rates. *Research in Social Stratification and Mobility, 11*, 17–202.

———(1995). *Flexible accumulation, the decline of contract, and social transformation*. *Research in Social Stratification and Mobility, 14*.

Rubin, B. A., Griffin, L., & Wallace, M. (1983). "Provided only that their voice was strong": Insurgency and organization of American labor from NRA to Taft-Hartley. *Work and Occupations, 10*, 307–324.

Rubin, B. A., & Smith, B. T. (1992). Forged ties: Cooperation and conflict in the metals industries. *Social Science Research, 21*(2), 115–132.

Rubin, B. A., Wright, J. D., & Devine, J. A. (1992). Unhousing the urban poor: The Reagan legacy. *Journal of Sociology and Social Welfare, 2*(3), 937–956.

Rubin, L. (1994). *Families on the fault line.* New York: Harper/Perennial.

Rumbaut, R. G. (1992). Passages to America. In A. Wolfe (Ed.), *America at century's end* (pp. 208–244). Berkeley, CA: University of California Press.

Sayer, A., & Walker, R. (1992). *The new social economy: Reworking the division of labor.* Cambridge: Basil Blackwell.

Schultz, B., & Schultz, R. (1989). *It did happen here: Recollections of political repression in America.* Berkeley, CA: University of California Press.

Scott, H. (1984). *Working your way to the bottom: The feminization of poverty.* London: Pandora Press.

Shaiken, H. (1984). *Work transformed.* New York: Holt, Rinehart & Winston.

Sidell, R. (1986). *Women and children last.* New York: Viking.

Simons, M. (March 15, 1994). Ban English? French bicker on barricades. *New York Times.*

Smith, J. (1982). Transforming households: Working-class women and economic crisis. *Social Problems, 34,* 416–436.

———(1984). The paradox of women's poverty: Wage-earning women and economic transformation. *Signs, 10,* 291–310.

Sokoloff, N. J. (1992). *Black and white women in the professions.* London: Routledge.

Stacey, J. (1990). *Brave new families.* New York: Basic Books.

Steinfels, P. (April 11, 1993). Enduring: Fundamentalists' traits span faiths. *Times-Picayune,* New Orleans.

Stepan-Norris, J., & Zeitlan, M. (1989). "Who gets the bird?" or, how the communists won power and trust in America's unions: The relative autonomy of intraclass political struggles. *American Sociological Review, 54,* 503–523.

Storper, M., & Walker, R. (1989). *The capitalist imperative.* New York: Basil Blackwell.

Sullivan, T. (1989). Women and minority workers in the new economy. *Work and Occupations, 16,* 393–415.

Toffler, A. (1991). *Powershift.* New York: Bantam Books.

Treas, J. (1983). Trickle down or transfers? Postwar determinants of family income inequality. *American Sociological Review, 48,* 546–559.

Tye, B. B., & Tye, K. A. (1992). *Global education.* Albany: State University of New York Press.

Uchitelle, L. (November 20, 1994). The rise of the losing class. *New York Times.*

U.S. Bureau of the Census. *Statistical Abstract of the United States* (selected years). Washington, DC.

U.S. Department of Commerce (Bureau of Economic Analysis). (1978, 1983). *Economic Report of the President.* Washington, DC: U.S. Government Printing Office.

Wallace, M., & Rothschild, J. (1988). Plant closing, capital flight, and worker dislocation: The long shadow of deindustrialization. *Research in Politics and Society, 3,* 1–36.

Wallace, M., Rubin, B. A., & Smith, B. T. (1988). American labor law: Its impact on working class militancy, 1901–1980. *Social Science History, 12,* 1–29.

Walters, P. B., & James, D. R. (1992). Schooling for some: Child labor and school enrollment and black and white children in the early twentieth-century South. *American Sociological Review, 57,* 635–650.

Walters, P. B., & O'Connell, P. O. (1988). The family economy, work and educational participation in the United States, 1890–1940. *American Journal of Sociology, 93,* 1116–1152.

Ward, K. (Ed.). (1990). *Women workers and global restructuring.* Ithaca, NY: ILR Press.

Weakliem, D. (1990). Relative wages and the radical theory of economic segmentation. *American Sociological Review, 55,* 574–590.

Weinstein, J. *The corporate ideal and the liberal state, 1900–1918.* Boston, MA: Beacon.

———(1973). Labor and socialism in America. *Labor History, 14*(3), 429–434.

Williams, W. A. (1970). *The shaping of American diplomacy, Vol. 1* (2nd ed.). Chicago: Rand McNally.

Wilson, W. J. (1987). *The truly disadvantaged.* Chicago: University of Chicago Press.

Wiltz, T. (March 5, 1995). Ill-defined racial lines growing even blurrier. *Times-Picayune,* New Orleans.

Wolfe, A. (1991). *America at century's end.* Berkeley, CA: University of California Press.

Wood, S. (1989). *Work transformed?* London: Unwin Hyman.

Wright, E. O. (1985). *Classes.* London: Verso.

Wright, J. D., & Devine J. (1994). Poverty among the elderly. *Journal of Long-Term Health Care, 13*(1), 5–6.

Wright, R. (February 18, 1993). Global revolution to bring problems, turmoil for Clinton. *Los Angeles Times.*

Zuboff, S. (1984). *The age of the smart machine.* New York: Basic Books.

GLOSSARY/INDEX

Acknowledgments

Grateful acknowledgement is given to the following for permission to reprint:

Fig. 1.2, from "New Realities of the American Family," by Dennis A. Ahlburg and Carol J. DeVita, 1992, *Population Bulletin* V. 47 (2): 5. Copyright 1992 by the Population Reference Bureau, Washington, D.C. Reprinted by permission.

Figs. 2.1 and 4.1, from CITIBASE, FAME Information Services, Inc. Copyright 1978 by Fame Information Services, Inc. Reprinted by permission.

Excerpt from "Hire Education" by Robert Reich from *Rolling Stone*, October 20, 1994. By Straight Arrow Publishers Company, L.P. 1994. All Rights Reserved. Reprinted by Permission.

Excerpt from "Rock Finds Religion Again" by Guy Garcia (2 January 1994). Copyright © 1994 by The New York Times Company. Reprinted by permission.

Excerpt from "Ban English? French Bicker on Barricades" by Marlise Simons (15 March 1994). Copyright © 1994 by The New York Times Company. Reprinted by permission.